INTO THE ABYSS

ALSO BY ROD MACDONALD

Dive Scapa Flow, Mainstream, Edinburgh, 1990. Third edition 1997
Dive Scotland's Greatest Wrecks, Mainstream, Edinburgh, 1993.
Second edition 2000
Dive England's Greatest Wrecks, Mainstream, Edinburgh, 2003

INTO THE ABYSS

Diving to Adventure in the Liquid World

Rod Macdonald

MAINSTREAM
PUBLISHING

EDINBURGH AND LONDON

Ki

First published in Great Britain in 2003 by
MAINSTREAM PUBLISHING (EDINBURGH) LTD
7 Albany Street
Edinburgh EH1 3UG

ISBN 1 84018 718 2

A catalogue record for this book is available from the British Library

Typeset in Century Gothic and Garamond

Printed in Great Britain by
Mackays of Chatham plc

He who fights with monsters might take care lest he thereby become a monster. And if you gaze for long into an abyss, the abyss gazes also into you.

Friedrich Nietzsche, *Beyond Good and Evil*

Contents

The Pinnacle, Corryvreckan Whirlpool, West Scotland

Our group of six divers struggled in the swirling currents to rendezvous at the appointed time on top of the Pinnacle, the column of solid rock that rises up from a depth of 200 metres to just 30 metres beneath the boiling surface of the Corryvreckan Whirlpool. The Pinnacle is both the cause and the very heart of the whirlpool, the third-largest whirlpool in the world.

The whirlpool lies in the Gulf of Corryvreckan, a half-mile wide channel between the islands of Scarba and Jura through which the whole might of the Atlantic floods and ebbs daily with incredible fury. Declared unnavigable by the Royal Navy, it is a hugely foreboding and intimidating place to be. On the surface, the powerful down currents produced by underwater waterfalls down the side of the Pinnacle create large standing waves and numerous swirling eddies. It is perhaps the most fearsome natural feature in British waters.

I gripped large rocky outcrops, my fingers searching for secure handholds to prevent me being picked up by the strengthening current and swept away into the abyss below. Apprehension upped my breathing rate – I tried to slow things down, taking several long draws on my breathing regulator.

I looked around the 100-foot wide Pinnacle summit. The underwater visibility was about 50 feet here and I could see the sheer sides of the Pinnacle dropping away all around me, disappearing vertically into the surrounding blackness of the Gulf.

My buddy diver Dave Hadden and I finned cautiously towards the side of the Pinnacle. The tide had now turned and I could feel the mass of water in which I was suspended starting to propel us over towards the edge. In just a few minutes the down currents would be so strong that this very edge would be a cascading underwater waterfall. Huge volumes of onrushing water were starting to thunder against the immovable Pinnacle, being pushed up one side to plunge and fall over the other side.

A gnawing fear gripped me as I moved over to the edge. If we lingered just a few more minutes the down currents would sweep us off the Pinnacle and drag us down into the depths – there would be little chance of breaking free of its grasp. To lose control here, in the face of the huge natural forces at work, would mean probable death.

Warily I kicked my fins and let the gentle current sweep me effortlessly and intoxicatingly over towards the sheer cliffs. I grabbed hold of any rocky handholds along the way that allowed me some semblance of control over my flight, finally anchoring myself with a handhold a few feet before the very edge itself. The current immediately swung my body round so that my feet were ahead of me, pointing towards the edge – and the abyss. The monster was trying to snare me and lure me to the point of no return, the point from which I could not escape its grasp.

Ducking into a small hollow behind a rock ledge at the very edge, I found some shelter from the current. Gingerly, flat on our chests, in the lee of the outcrop, Dave and I moved out and took hold of the smoothed edge of the pinnacle itself and peered down the sheer cliff face. We could see for perhaps 50 feet down the vertical walls. Beyond, the walls merged into the pure black chasm beneath us.

As we lay prone, peering over the cliff, I noticed that the rate of ascent of the exhaust bubbles floating up from my breathing regulator was slowing down. As I watched, the ascent of the bubbles got slower and slower – and then they stopped going up. In what was almost a surreal sight, they simply hung motionless before me, their natural upward buoyancy perfectly countered by the downward drag of the current. Then gradually, as the down currents got perceptibly stronger, my exhaust bubbles started disappearing downwards over the edge with increasing ferocity. It was time to leave this strange world – before we too were sucked into the abyss.

CHAPTER ONE

The Beckoning Depths

'There is nothing more powerful than this attraction toward an abyss'

Jules Verne, *Journey to the Centre of the Earth*

The chain of events that led me to dive into the heart of the Corryvreckan Whirlpool started in 1982 when I first turned up as a fresh-faced 20 year old at the Peterhead Scottish Sub Aqua Club's weekly dive training night.

I had snorkelled on holidays before on coral reefs, and seen barracuda and sharks in the wild, but I always felt that as a snorkellor you are something of a voyeur. You are on the outside looking in. I wanted to be a diver, getting down there and becoming part of the action happening below.

The difference between diving and snorkelling is similar to the distinction between riding a motorcycle and driving a car. Driving a car is a bit like playing a video game or watching TV. You are cocooned from the wind and rain outside and shielded from noises and smells that you would normally pick up subconsciously. Riding a motorcycle is a totally different experience. You feel more a part of what is happening. You get wet from the rain. You are rocked by wind and slipstreams as you pass large vehicles – you feel the effects on your skin. All your senses take in the environment around you. Sounds and smells are real – unlike the car-driving experience, where sounds are muffled by noise insulation and smells masked by whatever you have in the car. Such is the difference between diving and snorkelling.

My initial training covered endurance swimming tests to determine if I was physically fit enough. From there I moved on to the delights of practical tests – like duck diving to recover a rubber brick from the bottom of the 15-foot deep diving pool.

After some basic training and theory it was time to be introduced to the diving tool which would become such an important part of my life, the aqualung. I didn't, at this stage, truly understand how marvellous an idea it was, nor how it worked. I just knew that if you fitted the 1st Stage clamp of the aqualung onto the pillar valve on the top of a compressed air tank, and stuck the breathing regulator, the 2nd Stage, into your mouth, it gave you whatever air you needed, whenever you needed it.

Like practically every other novice diver in the world, my first experience of the aqualung was in a pool. Wearing just a T-shirt and swimming trunks, I sat down at the side of Peterhead pool and, with great relish, pulled on my new wetsuit boots and the incredibly robust black rubber Jet fins of the time. They have proved to be truly indestructible and are the only piece of my original dive equipment that I still have and use, 20 years later.

I picked up my mask and looped the strap over my head, perching the glass faceplate section on my forehead. I hesitantly slipped my arms through the straps of my back-mounted air tank harness and clasped the central belt across my stomach. After pulling my mask down over my face, I picked up the breathing regulator mouthpiece and put it into my mouth. Not knowing what to expect, I slipped into the water – and was immediately in love with a new sensation.

The cool water enveloped me and I sank down heavily to the bottom. Immediately, I saw a different aspect of the pool – from below up. There on the bottom, in little groups of two or three, were other novice divers being trained by instructors. I was able to swim around them easily and choose at what depth to swim; the feeling of weightlessness was akin to floating in space. I could move easily in every direction, up, down, left or right. I tried turning a few cartwheels which seemed hysterically funny until I realised that I had lost control of my buoyancy and floated up to break the surface. Red-faced I sank back down to my instructor.

I was hooked for life and continued at my training, turning up for weekly lectures. I began to understand the mechanics of how all my equipment worked and what it was for, and started to learn something of the physiology of diving – what was happening inside my body as I dived.

After six months of training and a move to Ellon, I joined the local branch of the British Sub Aqua Club (BSAC) there. There were a number of very experienced divers at this branch and the club dived regularly and went on expeditions to far-flung parts of Scotland. It all seemed extremely daring and exciting.

Soon after joining the BSAC in Ellon, I turned up at my local dive shop in Aberdeen, Sub Sea Services, to buy my first wetsuit. At that time everyone was still diving in wetsuits – the dry suit revolution had not yet happened in sport diving. With great relish I bought the biggest dive knife money could buy, a wetsuit, a 72 cu. ft dive tank and harness, weights and a weight belt and a Fenzy ABLJ (Adjustable Buoyancy Life Jacket). The ABLJ was a large, bright orange, horse-collar life jacket that went over your head and was secured by a couple of straps, one round your back and one under your crotch, so you didn't drop out of it.

Equipped with all this new gear, I went on to scrounge, or pick up cheaply, the other essential pieces of diving equipment: a torch, dive watch and an old-fashioned capillary depth gauge. This clever device was the size of a large watch and fitted over your wrist. It had a circular face with numbers all the way round. A thin pipe, open at one end, circled the outside of the face, and it worked very simply. The deeper you went, the more the increasing water pressure compressed the air in the thin tube. You read your depth from the number at the point where the air bubble was compressed to.

Even with all this equipment, under the prevailing club system of the time, it took me about six months before the time came for my first sea dive. Swimming around in the safe confines of the pool environment was one thing, but diving in the sea would be completely new to me.

My first sea dive was from Aberdour Beach, to the west of Fraserburgh on the north-easternmost corner of Scotland. The regular Sunday dive had been planned as an easy shore dive for the novices like myself coming through the club system. About 15 divers in total turned up, some experienced, some, like me, completely new to the sport and under instruction. I was paired up with an experienced club diver, Colin Rivers. Colin was a genial, tall, bearded diver, unassuming but very capable.

We got dressed into our wetsuits and rigged up with our dive gear. Colin, knowing that it was my first sea dive, had a good look over my shiny new kit to make sure that I hadn't forgotten anything obvious, like turning my air supply on.

I knew how buoyant my wetsuit was without weights and I wasn't entirely sure how much I should carry in my weight belt to counteract that buoyancy. Sea water is more buoyant than the pool water I had practised in so I knew I would need *some* more – but how much? I was also concerned at what might happen if the seemingly fragile plastic clamp on my weight belt were to fail or be knocked open.

To avoid such a calamity, I thought it would be a good idea to put a half hitch knot in the excess length of my weight belt to secure it to the main section. Colin saw this straight away and patiently explained to me the error of my ways. If he had to recover me from the water and had to get my weight belt off to get me into a boat or onto rocks at shore, he would be hampered as he would not be able to untie the knot quickly. He might have to resort to having to cut the belt off me. The weight belts were designed to be quick release for just such an eventuality, and I was complicating the situation.

13

With my buddy check completed I took a few trial breaths out of my breathing regulator. It was working fine, so, tank on back, mask on forehead, fins in hand and the all-important 'I'm a diver' knife strapped to my leg, I walked with Colin down from the car park to the water's edge over a shingle beach. Large rocky spurs ran out to sea from the beach for some way before disappearing underwater.

We walked into the water up to our chests then pulled our masks over our faces, ducked down, pulled our fins onto our feet and secured the straps over our heels. With trepidation I then let myself fall forward into the caress of the water wondering whether I would sink or float. As it turned out, with air in my ABLJ, I was quite buoyant.

We kicked our legs and snorkelled out from the beach on the surface until we got to a depth of about 20 feet. The sky was a rich summer blue and shimmering bright shafts of light were penetrating down through the water, lighting up a wondrous seascape below of sand, rocks and kelp forests. The north-east of Scotland has very clear seawater and I could easily make out the seabed and rocky spur in great detail.

Giving each other an 'OK' hand signal, I took the snorkel mouthpiece out of my mouth and stuck the breathing regulator 2nd Stage into my mouth. I took hold of the mouthpiece and corrugated hose from my ABLJ and held the mouthpiece up as high as I could. Pressing the dump valve on the end allowed all the air in the ABLJ to escape. The air rushed out and, from having been positively buoyant on the surface, I now became heavier – negatively buoyant.

I sank down, slowly at first but with increasing speed until I landed on the seabed, kicking up a cloud of white sand like a helicopter landing. Colin arrived down beside me gracefully and gestured that I should now get neutral buoyancy back. I took a long draw on my regulator and then took it out of my mouth and inserted the mouthpiece for my ABLJ in its place. Pressing the open/dump valve on it I then exhaled air into it and it puffed up a bit, but I was still too heavy. I replaced my breathing regulator, took another long draw, filling my lungs, and then repeated the laborious process of breathing out and into my ABLJ mouthpiece, giving it a bit more buoyancy. (In the following years this laborious process, something of an art form at the time, was ended when a direct-feed whip was introduced which ran from the 1st Stage straight into the ABLJ. Then, at the touch of a button, air could be bled directly into the ABLJ without having to remove your regulator from your mouth.)

After repeating this process a couple of times, I felt myself lift slightly as I breathed in, and sink slightly as I breathed out. I had achieved neutral buoyancy and it was time to head off on the dive.

Colin had a wrist-mounted dive compass and had taken a bearing for our route from the shore. While sorting out my buoyancy I had ignored my underwater bearings and, not having acquired a compass as yet, had no idea which way to go. Colin checked his compass, got our course and gestured for me to follow. We were off.

We swam over to the rocky spur, which had assumed a totally new perspective. Now there was a wall of rock, which ran all the way from the seabed up to the surface. It was an underwater cliff face and I was at once mesmerised by everything that could be found on it. Crabs and squat lobsters hid in the nooks and crannies. Large fronds of kelp drifted up from their fixings on rocky outcrops. Anemones and sponges competed for space. Large starfish lay on the bottom and fish drifted in and out of my vision. I was completely spellbound and followed Colin as we moved along the seabed beside the wall out into deeper water.

As our depth increased I could sense my surroundings getting a bit darker and could feel the cold of the water more. I realised that, even at this shallow depth, the weight of water above me was compressing my wetsuit, causing it to lose some of its thermal protection. Every now and then as I went deeper I felt the pressure increase in my ears and had to remember to 'pop' my ears, as you do on a plane, to equalise the pressure and relieve the pain.

Once we had swum out for about 20 minutes, Colin paused and took a new bearing on his compass at right angles to our previous path. We then headed off in that direction for five minutes before he reset his compass to take us on a return bearing back to the shore.

I arrived back in shallow water after some 45 minutes inwater and having got to a depth of about 15 metres. I had thoroughly enjoyed my first shore dive and the world of sea diving had been opened up to me.

The following week it was time for another first, my first boat dive. As with my first sea dive I simply had no idea what to expect when I eventually rolled off the side of a dive boat.

We arrived at Portsoy harbour and launched a battered old grey Zodiac inflatable. I watched, as if a spectator, as the old hands readied the boat for sea. Everyone except me seemed to know what had to be done. It was like a ritualistic occult practice. No one seemed to be giving any orders – they all just seemed to *know* somehow what to do, as if following some secret code unknown to me.

There were six divers diving off the boat that day, and all the divers' tanks, weight belts, fins and other gear had to be loaded into the boat as it was tied up alongside the pier. The engine, an old Johnston 35hp, was on tilt, its propeller out of the water.

Once all the kit was in, we jumped aboard. The engine was taken off tilt and the propeller and shaft were lowered down into the water. A few pumps of the fuel bulb and several pulls on the 'pull' start and the engine roared into life in a cloud of blue smoke.

The painter, the bow mooring line, was untied and the Zodiac moved ahead. We motored towards the harbour entrance and, as we did, a gnawing apprehension started to work on me subliminally. I had no idea whether I should be scared – I didn't know what there was to be scared of – but apprehension there definitely was. I suppose it was really just a fear of the unknown that was getting to me. The old hands chatted loudly above the roar of the outboard engine. There was a lot of manly banter. These guys didn't seem apprehensive at all. However, I couldn't help but think that this was a dangerous place to be going. It was one thing to do a dive from the shore. It was something totally different to head out into far deeper water, where there was no prospect of swimming back to shore if things went wrong.

We surged out of the harbour and throttled up. The boat pushed at its bow wave, driving a mass of water before it. We were heavy in the water with all these divers and their kit and the cox got us to clamber forward over the gear bags towards the bow.

The Zodiac got up to about nine knots, pushing at its bow wave. Then it seemed to conquer it and rode up and over. We were on the plane, and immediately our speed leapt up by about 10 knots, to between 15 and 20 knots. The cox then got us to return to our seats on the side tubes near the stern and throttled back as far as possible. He skilfully kept the inflatable boat up on the plane, conserving fuel – maximum speed for minimum fuel.

We roared along, bouncing from wave to wave, battered by wind and spray. With each impact onto a wave I was bounced upwards by the inflatable tube that was my seat. I held on for grim life with both hands to the lifelines along the top of the large grey side tube. At the same time I tried to wedge and secure my feet under heavy pieces of dive gear on the floor.

We headed out until we got into deeper water about a mile offshore. The boat didn't have an echo-sounder – they were not as popular and cheap in those days as they are now – so we didn't know exactly what depth we were going to be diving into.

After the short journey of 10–15 minutes out, the cox throttled back on the outboard tiller. We slowed and then the Zodiac dropped off the plane and wallowed to a halt before the pursuing wake caught up with us. The cox had the anchor ready and threw it over the side. We made an educated guess as to the depth we were in from the amount of anchor rope we paid out.

Once the anchor had snagged on something on the seabed the wind blew us round so that we were head on into the wind and waves. We now started getting kitted up and I soon noticed that the slow wallowing action of the stationary boat started to affect some of the divers – even the hard-looking guys in beards. One was sick over the side and one or two others started going a bit greenish-grey. I felt quite fine and, as if in some coming-of-age ritual, it made me feel as though perhaps I had the bottle for this after all.

My ABLJ went on, then my weight belt, then my air tank and harness, fins and mask. I was soon ready and sitting all kitted up on the tube of the Zodiac. I was to be diving with Colin Rivers again. We sat opposite each other and went through the standard buddy checks on each other's gear.

'Are you ready?' he enquired, staring straight at me.

'Yes,' I said hesitantly. I was on the brink of diving into deep water, and the gnawing apprehension I had felt at the harbour, which I had momentarily forgotten about as people got seasick, came flooding back.

'OK – let's get going,' he said. Slapping his regulator in his mouth and holding it and his facemask in place with one hand, he deftly rolled backwards off one side of the boat. I copied him and did my first back roll off a dive boat, splashing backwards into the water.

As my weighted mass hit the water, the surface erupted in a confusion of bubbles and white froth. Almost immediately the white foam of bubbles from my entry disappeared and I thrashed my legs and arms around to get myself upright from my upside-down entry position.

I looked downwards and was surprised that I could not see the seabed below. There was nothing but empty deep water as far as the eye could see. Below that was a seemingly bottomless, dark, inky void which filled me with foreboding. Was I really going down into that?

Looking around at either side of me, other than the boat I was holding onto there was also nothing that I could see apart from empty water. It struck me that this was something of a tenuous position to be in. I was far from shore clinging to a small inconsequential speck of rubber with an outboard attached to it, preparing to let go of even that meagre modicum of safety to plunge down into the depths.

I kicked my legs and finned to the front of the Zodiac where the anchor line dropped away down below. I looked down the line as far as I could and saw it disappearing into the inky void, seemingly into infinity. This was something totally new to me – I hadn't been in water this deep before and had not expected it to look so . . . well, deep.

Colin looked at me, eyes seemingly bulging through his facemask and gave me the OK question signal. I gave the OK signal back, belying my apprehension, and he then gave the thumbs down sign, the sign to start going down. He dipped his head and raised his feet high, and the weight pressing down helped him duck-dive. He started going down the line effortlessly and casually. I duck-dived and followed him down the line, hand over hand.

I was not to get far down. I had been unnerved by the depth of the water we were in – there was still no sign of the bottom. I then realised that I had not seated my mask properly on my face. The seal, which should clamp onto my skin, was sitting on *top* of a small section of my wetsuit hood, not *under* it. I did not have a watertight seal and so, as I went down, a steady trickle of water entered the mask and it started filling up. I was making the descent in a head down position so the water dribbling into my mask ended up on my faceplate. Everything below, including Colin, seemed to become slightly blurred and indistinct. Then everything swam completely out of focus so that I could not make anything out at all.

I knew that my mask was now almost completely filled with water. I had been trained in the pool how to 'mask clear' in a situation like this, but I was now in an 'incident pit', when one small thing triggers off a series of events and you lose the ability to sort it out. Each incident is manageable on its own but it is the combination of these individual factors that causes problems. A bit more common sense and experience and it would have been simple to resolve. As it was, I couldn't deal mentally with the depth or the mask flood and loss of vision. I was starting to lose it.

I tried a mask-clearing drill by holding the lower part of the mask off my face and blowing through my nose. You can only do that when you are in a 'head up' position, and I soon discovered this the hard way. As I was head down, the air I breathed out trying to clear the water from my mask disappeared, and more water flooded into my mask.

My mask was soon completely filled with water. As I breathed it was going up my nose and making me gag. My eyes were bulging wide open and were completely immersed in water. Why I didn't simply bring my legs and feet beneath me to repeat the drill I don't know.

On the verge of panic, I looked down with my blurred vision. I could barely make out my surroundings. I couldn't read my depth gauge and didn't know what depth I was in. I couldn't tell if I was going up or down and couldn't make out any sign of Colin below me. In the few seconds that it had taken for me to arrest my descent – and shoot from a semi-controlled state into abject terror – he had disappeared from view beneath me into the darkness. I grimly held onto the anchor rope and fought to deal with my mask flood.

In reality I was completely safe, but my novice's inexperience was playing havoc with my common sense. I was in an alien environment and things were going pear-shaped. I now perceived I was in trouble and was teetering on the edge of panic.

My first thought was to try and continue the descent and reach Colin who would now be well below me – out of sight but still holding onto the anchor line. I tried to tough it out and continue down blind but I got some more water up my nose and gagged – I couldn't go on.

I stopped this attempt at a blind descent and started to go back up the anchor line. I moved into a head up position and kicked my legs to start moving upwards. Why I didn't just clear my mask and recommence the descent I don't know. I had lost it and was bailing out whatever. Looking back, the main trigger for all of this was the simple fact that I was thrown by not being able to see the seabed below and not knowing what depth I was going into. That sealed how I behaved.

I reached the surface and my head broke through into daylight. I pulled my mask up and the water flooded out of it. I was back beside the Zodiac and safety. As I talked to the divers in the boat, reassuring them that I was fine, Colin appeared unexpectedly beside me. He swam over to me and asked if I was all right. It turned out that he had got right down to the bottom at 25 metres. When I hadn't appeared beside him he had followed the rules and made his way back up the line slowly.

I had given up on the idea of the dive completely and felt a fool. But Colin was very understanding and persuaded me to have another go. I agreed and we started the descent once again. This time Colin was right beside me, holding onto the strap of my ABLJ.

We pressed down and again I was disturbed at not being able to see the bottom. But then, when we got down to a depth of about 15 metres, it was as though a curtain had been pulled back and we moved through a visibility horizon. One moment I couldn't see the seabed. Next, there was an amazing underwater seascape about 10–20 metres beneath me. The white anchor line led down to the chain and anchor, which were just lying on the seabed.

We dropped down the last ten metres and landed on the seabed. I took time to look all around me at my new surroundings and get my buoyancy sorted out. Then, after an exchange of OK signals we moved off in one direction, swimming along just a few feet above the seabed.

All around me were flat slabs of rock, housing lobsters, edible crabs and lots of conger eels. I had never seen conger eels in the wild before and they hid in their dark bolt holes with their blue-black heads peering out at us, alien visitors in their underwater world. I had heard divers' stories of congers biting off fingers and so gave them a wide berth. At one point I saw a conger in the open, a rare sight during the day, moving over and under a large overhanging rock.

After a bottom time of about 20 minutes down at a depth of 25 metres it was time to start our ascent. My novice diver's inability had almost ruined the dive but Colin's stoic perseverance had saved the day and introduced me to the world of boat diving.

CHAPTER TWO

Learning Curve

'A little learning is a dang'rous thing'
Pope, *An Essay on Criticism*

For the next couple of years after my introduction to the amazing undersea world of Scottish coastal diving I turned up every Sunday for club dives around the north-east coast. My diving skills developed as I explored an underwater fairy-tale land of plunging cliffs, massive subsea canyons, gorges and caves amidst all the rich and varied sea life of Scotland's shores.

I moved down to Stonehaven, some ten miles south of Aberdeen, in 1984 but still kept my links with my dive buddies in the Ellon branch of the BSAC, now some 40 miles north of where I lived. I jointly took a small loan and invested in my own 5-metre orange inflatable dive boat, an Aberglen Gordon with a Johnson 35hp outboard engine.

Sundays consisted of an early wake-up to an alarm clock followed by a scrambled breakfast, before hitching my orange Aberglen onto my orange Renault 14, now rusting fast and covered in brown filler spots. In an orange blaze of polka dot car and boat, I would drive up to Ellon, arriving an hour later at my regular dive buddy Richard Cook's house. Richard was a strong, fair-haired and bearded old hand at the club. Somewhat older than me, he was an active and very capable diver with a great technical knowledge gleaned from working in the diving side of the oil industry for a long time. He knew his stuff and often helped me with my kit when things went wrong.

We would have tea and toast then go on for another 40 minutes up to one of our regular dive sites such as Sandhaven, Rosehearty or Gardenstown. It was this year that I had my first encounter with the somewhat strained relationships between fishermen and divers.

Fishermen at the time had a mindset that divers were diving with the sole purpose of taking lobsters from the sea and from their lobster creels. I was new to the sport and had never taken on the fast claws of a lobster or edible crab. But that didn't matter – I was a diver and that was enough. Some of them barely concealed their animosity.

I soon learned that there was a bit of a history in the north-east between my predecessor divers and fishermen. So much so that in the late '70s and early '80s, before I had started diving, there had been an attempt by locals in one of our now favourite dive spots to prevent divers using the harbour for launching and retrieving their dive boats. The BSAC had successfully taken the harbour trustees to court and got an order allowing divers access to the sea there.

My club soon discovered that the fishing town of Gardenstown, just a few miles to the east of Macduff, was situated in an area where there was little run-off from the land to bring silt down into the sea. Underwater, the sand was clean and white and, as a consequence, the whole area of sea around Gardenstown was truly blessed with fantastic underwater visibility, on average in excess of 20 metres. As a result our dive club found ourselves drawn there regularly for club dives.

I had not fully realised the strained relationship between divers and fishermen at that time – things are a lot better nowadays. But the history soon became clear when we returned to Gardenstown harbour in our dive boats after one dive. As we got changed out of the way at the end of the pier we saw a number of local youths in five or six cars driving along the harbour area towards the breakwater we were on. They then strung a barrier of their cars across the harbour pier, blocking in our cars and causing a bit of a stand-off as we tried to leave the harbour.

On another occasion our club had three boats out to sea from Gardenstown for a dive. As we arrived back at the harbour after the dive and I was jumping out of my Aberglen as we nudged up to the slip, a large splinter exploded off the side of a wooden creel boat tied up alongside. This was followed almost simultaneously by the crack of a rifle report. Our group had been shot at from the steep brae and houses above the harbour.

I reported the matter to the local police in the nearest large town some miles away but found that they were not interested in investigating the incident. No police officer bothered to come to see me about my formal complaint about the rifle shots. Perhaps they agreed we shouldn't be diving there as well.

Gardenstown itself is an idyllic, old fishing village. It is steeped in the sea and originally sprang up as a cluster of fishermen's cottages gathered around a favourable harbour site at the bottom of a steep, long hill, which shielded the houses from southerly and westerly winds. As is common with fisher houses along the north-east coast, many of the houses were built gable end on to the sea. This presented the smallest possible profile to the harsh northerly sea winds, which tried to strip the precious heat from the very stones with which they were built.

For us, as divers, to get down to Gardenstown towing a dive boat, was something of an art form. We had to manoeuvre down a hugely steep road off the main Elgin to Fraserburgh trunk road. This road meanders down through a confusion of old fishermen's houses with a couple of surprisingly tight hairpin turns which, towing a boat, we could only make by the barest of margins by taking a wide swing at it as slowly as possible.

Once down at the harbour we were able to launch our boats and then motor down the coast to the east, along plunging cliffs dotted with a white mass of seabirds, until we found a convenient sheltered cove to anchor in within a stone's throw of the cliffs.

Once kitted up, we would roll over the side of the boat into perfect visibility. It was often possible to see the seabed 20 metres below as soon as you entered the water. I never got over the sensation of weightlessness as I floated suspended in the sea, looking down some distance to the seabed below.

I was always amazed to be able to see other divers exploring far below in the distance. Their columns of brilliant white and silver exhaust bubbles belched and broke into smaller bubbles as they expanded and strained towards the surface.

As they reached the surface the large bubbles erupted in slow languid 'bloops', reminiscent of mud pools, before breaking into a shimmering mass of smaller bubbles and dissipating. Thousands of smaller bubbles accompanied the larger ones, shimmering and fizzing like a bottle of lemonade being opened. On oily, calm days you could hear the same noise if you listened carefully.

This area was rich in sea life and I became acquainted with all sorts of local fauna. I had my first encounter with a dogfish here. It looks like a small shark, about three to four feet long. Unlike most of the other sea life around it didn't seem to see my 6 ft 2 in. frame and that of my dive buddy Richard Cook as an immediate threat warranting flight. This dogfish just lay there on a large flat-topped boulder. Its cold, lifeless eyes looked at me but didn't flicker or show any emotion.

Richard swam up to it and it still didn't move so he put his hand high up at the back of its head and picked the fish up to show me how to handle it. It just remained impassive and unresponsive, waiting for us to tire of it and put it down. After he put it down again it moved off the boulder and with a flick of its long thin tail was gone. He told me later that if it was picked up in the wrong place it could quickly whip its tail around a diver's arm.

Diving around these parts I also came across my first monkfish, a thoroughly evil-looking flat fish which looks like a large naan bread from your local curry house. It has a huge semi-circular mouth, ringed with nasty teeth, that runs like a zip around the wide top of its head at the front. Its two small eyes sit behind, giving it good vision. As a child in Fraserburgh I had heard from fishermen how the jaws of this fish, once it has bitten something, lock fast and hold on – it just doesn't let go. Monkfish amongst a catch of fish were a continual hazard for local fishermen at sea. They would often put their hand randomly into the catch to pull out the next fish for gutting. If there was a monkfish in the pile of caught fish and it was still alive it could snap at them and cause serious damage to their fingers. I gave this one a wide berth, resisting the temptation to prod it with a stalk of kelp lest it come after me.

On another dive we came across an evil-looking wolf fish. This fish, enticingly called rock turbot in speciality seafood restaurants, has a very soft white flesh and is exquisite battered or fried. But in the wild these eel-like fish are blue-black, about five feet long, and have the meanest looking head and set of teeth and jaws you can imagine – designed to crush crabs and sea urchins.

On this same dive we next came across a rather less offensive-looking monkfish lying motionless on the bottom in a sandy clearing between several large boulders, which were covered in the waving fronds of a kelp forest.

My dive buddy on this dive decided to see what this monkfish could do, as it wasn't moving for us either. He pulled out his nine-inch long pencil torch, used for looking into nooks and crannies, and approached the fish menacingly . . . but obviously not menacingly enough to frighten this poor creature – it just stared at him. Emboldened, he got right up close to it and gave it a prod on its snout with his torch. It didn't move – probably hoping we would give up and go away.

Not deterred, my buddy gave the inoffensive and somewhat tolerant monkfish a harder prod on its nose. He had obviously overstepped some unwritten law and gone one prod too far. With blinding speed, the monkfish's inoffensive semi-circular mouth suddenly transformed into a large oval hole and, like lighting, it flicked off the bottom and attacked the offending torch.

The fish tried to take the whole torch into its mouth in one go, getting the whole one- to two-inch diameter width of it a few inches down its throat. However, when it bit down, it encountered, probably for the first time, man-made hard plastics. I expected to see its teeth all fracture and fall out like a *Tom & Jerry* cartoon scene, but even though the attempt to crack the torch in two wasn't a good idea for its dental care regime, it held on and simply wouldn't let go.

My buddy waved his torch about trying to dislodge the fish from the end of it but couldn't. It just hung on for grim life and he did not dare to try using his other hand to prise it off. If it could do this to his torch it could make a nasty job of a finger. Eventually, after a degree of thrashing around, the fish obviously decided that it had done enough to further our diver training on 'things not to touch underwater'. It let go and swam back down to the bottom where it turned round to face us and settled back down. 'You wanna try that again, laddie?' it seemed to be saying. If it was nursing a bad toothache it didn't show. We beat a retreat, Monkfish – 1, Divers – 0.

On another occasion we were swimming in a group of about four divers along the very bottom of some plunging cliffs looking into subsea caves when I saw my first bird flying underwater. This bird flapped its way down my bubble stream from the surface and swam right up to my mask homing in on the source of the bubbles, which it no doubt took for a shimmering feast of small fish. It got a shock when, unexpectedly, it came face to face with a 6 ft 2 in. Scotsman. It did an emergency brake in its flight through the water right in front of my face and stared at me for a second or two, no doubt trying to work out what this big, noisy, unusual visitor to its realm was doing. After working out that there was no food here, and that it may become food itself if it hung around, it beat its wings again and shot off towards the surface.

This bird was something of a vanguard, for as soon as it had disappeared, countless other birds came screaming into the water in quick succession, plunging downwards and speeding through our group leaving a small trail of bubbles to mark their passing – as if someone had been spraying machine gun bullets down through the water towards us.

On a shore dive towards the end of that summer of 1984, I had my first experience of something going wrong underwater. On a hot, lazy, blue summer day we had driven to a car park at a local beauty spot, Cullykhan Bay. This small, picturesque bay, only a few hundred yards across, is surrounded on both sides by high cliffs and jutting headlands. At one time there had been a medieval fort on top of the westmost headland, from which a cannon had been recovered by archaeologists. There was rumour of another cannon lying underwater in the rocks and gullies at the foot of the headland and we had decided to have a dive at the foot of the headland, out at its end, to see if anything was indeed there.

Our small group of six divers drove to a car park high up on the top of the plateau surrounding the small bay, arriving as usual at about 10 a.m. We got dressed into our dive suits in pleasantly warm conditions. The rolling farmland and woodland of the Buchan countryside seemed stunningly green, the water a deep blue. Once fully kitted up, we then walked gingerly and in a rather ungainly manner, weighed down by our heavy gear, along a small path that meandered across the hillside down to the rocky beach.

Once at the bottom we strolled past a few startled holiday makers sending their groups of children into an excited chatter about the 'deep sea divers' that were walking through them en route to what they thought was a terribly exciting adventure. Walking into the water to a depth which supported my body weight I bent down and pulled on my fins. One by one we flopped onto our fronts and started to snorkel out into deeper water, following the side of the cliffs on the west side of the bay.

Once we had got out to a depth of about ten metres and were approaching the end of the headland, we grouped up and then dumped all the air from our ABLJs. I sank slowly towards the bottom, a boulder field and kelp forest which, in the good visibility, I was able easily to see beneath me. Long kelp stalks were anchored to rocks, the fronds at their extremities waving in the gentle current.

As I sank I sensed the familiar increasing pressure on my sinuses but no matter how hard I tried to 'pop' my ears to equalise the pressure, I couldn't. As I dropped down to three metres it became uncomfortable. By five metres down it was sore and I struggled to pop my ears to alleviate the pain.

The pain grew worse and worse as I sank deeper, becoming numbing and intense and filling my forehead inside my skull. I didn't want to hold up the dive and with the 'save face at all costs' arrogance of youth, didn't signal to tell any of the others that I was having difficulty. Eventually we landed on the bottom. The pain was excruciating for me but I still managed to take a compass bearing to head out to the end of the headland where the cannon was rumoured to be.

We set off, heads down, finning out to sea. As we did so, the seabed dropped away and it got slowly deeper. As the depth increased, so did the water pressure – and the pain in my forehead. The pain became the focus of my thoughts, but as I worked down the shelving bottom as the dive progressed, I found that the pain slowly eased. Perhaps, I thought, the effort of finning vigorously had helped clear my ears – or perhaps the increased pressure of air had forced its way through whatever sinus blockage I had.

'Nature always tries to equalise' was a rule taught to me at secondary school. The higher water pressures now working on me had strained to equalise with the lower atmospheric pressure in my nasal cavity. Eventually, somehow, the higher-pressure air had forced its way past the blockage and the pain left me.

We finned forward, winding our way through the large boulders. Here and there we encountered large kelp forests blocking our way. The large ten-foot-long fronds at the uppermost ends of the kelp billowed in the gentle current and snagged at everything that protruded from our rigs, wrapping themselves around our knives or our tanks. We swam right down to the bottom of the kelp stalks and found that once you got below the waving fronds and in amongst the stalks, there was plenty of clear space between the stalks to swim through with your chest close down onto the rocks.

Although we searched in and around the large boulders and potholes at the end of the headland, we didn't find the fabled cannon. Eventually we turned and made our way back into the bay and headed towards the shore. As I moved back up into slightly shallower water the pain in my sinuses returned. This time it seemed that the air in my sinuses was at a higher pressure than the water pressure around me. It wanted to get out to equalise but couldn't because of the same blockage that had caused the trouble on the way down. It was exactly the opposite situation from the descent.

Once we got back into a depth of about ten metres, the dive leader decided that the group would surface, check where we were and snorkel back the last part to the shore. Rising straight up slowly from the seabed, the pain suddenly got so intense that I almost bit my mouthpiece off. In my silent agony I screamed into my mouthpiece.

As I slowly approached the surface, the pain suddenly disappeared in a palpable rush of air inside my sinuses. I felt as though my forehead was emptying of all its contents, including my brain. I felt light-headed at first and then I felt a wet, clammy sensation on my face inside my mask. There were lots of strange effects competing for my attention inside my head but the main problem, the intense pain, had gone. By the time I hit the surface however I was feeling distinctly dizzy and a little queasy.

The head of my buddy diver appeared beside me, water cascading from his wetsuit hood. He looked at me and immediately I registered concern in his face. Pulling his regulator out of his mouth he said casually, 'Your mask's full of blood, Rod. Are you OK?'

'I'm not sure . . .' I replied, my words hanging in the air as I tried to work out what was happening to me. The pain had gone, and as the time passed on the surface the faintness and dizziness were abating. At least I knew what the strange wet sensation inside my mask was. I had never had my face in a pool of blood before. The wetness of blood had a different, more clinging, oily feeling compared to water.

I lifted both my hands up and taking hold of both sides of my mask I gingerly lifted it off my face breaking the watertight seal. Instantly a pool of blood spilled from it into the water around me spreading outwards in a dark, red-black cloud like the ink of a startled octopus. A shock of panic ran through me as I watched the cloud spreading. This was beyond my limited experience and I didn't know if I was in trouble or not. I didn't feel in any great difficulty now, but the sight of so much of my own blood was disconcerting. I had perhaps a few hundred feet to snorkel back to shore, so even if it was serious, I wasn't in any immediate danger given that there were five other divers around me to assist.

My buddy, who was equally as inexperienced as me, didn't know what was up and called over the dive leader, a veteran diver. He took one look at me and said, 'You had pain going down in your sinuses, right?'

'Yes. As I got deeper it got worse, and then it went away. It's only as I came back up to the surface just now that something went high up inside my nose.'

'Don't worry about it, Rod – you're OK. You've just had some sort of blockage up there. Gas has gone in and got stuck. When you came up at the end of the dive, the air had to get out somehow and Boom! all those psi's had to go somewhere.' He thrust his hands upwards as he opened them, simulating an explosion with great eagerness.

'It's burst its way through some sort of membrane. It's not the end of the world and you ain't gonna die – so get your mask back on and let's get you ashore.' I must have looked unconvinced, or worried, because he then reassured me more sympathetically. 'It's OK, Rod, you're not in trouble.' And right enough, the rest of the snorkel back was easy.

Other than looking a bit white and drained (literally), back on the beach I didn't appear to suffer any other repercussions from the incident. But I had felt another of those surges of panic, the sort that shoots through you when something goes wrong and you don't know how to handle it – a gnawing fear that turns your stomach and makes you feel almost physically sick. It is a sensation that most divers will feel at some stage of their career.

In October that year I had my first dive on a shipwreck – not a Hollywood-style intact wreck, but more a mangled, flattened field of debris with two huge boilers standing proud in it.

Slains Castle, just north of Cruden Bay is known as being the inspiration for Bram Stoker's legendary tale of Dracula. Its now ruined, but imposing, remains sit right on the edge of sheer cliffs that plunge down for about a hundred feet to rocks and the sea. Several people have lost their lives on these cliffs – they are extremely dangerous.

Some of the more experienced club divers knew that there was a wreck smashed up hard in at the rocks right below the castle's remains. I was told that there was a rather perilous way down the cliffs to the rocks below, from the grassy area beside the castle where visitors park.

So, for our next club dive we agreed to meet at the car park – as ever at 10 a.m. At the dive site I parked my car alongside the others, who had arrived before me. I asked how we were to get down to the sea and someone beckoned me towards the sheer cliffs. I strolled over and had a look down. The sea surged and washed over a number of rocky spurs and ledges before draining away to reveal wet, seaweed-covered rocks plunging down into the sea. The main cliffs, down which we were apparently going to climb, looked seriously steep and I could see no obvious way down. Nevertheless I got kitted up into wetsuit, ABLJ and weights and slung my air tank onto my back.

Once we were all ready, clutching fins and torch in one hand, we all walked over towards the cliffs. This was going to be interesting.

I followed along behind the group as we meandered over to an almost imperceptible small gully that ran steeply down from the cliff edge. Here, cut in the rock, were rather precarious-looking roughly hewn steps over the difficult areas. One by one we started slowly down the solid but undulating rock of the track. I scrambled down the steep path, sometimes leaning so far back to keep my balance that I was holding myself off the rocks with my trailing hand. At other times I was almost sitting on the rock as I went down. We made our way down the 100-foot cliffs in this ungainly fashion but as we neared the bottom, the track became less steep and I could walk more easily. At the bottom, the track opened out onto a large tabletop slab of solid rock where there was a large rectangular hole, some 15 feet across and about 5 feet deep cut into the rocky shelf.

'That's the old castle pool for keeping lobsters and crabs in – nothing like fresh lobster' piped up one of the old hands.

So that was it – a hundred years or more ago some poor souls had been delegated by their superiors to cut these solid steps down the precarious cliffs and hack out a pool from the solid rock, just to keep shellfish fresh for the guests at the castle. Ingenious – and very functional. I tried to imagine the scene, my thoughts in black and white like an old picture. Castle servants in white granddad shirts with black waistcoats and caps bashing away at the solid rock to enlarge and shape what was probably partly an original feature.

We moved past the lobster pool and were soon standing at the side of the rocky shelf. From here there was a straight drop down some four or five feet to the deep water of a gully. The visibility looked quite good – I could see some large rocks under the surface sticking outwards.

Fully kitted, a diver is very heavy. I was going to have to make sure that I picked an entry point where I could leap far enough outwards to clear these submerged rocks. Looking around, I spotted a large rock further along that just protruded from the water, right at the bottom of the shelf. This would be my exit point and would allow me to clamber from there out of the water and back up onto the shelf where I was standing.

My dive buddy and I were ready. He moved up to the edge of the shelf and had a good look down. Clutching his mask to his face with one hand, his torch in the other, he strode and half-leapt well out from the edge, clearing the submerged rocks and splashing down heavily into the water. The sea seemed to part to swallow him up before closing over him with a large white splash. A second or two later his head popped up again and rolling onto his back he kicked his fins and moved away from my entry point, keeping an eye on me.

Heart pounding, I moved up to the edge and held my mask to my face. I looked down once to check where in the water I was aiming to land, and then raised my head to look at the horizon. I had heard of faceplates cracking on stride entries if a diver was staring straight downwards. The glass took the force of the impact with the water and sometimes yielded to it.

Striding outwards strongly and pushing off with my trailing leg I was suddenly airborne. The combined weight of my dive kit and myself took me downwards like a Disney ride and I splashed into the sea in an explosion of white water and bubbles. As the foam of my entry dissipated, I looked downwards and saw the seabed at the bottom of the gully running off out to seaward. I looked back at my buddy and he signalled for us to dive so down we went. I followed him as we meandered out along the bottom of the gully before we cleared a large rocky shelf and the seabed dropped away deeper.

As we moved deeper, I started to see some mangled bits of ship debris. Some rotted plates were lying in the sand alongside a pile of anchor chain. As we moved further out the debris got thicker and more crowded. Very soon the whole seabed was covered in the debris of a ship's demise.

The seabed was an almost uniform litter of flattened bits of ship. Sections of ship's side plating, beams and struts lay all around, sometimes partly covered by rippled sandbanks driven there by winter storms. Then in the distance appeared two large black circles, some five metres high. As we approached them I saw that they were boilers, about seven metres in length. I swam around them trying to work out how they had functioned in life. All around them were the remains of an engine room. Large steam pipes competed for space with mangled bits of catwalks and other unidentifiable pieces of machinery. And all around in the nooks and crannies provided by this mass of bent and buckled steel, the seabed teemed with all manner of crabs, lobsters and the occasional conger eel.

I was also surprised to find several golf balls in varying states of decay amongst the debris. Cruden Bay, a small coastal village a few miles down the coast, has a very fine and well-respected championship golf course, which I had played, right down at the seaside. These golf balls had been lost years ago and had been driven here along the sandy seabed by the current, before they had become trapped in the wreckage.

Once the dive was over we retraced our steps back through the mangled mess of steel and I was very impressed at my dive buddy's precision in difficult surroundings in being able to navigate straight back to the same gully where we had entered. When we had struggled back up the steep path cut in the cliffs to the cars high above us, we all chatted about the wreck. This had been my first taste of wreck diving and although there was no recognisable ship shape left to the vessel, the submerged devastation had been fascinating. I tried to envisage the awesome power of winter easterly storms that could reduce a large ship to pieces no larger than a dining-room table. I enquired if anyone knew the name of the vessel, but no one did.

In the coming weeks I read up on a few publications about shipwrecks in the north of Scotland. In an old dive magazine I came across an article on shipwrecks around these shores. Interestingly, there was brief mention of the SS *Chicago*, which had run aground right beneath Slains Castle. She was a large vessel and the more I read the more I realised that this was surely the identity of our wreck. This was my first experience of amateur wreck detective work and soon I was regaling the club with the identity of the wreck and the story of its sinking.

Just identifying the wreck and learning its story had brought it to life for me. No longer was it a mangled pile of junk on the seabed. I could tell where the vessel had been built and by whom. But the most intriguing aspect of all was the tale of how this vessel came to lie at the foot of Slains Castle.

The SS *Chicago* had been a Sunderland-registered schooner-rigged steamship owned by the Neptune Steam Navigation Company. She had sailed on 9 October 1894 from her homeport of Sunderland, bound for Baltimore with a small general cargo of 130 tons. She had safely run up the east coast of England and then moved past the Firth of Forth and on to Dundee and the River Tay. Moving further north, Aberdeen had passed by on her port beam. Shortly after midnight she had passed by Cruden Bay and the feared Cruden Skerries, a very dangerous collection of rocks and reefs, already a graveyard for many a ship.

A stiff southerly wind was blowing, helping her northerly progress. The second officer, who was on watch, saw an unidentified light ahead and called for the captain to come to the bridge. Suddenly they realised that they were heading for rocks and the shore. The engines were put full astern – but it was too late. Her momentum and the southerly winds contrived to drive her onto the rocks right beneath the castle.

Her three forward holds were punctured and she stuck fast on a submerged rock ledge. Her engines were run astern for two hours to see if she could be pulled off the rocks and saved, but all the time, the once-friendly southerly wind contrived to become her enemy, working against her engines, on her hull and masts to pin her on the shelf. Eventually the crew was taken off by the local Rocket Brigade, watched by a large audience of those who had been attending a servants' ball in the castle but who found this compelling drama far more entertaining. The *Chicago* became a complete write-off.

I had found something new in diving. I found this combination of wreck diving, research and acquisition of knowledge irresistible, and I soon found myself being drawn towards further wreck dives. Little did I know how this passion would develop.

CHAPTER THREE

Kyle of Lochalsh and HMS *Port Napier*

'And make your chronicle as rich with praise,
As is the ooze and bottom of the sea,
With sunken wreck and sumless treasures'
Shakespeare, *Henry V*

Later that same year, 1984, as a veteran (well, in my own mind at least!) of some 25 dives, I booked myself onto the Ellon BSAC weekend dive trip to Kyle of Lochalsh on the west coast of Scotland. I was keen to dive my first proper shipwreck, something that looked like the Hollywood version of a shipwreck.

At dive club meetings I had heard much talk of the wreck of the *Port Napier* at Kyle. Kyle is a small coastal town, the gateway from mainland Scotland to the romantic Isle of Skye. It is only about half a mile across Loch Alsh to the Isle of Skye. Looking across to Skye from Kyle, the dark brooding mountains of the Cuillin Hills, famous amongst mountaineers, dominate the lower lands around. At this time, Skye was only reachable by the local ferry – now, of course, it is served by the controversial Skye Bridge.

The plan was to dive the relatively intact wreck of the Second World War mine layer, HMS *Port Napier*, twice on the Saturday, stay overnight and dive another location twice on the Sunday. We would then head back home to the east coast of Scotland. This would involve a five-hour drive across the whole width of Scotland, directly after work on a dark November Friday night.

The club had booked into a small cluster of about five wooden log chalets at Duirinish, a sleepy hamlet through which sheep wander freely. Some of the cottages still have the old-fashioned corrugated tin roofs. It lies a couple of miles from the small town of Plockton, along a narrow road with passing places.

Plockton, which is about ten miles from Kyle, is perhaps one of the most picturesque villages in Scotland, famous for its palm trees, warm waters and coral beaches, a product of the warming Gulf Stream that runs along the west coast of Scotland. Plockton consists mainly of several rows of houses and a couple of hotels which are strung along a pretty, small sea loch – and boasts its very own small island just 200 yards off the main sea frontage. This island dries out at low water allowing locals, tourists and the local free-range Highland cows to walk out to it and explore.

I left work at 5 p.m. on the Friday night and quickly loaded my dive gear into my rapidly disintegrating, patched up, rusted and now-not-so-bright-orange Renault 14. This now boasted a front nearside wing in purple, which I had recovered from a scrap car dealer and fitted myself, along with racing-style bonnet catches. The bonnet front and its usual fixings had all rotted away and the bonnet was in danger of flying up in windy conditions.

I set off for Kyle on my own in the dark. The miles sped by and in the darkness I became inured to the constant trail of headlamps coming the other way as I crossed the busy contraflow section of road from Aberdeen to Inverness. Once past Inverness, I drove down the road that meanders along the shores of Loch Ness and the haunting ruins of Urquhart Castle passed by me as a ghostly silhouette in the darkness. Soon I had turned off onto the road through Kintail to the west coast, and Kyle.

I had never spent time on the extreme west coast of Scotland before and had no idea what to expect after Loch Ness. The contraflow road soon gave way to a single-track Highland road with passing places. As it was well into the evening, the road was quiet and I could see the lights of occasional approaching cars miles ahead in the dark distance.

I moved quickly and smoothly through the twisting forested section before the forest ended and I was in the open valleys and lands of Kintail. In the darkness I had no idea of the beauty and majesty of the mountains that were now flashing by me. The limit of my world was the dim cocoon of light around me from the dashboard instruments, and the brilliant beams of light from my headlamps.

Kyle soon approached and I took the turning off to the north, to Plockton. Ten minutes later I was completely lost in pitch darkness amongst heather-covered hills. The single-track roads I was following meandered all over the place in the ten miles between Plockton and Kyle. They were poorly signposted, presumably intentionally to confuse German paratroopers – and the odd visiting diver. I reached several unsignposted junctions where the road split. It was potluck.

It turned out that the chalets were off the beaten track, down a small tree-shrouded and unsignposted entrance, itself off a small road, which in turn led off from the single-track road that linked Kyle to Plockton.

Eventually, after circling the area several times and ruling out all of the possibilities one by one, I drove down a small road, over a cattle grid and turned down the small entranceway to the Duirinish chalets and over another cattle grid. The small cluster of chalets was at last revealed in the glare of my headlamps. Here and there light spilled from windows running with condensation. Cars and grey rubber Zodiac dive boats on trailers were clustered around a few of them.

In the darkness I was drawn to the welcoming chinks of light escaping past drawn curtains. I parked the car, took out my dry gear bag and a sleeping bag and jumping up a few slippery wooden steps, opened the door of one of the chalets. I was immediately enveloped by a hubbub of conversation and activity. After five hours of darkness in my car the harsh glare of fluorescent strip lights assaulted my eyes as if someone had just switched on a set of football stadium floodlights. A kettle was coming to the boil on one of the units and the smell of brewed tea, toast and peanut butter hung in the air. I made myself a welcome cup of tea and sat down to chat to the rest of my club members. There was an excited animation to the conversation, common to any sort of expedition, mainly centred on planning the next day's diving.

The dive marshals for the trip had scheduled two dives, both on HMS *Port Napier*, the first at about 9 a.m. The maximum depth for the dive, the depth to the seabed, was about 20 metres. In keeping with the BSAC recommendations of the time for repeat diving, there would then be a six-hour decompression surface interval, before the second dive of the day, later in the afternoon.

In anticipation of the trip I had avidly read all the information I could gather on the wreck. *Port Napier* was a huge mine-laying vessel, some 550-feet long and weighing in at 9,600 tons. On the night of 27 November 1940, she had been berthed at the railhead at Kyle, just a few hundred yards from where we would be launching. At that time, Kyle, with its deep water and easy access to the Inner Sound and out to the Minch, the Hebrides and Northern Isles, was a significant naval base. Kyle was also the railway head, the end of the railway line that snaked here from Inverness. The harbour was deep enough to accommodate large vessels of *Port Napier*'s size.

For days her crew had laboured hard, loading her with 550 mines that had arrived by rail. They were carefully passed down through the small loading hatch in the deck near the stern. From there, the crew ran the mines along narrow-gauge railways inside the vessel, which ran her full length and connected her six cavernous holds where the mines would be stored.

The railway lines ended at the very stern where there were four mine-laying doors cut in the hull. The mines, on their trolleys, were simply pushed out of the large doors. Each trolley was very heavy and immediately sank quickly. The buoyant mine was secured to the trolley by a long chain and cable, which had been cut to exactly the right length for the waters it was to be deployed in. The buoyant mine would be anchored to its trolley about 30 feet beneath the surface, deep enough not to be wasted on small vessels, but at a depth where it would be struck by larger, more precious ships with a bigger cargo.

The loading operation had gone smoothly at first but then someone spotted that a fire had broken out aboard her. At first, frantic attempts were made to extinguish the flames, but without success. Despite the efforts of the firefighters the flames spread remorselessly and it soon became apparent to those aboard that the fire could not be controlled.

The intensity of the fire grew and grew, as did the realisation that if the fires reached her cargo of 550 mines there would be a cataclysmic explosion which would destroy *Port Napier* – and which would also flatten Kyle. The priority now became moving the burning vessel as far away from the town as possible. The fire could not be extinguished and would be left to run its full course. Only time would tell how this drama would unfold.

The red glow from the flames grew in intensity, lighting up the darkness of the night sky. Many of the residents of Kyle noticed the fire and general commotion down at the pier, and congregated at the dock curious to see what was going on. As they pressed forward to watch the fire, not knowing the danger they were in, they had to be held back by the local police.

In order to protect the inhabitants and buildings of the town, frantic arrangements were made for Kyle to be evacuated. HMS *Port Napier* was cast loose from her moorings and towed away from the town by another naval vessel. Initially, of necessity, she was towed in the direction of the small village of Kyleakin on the other side of Loch Alsh, on Skye. Hurried plans were made for Kyleakin to be evacuated and for the inhabitants of Portree, Skye's main town, 30 miles to the north, to take in the evacuees.

Whilst under tow, the fires continued to intensify and eventually in Loch na Beiste, a small bay about a mile south-east of Kyleakin and well away from habitation, the burning vessel was let loose and cast adrift. Shortly afterwards, there was a flash that lit up the night sky momentarily, followed by a loud explosion which resonated around the nearby hills of Skye. Part of the central superstructure was blown off the vessel several hundred feet in the air and all the way to the shores of Skye about 300 yards away. The superstructure landed on the beach, complete with one gun-mounting and a bath. Some of the fragments ended halfway up the hill beyond, where they still sit among the trees today. Surprisingly, despite the magnitude of the explosion, none of the mines detonated even though *Port Napier*'s midships area was badly mangled by the explosion.

She rapidly flooded with water and started to keel over onto her starboard side as she sank. The sea consumed her and she came to rest on her starboard side in about 20 metres of water, complete with her entire cargo of newly loaded mines. *Port Napier*'s beam was 68 feet, which meant that her port side showed above the water at most states of the tide.

That night, because of some German bombing over Ayrshire, some 200 miles to the south, a strict security blackout was imposed to keep the loss secret. As a result, nothing appeared in any local or national newspapers. As with many other sea losses in both world wars, rumours of sabotage were rife, and the security blackout probably fuelled these rumours. In the absence of any official explanation people speculated wildly about what had happened and these rumours became more and more exaggerated as they passed around.

After the war had ended, thoughts turned to lifting the dangerous cargo of mines. In 1950, the Royal Navy decided to clear the mines but things moved slowly. It took until 1955 before a Royal Navy salvage team from HMS *Barglow* started working on her, removing the entire upmost port side plating of her hull and exposing her inner ribs, bulkheads and double bottom. By opening up her innards, Royal Navy clearance divers were able to rig up a lifting system and lift the mines vertically from the bowels of the wreck to the surface between each of the decks. In all, 526 mines were removed and 16 had to be detonated *in situ* for safety reasons. The Admiralty was never sure of the exact number of mines aboard her and there had been rumours within the diving community for years that you could still see the 'missing mines' in deep, hidden recesses of the wreck.

We talked long into the night until I found a bunk, uncurled my sleeping bag and wriggled in. I lay in the darkness of the cold room, facing the heavily varnished wood logs of the cabin wall, wondering what it would be like to dive a shipwreck for the first time. Gradually, I drifted off into sleep's warm embrace.

Within what seemed like just a few minutes of going to bed, alarm clocks were going off all over the place – it was 7 a.m. and time to rise. The six sleepy inhabitants of my chalet roused themselves and, peering out through single-glazed windows running with condensation, we were greeted by a typical west-coast morning: chillingly cold, with a clinging damp grey mist that cast a veil of secrecy over anything more than 50 feet away. I looked at the Zodiac parked on its trailer outside and saw large droplets of water forming from the mist and running down the large grey side tubes. The two dives we planned were going to be interesting in these conditions.

I hopped out of bed as a delicious aroma of coffee and bacon wafted over the cabin – a smell that has become synonymous with dive expeditions for me. I pulled on some thick clothes and ventured into the lounge which was a hive of activity, with everyone trying to cram in as much food as they could. Very soon I had a bowl of cereal down me and was munching on a bacon roll. Bacon rolls never taste as good as they do on a cold morning, somewhere remote, on a dive trip.

Soon, it was time to get going and we all loaded ourselves and our kit into cars. Engines roared into life, shattering the silence of the heavily wooded surroundings. Fan heaters were switched up to maximum to dispel the clinging dankness and condensation on windscreens. The two cars towing Zodiacs went off first, followed by a succession of other cars in convoy.

We meandered along the narrow single-track roads, which were deathly quiet at that time of the morning. I started to notice the magnificent scenery through which I had blindly blundered the night before. As we headed to Kyle, on our right-hand side, the azure waters of Loch Alsh as it opened into the Inner Sound were dotted by small islands so typical of west-coast scenery. Across Loch Alsh, I could see the shores of Skye, a name I had only ever seen written in childhood adventure books recounting the romantic and daring deeds of the 1745 Jacobite rebellion. In the distance the majestic mountains of the Cuillin Hills on Skye reared up, black, foreboding and ominous, with a seemingly perpetual cloud system hovering over them.

Our procession snaked its way to the outskirts of Kyle, the old hands leading us down to the ferry slip, where the cars towing boats turned around and then reversed down the slip until the sterns of the two Zodiacs were almost at the water line. This slip used to serve the old ferry but had fallen into disuse when the larger roll on/roll off ferry had come into service, with the new large concrete landing ramp that was created for it. The two boat drivers jumped out of their cars and deftly started stripping off lighting boards and securing straps, readying the boats for sea.

The other divers, including me, busied ourselves, getting air tanks, weights and heavy gear out of the cars and ferrying it all down to the edge of the slip, where the Zodiacs were to be tied up once launched. In what seemed like just a few minutes the boats were ready and the boat coxes were getting into their wetsuits – seemingly able to prep a boat for sea and yet still be ahead of me getting rigged up in their own dive kit.

Very soon a cluster of divers rigged in wetsuits, and some in the new hotly debated drysuits, stood around both Zodiacs as the drivers reversed their cars down the slip towards the water. The trailers were reversed into the water right up to their axles, their wheels part submerged. Attendant divers then pulled the Zodiacs, floating them easily off the trailers, and moving them around to the side of the slip where they were tied off.

The remaining divers started loading their gear into the two boats as the cars surged forward, pulling the trailers behind in a white wash of water at the trailer wheels, out of harm's way to leave the slip clear.

As we waited at the slip for the coxes to return, we talked excitedly about the *Port Napier*. She lies on her starboard side in about 20 metres of water (msw) just 300 yards offshore from an uninhabited part of Skye, facing towards the Scottish mainland. It is only a short ride of some ten minutes out from Kyle in a dive boat.

With such a large, substantially intact wreck lying in relatively shallow water so close to mainland Scotland she has become one of Scotland's most popular wreck sites, drawing thousands of divers to her slowly rotting remains each year. She is regarded as a safe wreck dive, because of the relatively shallow depth and also because the Royal Navy obligingly removed her uppermost port-side hull plating during the mine-recovery operation. If divers penetrate into her interior down at depth and something goes wrong they can rise up to a clear surface inside her – instead of being trapped inside. Additionally, the open side of her hull lets lots of ambient light penetrate down into her innards, lighting up her inner recesses which would otherwise be cocooned in eternal darkness. She is many a diver's first taste of wreck diving, as well as my first taste of a relatively intact wreck. While I listened to the divers' tales my imagination ran riot as to what it would be like.

I was soon snapped out of this reverie by the return of the two coxes. I was to be in Richard Cook's boat today. He showed me where I should stash my gear and where I should sit and then went on to organise all the other kit coming aboard and to allocate spaces for the other divers to sit to keep the boat balanced up and trim. Once both boats and their human cargo of divers were ready for sea the mooring ropes were cast off. The two Zodiacs powered up and roared out from Kyle harbour across towards Skye, pushing at their bow waves before riding up on top of them and onto the plane. I watched as we flashed at full speed past two small rocky islands. Richard shouted over the roar of the outboard that there was a smashed up wreck in between.

The strip of water here that divides Skye from the mainland, Loch Alsh, is only about half a mile wide and is protected by high land on both sides so it can be a very settled piece of water. Today, in the early stillness of a crisp November morning, the water shone and glistened like a millpond, the foaming, white wash of our wakes cutting an ever-increasing V shape as it rippled and spread out unceasingly from our stern across the oily surface of the water.

We continued on our way to Skye, turning slightly to head towards the south. Soon, in the distance, I could see what looked like a long line of rocks sticking out of the water dead ahead of us.

'That's the *Port Napier* over there,' said one of the old hands over the roar of the outboard. 'It looks like a pile of rocks but what you're really seeing is the kelp- and barnacle-covered ribs of her hull sticking up.'

'Look at the shore,' said another, eager to share the knowledge with me. 'Can you see the large square sections of rusted metal at the water's edge? That's the deck-housing off her – it blew there when she exploded. Look further up the hill behind – yeah, up there. See the large grey overhead electricity pylon? If you look carefully at the bottom of it you'll see some more of the deck-housing. That's the furthest it went – it must have been a helluva bang!' he laughed as he spread his hands out recreating the explosion manually. My mind boggled at the enormity of the explosive force that must have been needed to propel a section of steel deck-housing that big over such a distance.

As our Zodiac closed on the dark, kelp-covered line of rocks I was told was the *Port Napier*, a few sea birds lifted off its ribs, screaming at our intrusion into their domain. Richard took the Zodiac down off the plane and deftly let the boats' momentum carry us up to a small white buoy that bobbed in the water some way from the wreck itself. As we glided up to it he untied the bow painter rope from one of the side tube grablines, deftly snared the white buoy and tied off to it. The other Zodiac nudged to a stop beside us. 'The buoy here is tied off about 30 feet along the foremast,' explained one of the divers who had dived her before. 'The mast still sticks right out from the hull about halfway down the deck – that's ten metres down to it – and another ten metres down from there to the seabed.'

There were to be two waves of divers going in from our boat today. The first wave would dive, leaving those diving in the second wave in the Zodiac to give boat cover. Once the first wave of divers were back in the boat, the second wave of divers would go in.

I was by now extremely eager to get in the water but found that most of the old hands indicated that they wanted to dive in the second wave. Too late, it dawned on me that they would be able to sit warm and dry throughout the first wave's dive. The first wave, the wave I was told I was to be in, would get back into the boat and then have to shiver through the long wait whilst the second wave went in. Being wet, with a November wind slicing effortlessly through my wetsuit, would soon have the cold gnawing at my bones. There's no substitute for experience.

I had already learned to take a waterproof out to sea on boat dives, to slip over my wetsuit to lessen the wind chill. Although no one dives in wetsuits these days, then they were the prevailing way to dive. They worked quite well in shallow Scottish waters. Once above water however, the layer of water trapped between wetsuit and skin, which is what keeps the diver warm, drains down into your boots and robs the wetsuit of its thermal qualities. A cold wind seems to slice right through you.

I was to be diving in a threesome that day with the experienced Richard and one other diver, slightly more experienced than me. Sitting on the side tube of the Zodiac I popped my Fenzy ABLJ horse collar over my head and clipped off the two fixing straps. I pulled on my weight belt, fastened the quick release clasp, pulled up my integral wetsuit hood and slipped my mask onto my forehead.

Picking up my single air tank I hefted its black rubber-encased bottom onto the large grey Zodiac side tube. Holding it steady, I squatted down almost onto my knees, got my arms under the shoulder harnesses and stood up and tied the waist fastener around me, letting the tank sit securely and snugly. Sitting down on the tube again, I rested the tank on the grey tube, letting it take the weight whilst I pulled on my black rubber Jet fins. Finally I was ready to dive.

My two dive buddies for the morning were also just about ready. With a few minutes' grace, I turned round and studied the buoy and followed the line as it plunged beneath the water down towards the foremast of the wreck. The visibility looked quite good, as I could see a long way down the line from here above the surface, but there was no sign of the foremast itself.

The ominous clouds over Skye to the west seemed to be getting larger and slowly moving our way. There was a darkness which promised rain – or even snow – later in the day.

My two companions signalled that they were ready, and we did a quick buddy check on each other's rigs to make sure that there had not been a stupid omission, like forgetting to switch open the pillar valve on an air tank. Everything was in order and we all rolled simultaneously off the two sides of the Zodiac into the dark water.

As the first explosion of white water and bubbles from my entry disappeared I looked downwards and saw my legs and black fins suspended above an inky void. There was no sign of any wreck at all. I got myself into a prone position and kicked my legs, the Jet fins propelling me easily up to the bow where the painter was tied off to the white buoy. Once I got there I could see the buoy line leading below and, at the limit of my vision, I could make out a blurred shape, which turned out to be the foremast down at a depth of about ten metres.

The three of us clustered around the down line and after a round of OK signals the dive started. I dumped some air out of my ABLJ and duck-dived, getting my head well down and my feet high above me out of the water. The weight high up sent me moving downwards and as my fins slipped beneath the water, I kicked my legs and moved further down, keeping a wary hand on the down line. Very soon the foremast materialised out of the gloom, covered with marine growth, with swathes of long kelp fronds attached to it. Some of the original cross rigging hung about in places, providing footholds for sea life to begin colonisation.

I moved onto the foremast and looked horizontally along it towards the wreck itself. It was only barely discernible at this distance. All I could see of it was a sinister, black silhouette, a dark shape that rose right up to the surface. I followed the foremast horizontally towards the now vertical main deck of the wreck. As I moved along the mast, the blurred image of the wreck seemed to loom out of the gloom ahead. Suddenly, as I came within the horizon of underwater visibility, everything swam sharply into focus.

A large section of the shipwreck was laid out before me and I could see that the foremast rose out of a small deck-house which had three rooms side by side in it and an aft-facing door into each room. Now this was interesting – what was inside? I moved over to the door of the first room and, switching on the powerful beam of my dive torch, swept the interior of the room. The uppermost and rearmost walls were covered in all sorts of old-fashioned electrical switches, junctions and white Bakelite fittings. I learned later that this was the switch room. The bottom of the room was filled with silt, shale and all sorts of shell life. There was so much to see in just this one small room that I almost forgot that there was the rest of the 550-foot wreck to explore.

Richard was the dive-leader for our group and beckoned for us to follow him. We kicked our fins and moved slowly forward, past the foremast to the open expanse of the foredeck holds, which had been covered over when she was converted to a mine-layer. Wooden deck planking was still visible, something I had not expected.

As we moved forward the lower of two side-by-side four-inch deck guns came into view, its huge barrel still pointing defiantly dead ahead. I had never seen a wartime big gun like this underwater before and I was able to drift around it and get a feel for its dimensions.

Looking upwards, I could see the silhouette of the uppermost four-inch gun, but it lies in much shallower water, nearer the surface where the kelp is thick and strong, so it was partially obscured by a carpet of kelp fronds.

Just forward of the four-inch guns, anchor chains rose out of a chain locker below decks and ran to an anchor winch, before snaking off in great suspended loops to the anchor hawse pipes. Beyond the hawse pipes, the hull started to sweep together and narrow as we headed to the very tip of the bow itself. At the bow I kicked out and moved away from the wreck, before turning round to look at the whole bow section of this massive vessel, lying on its side. The sharp stem looked as though it was still ready to slice through the waves. Even to my untrained eye she looked a fast vessel, well-designed for the open sea and mine-laying.

The stem gave way to the lower starboard side of her hull, which swept down towards the bottom. This was the first time I realised that the visibility here was so good that I could see the seabed, ten metres below me. I hung there, suspended and motionless, for a minute or so just taking in this spectacle and enjoying the sensation of weightlessness and the feeling of being so small and insignificant beside the imposing majesty and scale of this huge shipwreck. I saw too that the starboard side anchor chain was run out through its hawse pipe and looped away down to the seabed below. The seabed was covered with a carpet of scallop and razor shells, no longer inhabited.

On the seabed all around was the debris field, which is always found beside a shipwreck – the casualties of a ship slowly rotting and falling to pieces in the depths. Sections of the ship's plating, spars and pipes lay scattered about on the seabed. Cables, pieces of deck gear and remnants of handrails added to the mess. The wreck itself was well covered in a ghostly carpet of sponges, anemones and the soft coral called 'dead man's fingers' by divers because of the white, bulbous, skin-like look of its clumps. They look exactly like a dead man's fingers would look after long immersion.

Richard motioned to me to come back towards him and he led us downwards, following the sweep of the starboard side of the deck until we were just a metre or two off the seabed. We moved back along the ship, retracing the way we had passed earlier, higher up the wreck. I saw the silhouette of the lower four-inch gun pass overhead and then we were back at the small deck-house where the dive had started, a seeming eternity ago. I looked at my dive watch and found that we were only ten minutes into the dive. We were planning a run time of about 45 minutes so we had a lot of time left to explore. I was exhilarated by the dive so far. What else would this fantastic wreck reveal to me?

We finned around the deck-house and moved over the covered-over remains of another hold until we arrived at a flat wall of a far larger deck-house – this was clearly the main bridge and midships superstructure. Richard moved on downwards towards a small hole just above the seabed which looked as though a diver could pass into it, although it would be a tight squeeze. It appeared that he was going to lead us in. The thrilling prospect of going inside my first intact wreck was overwhelming.

Without hesitating, Richard moved through the hole and was gone into the blackness. I knew he was pretty familiar with the wreck and guessed he had been through here before, so we kicked our legs and followed him into the darkness.

Once inside I swept my torch around and found that I was in a walkway, one of which used to run along either side of this superstructure. Below me was the seabed and the ever-present carpet of shells. Above me was the flat seaward-facing starboard side of the superstructure, dotted with portholes. It didn't even occur to me to consider the enormous weight of metal that was now sitting above me.

About 100 feet ahead of me I could see that the walkway ended. A large rectangular opening was a brilliant green glare of clear, open water. I could see Richard's silhouette, framed in the bright rectangle ahead of me, finning slowly and carefully as he moved forward along the walkway tunnel. As I kicked after him I discovered a doorway above my head. Now this was interesting, but to venture inside would be serious wreck penetration, for which I was not equipped. As dive leader, Richard would be expecting me to follow him, and would not take kindly to turning round and finding that I had disappeared without warning into the very bowels of the wreck.

I decided to just have a quick peek, and popped my head in through the doorway and shone my torch around. It was a large room, the bottom of which was carpeted in a fine grey silt. Above me, another doorway led off somewhere deeper into the wreck enticing me to explore further, but caution overcame the urge to explore inside. I dropped back down into the corridor-like walkway and finned quickly after Richard. I caught up with him just as the three of us emerged from the gloomy corridor into open water again.

Below me, on the seabed, was a large flat section of metal, which ran out from the deck-house and was studded with rivets. As I looked at it, trying to work out from its size what it must have been, it suddenly dawned on me that this was the massive funnel of the 550-foot-long ship. When she sank, it would have jutted out of the deck-house. Made of lightweight steel to keep weight down, the funnel would soon have rotted and collapsed to the seabed, crumpled and flattened.

Exploring further I came across a small rectangular opening set in the hull. In full exploration mode, I swam into this opening and found that I was inside a room or space, which went down below the level of the seabed. There was little of interest in here, but as I turned to ascend towards the bright light of the entranceway, now above me, I saw that there were a few antique-looking medicine bottles, still part-filled but buoyant from the air inside them. The bottles with their mysterious contents seemed to dance in the invisible current of disturbed water from my passing. I wondered when these bottles had floated free to be trapped against the roof – had they been suspended here since the Second World War?

After leaving this room we pressed further aft. Here we came across another, far larger opening into the hull. All three of us swam inside together and moved into the wreck itself, heading astern. In the distance I could see a small, bright green rectangular opening and bright green free water outside.

In front of me were the rails of a narrow-gauge railway now set one above the other in this on-its-side world. I realised that we were in one of the four fabled railway lines for the mine trolleys that ran through the entire length of the ship, connecting all the holds throughout it together.

We must have swum for about 100 feet along this corridor in complete darkness, following the rails as they led us astern. As we did, the bright green patch of open seawater at the end of the line got larger and larger. Before long we were popping out of the corridor cut in the rounded stern of the ship itself. The exits for the three other corridors were all open for inspection here, one of which had guide ropes rigged in it by some serious wreckies.

Richard led us up into shallower water and then guided us back along the length of the ship, passing a devastated area where the wreck lost its ship shape. This was where the explosion had taken place. Very soon we were back at the foremast and moving out along it to find the buoy line to ascend. Once back on the surface I checked my dive watch. The dive time had been 45 minutes, and in that time we had completely circumnavigated the whole 550-foot long wreck. That was a big swim indeed in our heavy cumbersome gear.

As my head broke the surface beside the dive boat, I took off my air tank and willing hands in the Zodiac, eager to get in the water, hauled it inboard. Unclipping my weight belt I held it up and it too was grabbed and taken into the boat. Grabbing hold of the life lines running along the tube top of the Zodiac I kicked my feet and propelled myself upwards, getting my chest onto the tube like a beached whale. In a rather ungainly fashion, I rolled into the Zodiac and pulled off my mask. The three of us sprang into excited chatter about what we had seen and where we had been.

The warm water slowly drained from my wetsuit and I started to feel the wind chill. Reaching into my gear bag, I pulled out a long cagoule and got that on to get the wind off me. A mug of hot tea was thrust into my hands, which shivered and shook with the cold as the hot tea burned my numbed lips.

This had been my first wreck dive proper and it had been a formative experience. I was turned on there and then to a branch of diving, wreck diving, which would last me throughout my whole diving career without ever ebbing. The thrill of exploring a relic of a time gone by, preserved underwater and hidden from general view, was amazing.

The second wave of divers splashed into the water and the three of us sat and chatted the next hour away, oblivious to the cold until the other divers returned and we could make the short dash back across the loch to Kyle. There, I stripped off my wetsuit on the pier and got into some warm clothes, before a welcome lunch at one of the local cafés. We strolled along to the front of Kyle's main hotel beside the ferry ramp, which has stunning views out across to Skye. There, a wartime mine and trolley system has been preserved and displayed – a fitting reminder of Kyle's importance to the Royal Navy as a mine-laying base for the Western Approaches during the Second World War.

That afternoon, the second dive was on *Port Napier* again. My memories of that dive consist solely of the trouble I had getting on a now freezing, wet wetsuit, in bare feet on the wet tarmac of an open, wind-swept car park above the pier. The wind had picked up since the morning and the promised rain had materialised. The old hands, used to this form of sadomasochism, produced a thermos of hot water, which was poured into my wetsuit before I put it on, easing the initial shock. I struggled vainly to get the wet wetsuit up my legs. A dry wetsuit is far easier to pull on than a wet one and my tight-fitting second skin seemed to have turned into a version of superglue inside.

Whilst wreck diving was it for me from now on, I was realising the limitations of diving in a wetsuit in Scotland. Although it was the prevailing way of diving, the new breed of drysuits was just hitting the shops and promised warmth both underwater and in dive boats. Until then, a few people had used old black rubber Nato Avon suits which were usually very easily holed and had to be held together by Isoflex patches.

Drysuits were being very heavily criticised by the establishment at the time; the diving magazines were full of articles about how dangerous they were and how 'real' divers would never use them. There was one headline I remember well: 'Throw the drybaggers out of the BSAC'. But right now, standing soaked and cold on a windswept car park on the west coast of Scotland in what seemed like sub-zero temperatures, in the driving rain, it seemed the way to go.

As the dive boats arrived back at the slip at Kyle after the afternoon dive, it was already starting to get dark. The trailers were backed down the slip and each boat was pulled onto its part-submerged trailer and strapped down before the car drove forward. Wetsuits were gleefully pulled off and warm clothes pulled on. Lukewarm tea from thermos flasks was passed around before we loaded up the cars once more and snaked our way back to the Duirinish chalets.

Back at our base, we all piled into our chalets and started cooking up all manner of food in the kitchens. Outside, the air compressor we used for filling air tanks, which we had towed from Ellon, was fired up and empty tanks were put in line to be filled one after the other. Whilst this was going on someone, amid the cacophony of sounds, piped up: 'Anyone fancy a night dive?'

All sound in the chalet stopped at that. A night dive was something rarely done on our native east coast because of the distance of getting to the coast combined with the difficulties of getting access to the sea. There were often rocks that were difficult to clamber over in the darkness, fully laden with tanks and weights, as well as the difficulty of finding an exit point and getting back ashore. That, coupled with strong local currents, which could sweep divers a long way away very quickly, all prevailed against local night diving.

'OK,' the omniscient voice said, brightly, 'so we're all cold and wet. But we are all here, as is our kit. The slip at the pier would be a great entry point for a shore dive. We could then swim round to the left following the built-up side of the roadway towards the harbour. There will be light around from street lamps and we'd know to keep the land on our left side as we go out. Then to come back, we turn around, until everything is on our right hand side, and just come back. Easy enough.'

The prospect of pulling on a cold, wet wetsuit for the third time that day didn't appeal to many of the divers but three of them thought it was a good idea. Intrigued – I'd never done a night dive before – I volunteered to go as well.

By about 8 p.m. we had finished a DIY dinner and cleared up. The four of us loaded our kit into a couple of cars and headed down to Kyle once again. A couple of others came for the life experience and to give shore cover. If we got into trouble or got carried away we could signal to them with our torches and they would know to put a rescue into effect.

Back down at the slip at Kyle, every brick and nuance of which I was now becoming intimately familiar with, we once again parked in the darkness of the car park, half lit by the orange glow of a solitary streetlamp. The afternoon wind and rain squall had given way to the stillness of a west coast evening, with a steady drizzle that fell vertically from the darkness above. Beyond the cocoon of light from the street lamp it was black all around. Across Loch Alsh we could see the orange lights of the small village of Kyleakin, the other side of the ferry route.

I walked down the slip to the water's edge and looked in. The water was still, the oily surface dappled almost mesmerically by the light drizzle. The water was black as the darkest night, but still seemed as though it would be clear enough once we were in.

Once the four of us were rigged, we all walked down to the end of the slip along with the two non-divers doing surface cover. I looked at my newly acquired Suunto wrist compass and took a bearing along the heavily built-up embankment that ran off towards the distant harbour. I wanted to know which way I was heading out so that if we got disorientated in the darkness I'd know which way I had to go to get back.

We would dive in two buddy pairs, but keep together in a loose foursome grouping. We ran through a few underwater torch signals. Divers normally communicate by hand signals during daylight. At night there are signals that can be made to each other with the torches. For example, the easiest way of giving another diver the OK signal is to get the torch behind your hand and silhouette your signal to the other diver with the torch. Alternatively, sweeping your torch round in a large 'O' signals that you are OK.

Once we had agreed our signals, I turned round and shuffled backwards and flopped into the water. The shocking cold trickle of water down my back sent a shiver through my body. One by one, the other divers flopped into the water beside me. I rolled over onto my front and looked down, not knowing what to expect. Of course, the water was pitch black and I couldn't even see my own feet. I pulled up my dive torch and switched on the beam. A powerful light sabre shattered the darkness, glaringly lighting up everything in the foreground and stretching away more dimly for about 15 feet. Outside this ribbon of light was a seemingly impenetrable barrier of darkness.

The others switched on their torches and three more light sabres danced around. I was still head down on the surface of the water at this time so I lifted my head and had one last look at the lie of the land to orientate myself. Dropping my face back down in the water I kicked my fins to propel me along towards the end of the slip.

Once I got there, the slip stopped abruptly and dropped straight down for another six or so feet. We all duck-dived here and made our way down to the bottom. It was a novel sensation for me to be diving in complete darkness, not able to see my companions. I could only see their torch beams dancing around, seemingly emanating from nowhere.

I reached the bottom at about five metres and we swam along, keeping the embankment on our left. The water got deeper and deeper shelving off slowly until we got into about 15 metres. As we moved along, we came across a point that obviously was, or had been, used as an unofficial dumping ground. All sorts of debris lay around, including a selection of emblazoned crockery plates from one of the local hotels. We tried using these as underwater Frisbees for a while until the novelty wore off.

We moved on along the embankment and about ten minutes into the dive the embankment gave way to a proper harbour wall. My torch lit up large square sandstone blocks roughly cemented together many years ago, with most of the cement having fallen out or turned to dust long ago. At one point I swept my torch upwards along the harbour wall that was passing by on my left-hand side. Two enormous conger eels were sticking half out of their holes in between the blocks. These eels are about 3–6 feet long on average and as wide as the circle formed by a grown man's two hands held apart with fingers and thumbs touching. They are a foreboding blue-black colour with the most cold, lifeless, jet black eyes imaginable.

Thankfully these seeming monsters didn't come out of their holes to investigate us. We swam along beneath these congers but as we continued to swim more of them appeared – the whole place was well stocked with congers.

About 20 minutes into the dive and the harbour wall made a sharp right-angled turn to seaward. As we continued along I swept my torch upwards and was surprised to see the steel hull and large brass propeller of some sort of merchant ship about ten feet away, directly above us. There was no sound of any engine, only the stillness and quiet that you get used to as a diver – a silence only broken by the mechanical sounds of your aqualung and the gurgle of your exhaust bubbles as you exhale.

We collected and closed in on one another. Once we were close enough, we had a silent underwater conversation using light signals and agreed to turn the dive here. We made an about turn until the harbour wall was on our right-hand side and the hull of the large vessel overhead was pointing in the opposite direction. Forty-five minutes into the dive, we arrived back at the slip and broke the water, rising up like silent predators from a swamp.

Once on the safety of the slip I turned and looked across the water towards the harbour and managed to make out an orange freighter tied up against the harbour wall. I was staggered at its distance from us and at how great a distance we had covered in that time. I was shivering again from the cold and dashed to the car to change into warm clothes before heading back to Duirinish. When we were warmed and showered we all piled into a car and headed down the couple of miles to The Plockton Hotel where we met the rest of our expedition and drank far more beer than was good for us.

Sunday morning welcomed us without the mist of the preceding day. Conditions looked better and by 9 a.m. we were back down at the Kyle slip launching the two boats. The Admiralty chart of the area had shown that there was a wreck well up the small Loch na Beiste sea loch, towards the southern side. We thought it would be an idea to have a look for it.

We zipped flat out across Loch Alsh in the two boats, testing one against the other for performance, and darted into Loch na Beiste itself. The other boat had a rudimentary echo-sounder and, rather haphazardly, we went to work scouring up and down the loch for a snag.

'Got something here,' shouted the cox of the other boat excitedly after just a few minutes. Wreck finding couldn't be this easy.

'Depth is about 25 metres to the seabed and it rises up about 5 metres. There's something big down there.'

Whilst we had all sat quietly listening to the most exciting words a diver can hear, as soon as the cox had finished speaking there was an almighty explosion of activity in our boat. We gunned the boat over towards theirs, which was now dropping an anchor down onto the possible wreck and tied off to it.

As we were doing that, we raced to get kitted up into our dive gear, each pair of divers trying to get kitted up as quickly as possible. I was discovering the allure of being the first man down on a new wreck. We had no idea what we were away to dive on – but there was something to explore just waiting for us only 25 metres directly beneath us.

About two minutes later I and my buddy for the day were ready to dive.

We sat opposite each other grinning like Cheshire cats. Sticking regulators in mouths we gave each other an OK signal and rolled backwards off the Zodiac splashing into the still waters. There was no trace of a current here.

Righting myself I started dumping air from my Fenzy ABLJ and looked under the boat. My dive buddy was ahead of me and already making his way down the anchor line, which snaked down into rather murky waters below. I kicked my legs and headed off downwards, diagonally across to intersect with the line and follow him down.

Once I was about 15 metres down, the unmistakable outline of a long thin barge materialised out of the gloom below. The underwater visibility was only about five metres on the bottom but I could see that we were at the stern. There was a three-feet-square open hatch leading below the main deck and I could see the start of a rectangular hold, some 10–15 feet wide, leading off in the distance into the darkness. With the poor visibility the end of the hold was out of sight in the gloom.

Without hesitating, my buddy made a bee line for the open hatch, swept upwards into a standing position and let himself drop down feet first into it, slowly being consumed by the vessel until he was gone from my sight.

I followed over and grabbed the rim of the hatch and looked down. I could see nothing but darkness. I started to fumble with my hand for my torch but as I did so a large cloud of fine, grey silt suddenly started emanating from the hatch followed by my buddy's grinning face. He produced a large, old, aluminium teapot and set it down on the deck. Hardly a collector's item but still, one man's rubbish is another man's treasure, as the saying goes.

We left the teapot there on the deck for posterity and started to move forward towards the hold. As I reached it, I could see that there was a silt-covered cargo heaped in it, the heap rising to a high peak in the middle. Dropping down onto it I landed on my knees and pushed my hand into the heap and felt roughly hewn pieces of stone. I pulled out a piece and as it came towards me, the covering of silt trailed off it like a wake to reveal shiny black coal. We had found a coal barge.

We kicked our feet and moved along the side of the hold, keeping away from the silty cargo, which was also billowing up black coal dust when disturbed. After about 20 or so feet, the hold ended and there was a small strip of decking. Passing over this strip another hold of similar dimensions was found similarly filled with coal. This hold gave way very abruptly to a snub bow.

At the bow we dropped over the side and down onto the seabed. I swept my torch along the gap beneath the sweep of the keel and found this refuge jam-packed with conger eels, a few lobsters, squat lobsters and a host of crabs. In all I estimated that this barge was about 75–90 feet long with a beam of 15–20 feet. (I returned to dive this barge again in 2001 after a gap of some 15 years and found that both holds had been cleared of their cargo of coal very professionally. Hardly a single lump of coal was left in the wreck.)

After the morning dive we rendezvoused back at the Kyle slip for a surface interval and an early lunch. The morning dive had been fantastic and I thought that I had had all the excitement that would be coming my way that weekend. However, whilst standing on the slip sipping tea, one of our divers, who worked in the oil industry, mentioned that he had been involved in the laying of a power cable across Loch Alsh from Kyle to Skye. The cable had come ashore on the remote northmost rocky corner of Loch na Beiste about half a mile from where we had dived in the morning.

Once the cable was laid, he told us, it had become clear that the cable had been snagged on some underwater obstruction. A Remotely Operated Vehicle (ROV) had been sent down to check out the obstruction and it had found that the cable had been laid right over an old wreck just 50–100 metres off the rocks in about 15 metres of water. Wreck fever gripped us again and we agreed to have a go at locating this new wreck and diving it in the afternoon. If we couldn't find it we could just enjoy a pleasant shallow dive to wrap up what had been a stunning weekend.

Once again our two Zodiacs were loaded up with kit and divers and were zipping across Loch Alsh. When we got to the rocky promontory, the route of the cable was clearly marked by a large yellow Power Cable Marker sign erected on the rocks. We rounded the point into a sheltered spot of water and dropped our anchors about 25 feet off the rocks.

Dropping over the side, I was immediately in about ten metres of water and my dive buddy and I let ourselves sink slowly to the bottom. Getting a compass bearing out into deeper water we started finning down a slowly shelving seabed, covered in shells and large rocks.

Gradually I began to see evidence of several ships having been moored in this area as the seabed became increasingly littered with all manner of bottles, crockery and rubbish that appeared to date back to the Second World War. I realised that this was an ideal place, a sheltered spot protected from northerly and westerly winds, the prevailing winds for this area. Perhaps that would explain why a wreck lay on the bottom in this exact location amidst this sort of debris.

My dive partner and I moved slowly down the shelving slope for a hundred feet or so. As we did, my eyes strained through my faceplate for the looming ghostly silhouette of a wreck to materialise out of the gloom down the slope. As the minutes went by and nothing appeared, I started to think that we had missed it. However, almost imperceptibly at first, I started to see that the way ahead of me was darker. About 25 feet down the slope, at the periphery of my visual field, there was an ominous, dark-looking shape, much like a black cloud. As I moved towards it the shape got darker and more solid until finally the looming presence of a wreck materialised out of the gloom. It was thrilling that our initial excitement had not been misplaced.

We kicked our fins and careered down the slope towards the wreck, which was clearly of a sizeable vessel and was sitting on an even keel. Its side seemed to rise upwards for about five metres. As we arrived at the bottom of the keel, I found that, where the hull ran underneath the vessel towards the keel, there was a small gap between it and the seabed, similar to the barge we had dived on earlier. All manner of startled sea creatures peered out at us, unusual intruders to their realm. Here and there a ling, an odd eel-like, sand-coloured fish with a hook of skin beneath its bottom lip, tucked itself away. A few conger eels were also dotted about amongst less threatening edible crabs, lobsters and the smaller squat lobsters.

The steel hull itself was very box-like, well-corroded and covered in marine growth. The vessel had been down here a long time. We kicked our fins and moved up. As we reached the top of the side of the hull, the gunwale, we were at a depth of about ten metres. Moving over the side of the hull onto the deck, there were a few feet of deck space before a large open cargo hold, which beckoned me inside. Pushing myself forward from the rim of the hatch I moved out into open water in the middle of the hatch opening, and started to drop down into the hold. I wanted to find out what, if any, cargo this vessel had been carrying. I soon landed on what turned out to be a flat, silty but unyielding hold bottom. The hold was disappointingly empty – but as I kicked to move forward, a small Queenie scallop, a clam-shaped shell about three inches across, opened and snapped shut, propelling itself upwards from the silt into the water in front of me. It continued to open and close as it made off comically like an outsized pair of false teeth. As it did so, a cloud of perhaps ten or twenty Queenies in turn rose up from the silt in a confusion of opening and closing false teeth as they tried to make good their escape.

We swam down the inside of the hull passing from one hold to the next through what would once have been a bulkhead, but which was now largely corroded away. We arrived abruptly at the furthermost end of the next hold. This was a solid wall of steel and we couldn't go any further. We kicked our fins and moved up out of the holds and onto the deck. Here I found that, other than a small deck winch and a hatch down into some storage spaces, there was precious little deck space before the sides of the vessel swept round to a very blunt bow. With no prop at the other end of the hull, and no superstructure at all, it was now clear that this was a small barge we had been diving, some 95 feet long with a beam of approximately 25 feet. Not the greatest of shipwrecks – but still exciting, and another wreck for my logbook.

Back in our boats we chatted about what we had found and promptly christened the unknown barge the *Power Cable Barge* because of the large armoured power cable that lay right over and across the wreck amidships. To this day this wreck is still known amongst divers simply as the *Power Cable Barge*.

The weekend's diving finished, we made our way back across the loch to Kyle to retrieve the boats, stack the cars and head off for the long five-hour drive back to the east coast. The world of wreck diving and the thrill of finding and diving virgin wrecks had been revealed to me. I would no longer be content shore-diving on reefs and rocks. The wrecks themselves were full of interest and challenges – and attracted more sea life than elsewhere. I would now focus on wreck diving – and I vowed after the cold of this weekend to get myself one of the new drysuits. I had just grown out of Scottish wetsuit diving.

CHAPTER FOUR

Circles Within Circles

'BOND-LIKE BOAT CHASE'

Sunday Post, 15 June 1986

From my initial training in 1982 onwards, I had been spending progressively more time out at sea, diving. Other than a panic attack on my first deep boat dive and a few other minor mishaps, I had not managed to get myself into any particularly dangerous or life-threatening situations. That was about to change in a way that would have been comical – had it not been so deadly serious. Curiously, the incident was in no way connected to diving.

Since purchasing my Aberglen Gordon five-metre inflatable dive boat in 1984, I had learned quickly how to handle it, how to launch and retrieve it, how to drop divers in the right place and how to recover them safely from the water. But, with hindsight, my sea craft was still in its infancy and I had had no formal training. None is legally required in the UK, although the Royal Yachting Association does offer very good courses.

I bought a pair of second-hand wooden waterskis and soon found that learning to waterski was hard work, but exhilarating. At first I spent a lot of time floating in the water, being pulled up eventually to last upright for only a second or two, before crashing back down into the water in an explosion of froth and foam.

The theory was simple enough. Float in a sitting position, knees up at chest and get the tips of the skis out of the water. The boat should circle, towing the waterski rope, which would gradually close in. The rope could be flicked over a ski until it was in a comfortable central position between the skis. The boat would move forward slowly until the slack was taken up, then a lusty cry of 'Hit it!' was the signal for the cox to gun the throttle. The boat would surge through the water, pulling at the skier. The effect of the skis pushing against the oncoming water would start to raise the skier out of the water.

Once I got to this point, I would push down hard with my legs, thrusting upwards and lifting my body into a standing position. More often than not however, this standing position lasted for only a few seconds before I leant back and fell in, or fell forward, or fell to the side, or pulled the rope handle too close to me, losing speed before wiping out in a white explosion of spray. Evolution is a slow process, as the saying goes, but eventually my style did evolve and I began to master the art of staying upright.

Before long I could stay upright indefinitely and started learning how to turn way out to one side before swinging backwards across the wake of the boat, sometimes getting airborne as I took off from the wake. Emboldened, I then tried monoskiing. I found it impossible to get up on just one ski, and even though I tried getting up on both skis before kicking one off, as soon as I was on one ski, the water would inexplicably rise up to engulf me. But at least I had mastered two skis.

On a sunny Saturday morning, 14 June 1986, I telephoned my friend and former flatmate Derek Sangster, who had expressed an interest in getting out to try learning to waterski. We arranged to meet down at Stonehaven harbour around 12 p.m. My wife Claire and Derek's girlfriend Eileen decided to come down to the harbour to do a bit of sunbathing on the sand, in the shelter of the harbour wall. As Derek and I launched the boat, Claire went into the Ship Inn and came out with a couple of drinks for the girls.

Once we had my Aberglen launched, as we slowly motored out of the harbour to sea, I ran over the procedure with Derek. I agreed with him that I would drive the boat first to let him have a go at skiing, and then after that, he could do a bit of driving for me in the boat. Once we got about half a mile to a mile offshore, I took the boat down off the plane and we slowed to a halt. Derek was in a full wetsuit. He slipped into the water and got into the start position.

I motored round him and played out the waterski rope. Once he had grabbed it I took up the slack – until the rope was taut. At his shouted command, I gunned the outboard engine and the boat surged forward. Although he clung on manfully he didn't get up. Of all the times I had taken first-time waterskiers out I had never seen anyone learn to get up and going very quickly.

After a few more attempts, he started to get up and then tried to master the art of staying up. Having found this hard to do myself I realised how tough he would be finding it. Bravely he persevered and after a while was able to stay up for longer and longer periods. After about 45 minutes of this rather arduous work he signalled that he had had enough. I pulled in the waterski rope and came alongside him. He pulled off the skis and handed them up to me and then pulled himself up over the tube into the boat.

The wind by now had picked up a bit, and there was a bit of a swell to the sea. But I still thought I could ski in the conditions and, pulling on the skis, slipped over the side. Derek motored round me perfectly, just as I had told him. The rope closed in and as it came past me I grabbed hold of it and he slowly took up the slack. I flipped the rope over one ski and got myself into the start position: skis upright, arms outstretched and rope between the skis.

Once I was ready I looked up and saw Derek standing up at the stern of the boat looking at me, waiting until I was ready. He had one hand on the tiller throttle of the engine. I looked at my skis and shouted out 'Hit it!' I heard the engine roar and I was pulled forward, but not with enough torque to get up. I was dragged through the water in a mass of white water for a second or two. My arms felt as though they were being pulled right out of their sockets and I realised I wasn't going to get up on this occasion. I let go of the ski rope handle and sank down into the water.

Once the motion subsided I looked up to see what had happened and saw the boat careering off to one side and there was no sign of Derek. My God, I thought, what has happened? Where is Derek? Has he slipped and fallen?

I stared fixedly at my boat, which had now started going round in circles. It seemed to be flat out. It was going so fast that it was bouncing off small waves almost to the point of getting airborne. I watched as it seemed to come full circle and start towards me. As it came to its closest point I could clearly see that the boat was empty. The tiller was hard over, which was what was causing it to go round in circles. The throttle on my Johnston 35hp outboard stayed open at the point you throttled up to, to avoid having to hold the throttle open on long journeys the whole time.

As the boat came past me, there was at first a feeling of disbelief – denial even – that this was really happening to me. As the boat bounced and sped past me I suddenly saw Derek in the water, head up and gesticulating at me. I couldn't hear his cries for the noise of the outboard.

We started swimming towards each other. In my full wetsuit with wetsuit boots on, it was hard to make any distance at all on my front. I flopped over onto my back and sculled over to him. As I did so, I looked towards the distant shore. We were an awful long way offshore and I felt that there was no way I could swim it in the restrictive 7mm wetsuit.

As I reached Derek, I was relieved to learn that he was not hurt. He told me that he had been standing at the engine, and when I had shouted, 'Hit it!' he had opened the throttle fully. The engine had been more powerful than he had expected and as the boat had surged forward he had been flung over the top of the engine and into the water.

As he explained I realised that he was not wearing his wetsuit top and had only the long johns on. His upper chest and arms were bare. Whilst I was in the water getting ready he had taken off his wetsuit jacket as he was hot. Although this was the middle of the summer, it was still the North Sea, and the water was icy cold to the touch.

'I'm getting cold,' he said. 'I'm going to have to swim for the shore.' With his arms unencumbered by a wetsuit he would be able to crawl on his front.

'I can't swim it in this wetsuit, Derek,' I replied. 'I'll have to wait here. When you get ashore get help as quickly as you can.'

Derek, thankfully, was a very strong swimmer and he struck off in a crawl towards the shore. Later, he would recount that as he headed towards the shore a wind surfer had come up to him. He had asked for help but the surfer had said he couldn't help and just sped off into the distance.

With Derek a receding figure I looked around me. In the distance I could see another white speedboat. I tried yelling as hard as I could and splashing and throwing white water high into the air. But my cries and efforts were futile. They were simply too far off, and my blue wetsuit blended in all too well with the surrounding water. The speedboat soon disappeared towards the harbour. I was left completely alone, far offshore, trying to come to terms with my predicament.

I started to try to think of a solution. The boat was continuing to career round and round in circles not far from me. As I floated there upright in the water I watched the boat. Every now and then it would strike a wave at an awkward angle as it circled and this would change its direction slightly, so the area it was circling was changing over time.

As I watched the boat, it took a big hit on a wave which altered its direction significantly. It suddenly dawned on me that the boat may well now circle fairly close to me. Sure enough, the bow of the boat started to turn towards me and soon the bow was heading right at me. But the boat was continuing to turn and it wasn't going to hit me – this time.

As the boat continued rushing round in its seemingly eternal circle, I saw the waterski rope still trailing out behind it. The rope wasn't particularly long, perhaps about 20–25 ft. The off switch for the outboard was mounted very close to where the rope was attached to the waterski hook – if I could pull myself up the rope I could perhaps get my hand up and switch off the engine.

I know now never to react in the first flush of emotion – it usually isn't wise and can lead to more trouble. If I did nothing I would float out here not coming to any harm until either Derek got ashore and raised help, or the girls realised that we were overdue. Either way, in my 7-mm full diving wetsuit I wasn't going to come to any harm – I could float out there in relative warmth and comfort for 24 hours if need be. The coastguard would know the currents and which way I would be swept. They would know where to look for me.

But that's not how the brain works in moments of crisis. I reached out my hand and grabbed hold of the waterski rope as it whisked past. I thought this might be my one and only chance to get myself out of this situation under my own steam. As soon as I grabbed the rope I realised this was a seriously bad move. The boat was probably only doing 10–15 knots but it was still a high speed to move instantly to from a waterlogged standing start. My arm seemed to stretch out cartoon style as it tried to remove itself from its socket. I had to let go quickly or risk injury.

The boat sped away in another circle, bouncing off waves before turning round and starting to head towards me. This time I felt sure the boat was going to hit me. In my full wetsuit I wasn't able to move with any speed and couldn't get out of its way. With no weight belt on, I was hugely buoyant and couldn't duck-dive beneath the boat. Remorselessly, the bow of the boat got closer and closer, and as it approached the bow was turning towards me all the time. Then it sped past me – so close that I could almost touch it. With each circle the boat had come closer to me and I was now hugely concerned about the next circle.

I kicked my feet and tried to propel myself away from what I guessed would be the next circle of the boat. As I did so I looked up to see the boat moving away into the distance engine roaring but all the time starting to wheel round towards my direction. No matter how hard I kicked my legs, I just didn't seem to move with any speed through the water. I looked up again and was horrified to see the bow of my own boat bearing right down onto me.

In a slightly surreal moment I was fixed on the big square orange section of tubing at the front of the boat, never having seen the boat in this way. But it wasn't the bow I was worried about – it was the stern and the thrashing propeller which could do me an awful lot of harm.

The bow came at me – closer and closer – and as it did, it turned slightly to my left-hand side. I flung my arms up, crossed them in front of my face and kept my hands well out of the water before the port side tube whacked me. I was swept down the port side of the tube. Luckily the boat didn't ride up over me.

Suddenly, my head was in the water. Eyes wide open with fear, I saw the white thrashing of the propeller flash past me in an instant. The propeller missed my torso by about two feet – had it hit me I have no doubt that it would have ripped me to pieces.

The whole thing was over in a second and the boat was away again. Perhaps it hit another wave that changed its course, or perhaps it was hitting me that changed its course, as, although it continued its wild circling, it was now starting to move slowly out to sea and away from me.

I bobbed in the water helplessly as my boat started to get smaller and smaller and moved well away from me.

I don't know how long I floated in the water for – it seemed to be forever but was in reality probably only half an hour or so. There was no one else out on the sea and I had resigned myself to a long float before any rescue.

Eventually, as I turned to look forlornly at the distant shore, suddenly my spirits jumped from utter dejection to utter elation. For there, charging out of the harbour was the large bow and white bow wash of one of the Maritime Rescue International training vessels, one of several fast rescue vessels that were used for training out of Stonehaven harbour.

As the boat sped over nearer the shore, I realised that they were getting Derek out of the water. Before long the boat was charging over to me and slowing down to let me clamber aboard. We then went over and picked up the waterskis, which were floating not that far away from me.

The skipper of the boat, Hamish McDonald, then had me recount what had happened, and asked some searching questions about the set-up on my boat. He wanted to know how much petrol was left in it – if it was low then he would simply wait until it ran out of fuel and stopped of its own accord.

'It's got a full tank,' I said. 'We've only been out on the water for about an hour – the engine will run all day.'

He then asked about my engine: did it have a long shaft or a short shaft? Did it have a shear pin? I replied that it had a long shaft but that I didn't know if it was fitted with a shear pin or not. He decided to try and lay a rope across the track my boat would take in the hope that we would foul the propeller and the engine would stall, or else the shear pin would disable the engine.

Having agreed the plan of action he throttled up his boat and we raced out to sea, in the direction my boat was headed. Very soon, we were closing in on it as he rigged up a sturdy rope to a large pink Dan Buoy. We motored across the path my boat would take. Hamish threw out the Dan Buoy and attached rope and, as he motored forward, the rope floated up to the surface in a long line stretched across the path of my boat.

My boat came charging round and motored right up to and onto the rope. The rope went taut. We had hooked it all right. However, the rope had caught above the prop and not fouled it or sheared it off. We now had my boat straining to go in one direction like a hooked fish. It wasn't going anywhere against the weight and power of Hamish's far larger boat – but we couldn't do anything with it.

Eventually Hamish cast off the rope and my boat immediately leapt forward and went about its way again. We pulled in the rope and buoy, wondering what to do next.

A large dredger platform had been moored just outside the entrance to the harbour over the course of the preceding week. I now became aware of a small grey Rigid Inflatable Boat (RIB) heading off from it and making a beeline for our position at great speed. They must have seen what had happened and were coming over to have a go at bringing the boat under control.

There were three crew in the RIB, all in boiler suits, peaked caps and steel-capped work boots. They handled their boat well and with ease as it sped past us and headed straight for my boat. As they approached, the cox started to track my boat as it circled. Gradually, after sizing up the situation, he started to edge his RIB closer and closer to my careering inflatable. Before long the RIB was side by side with the boat, tracking it perfectly as it circled. I was hugely impressed by the skill and seamanship shown by the cox, as my boat wasn't taking a true course and was bumping and changing course every now and then. The cox had to react immediately to all these sudden changes in direction but did so as if he had been doing it all his life.

The cox closed in one more time on my boat and one of the crew calmly jumped into it, moved to the stern and killed the engine. It was over.

Hamish took us alongside and I thanked the crew of the RIB. They graciously made light of it and zipped off back to work on the dredger. I jumped back onto my own boat and pulled in the waterski rope. I started the engine again and followed Hamish's boat as we headed back to the harbour at a sedate, safe speed. I had had enough thrills for one day.

Meanwhile, back at the harbour, Claire and Derek's girlfriend had enjoyed a leisurely couple of drinks down on the sand by the slip. It had crossed their minds that Derek and I were taking a long time to come back, but that's not unusual when you go to sea. They were just enjoying the pleasant sunny conditions.

As they sat, glass in hand on the sand, they had watched bemused as the Maritime Rescue International's fast rescue boat powered up, cast off and sped out of the harbour. They watched innocently as an ambulance arrived down at the harbour, followed by a police car. What could all the commotion be about? Their view of the sea was screened by the harbour walls and it never crossed their minds that we could be in trouble. It was only when Derek stepped off the rescue boat back in the harbour, and I arrived back shortly afterwards alone in my boat, that the penny dropped.

I was interviewed by the ambulanceman to make sure I wasn't suffering any adverse effects from my immersion, such as hypothermia. I was then interviewed by a police officer who took my details, for the record. They told me that someone in the small coastal village of Cowie, adjacent to Stonehaven, had spotted our plight and alerted the rescue services.

I also learned later that my predicament had stopped play up on Stonehaven Golf Course, which sits high on the cliffs looking down over

Stonehaven Bay. The golfers had a grandstand view of the events as they unfolded from up there. It was even written up in the *Sunday Post*, as a 'Bond-like boat chase'!

Needless to say, I made a suitable donation to the RNLI in the weeks following as a thank-you token. I had been very impressed by the cool professionalism displayed by Hamish and by the crew from the dredger.

Thankfully no one got hurt but it had been a close thing and I learned a number of invaluable lessons in those short hours on the water. Like everything else in life, you learn your hardest lessons from experience. But I would try to never leave anyone alone in a boat again and I would always have a means of attracting attention to myself in the water. For years afterwards, I dived carrying a small watertight plastic container that held personal distress flares and a launcher.

CHAPTER FIVE

Scapa Flow

'The British Battle Fleet is like the Queen on the chessboard;
it may remain at the base but it still dominates the game'
Lord Chatfield, *Admiral of the Fleet*

As the 1980s progressed, my interest in wreck diving became more intense. The allure, mystique and hidden wonder of wrecks beckoned me into the depths. Almost exclusively I was diving wrecks, and no longer dived for the simple pleasure of floating weightless and exploring the rich marine seascape of Scotland's shores.

In 1984 a friend and I towed my Aberglen Gordon up to Orkney to dive the fabled wrecks of Scapa Flow for a week. These wrecks were in relatively deep water of up to 45 metres. The water was cold and dark, but the massive wrecks lying at the bottom of Scapa Flow were worth the effort. The lure of the German wrecks would bring me back to Scapa Flow each year for many years thereafter.

Scapa Flow itself is a dramatic and windswept expanse of water some 12 miles across, which is almost completely encircled by the islands of Orkney. To get there from mainland Scotland entails a long drive up to the ferry port of Scrabster, near Thurso. This is followed by a two-hour sea crossing on the P&O ferry (then the *St Ola*), past the rugged sheer cliffs of the island of Hoy, home to the fabled Old Man of Hoy, a 200-metre-high rock pinnacle.

On the land all around Orkney there are poignant reminders of its war-torn past. Long deserted military bases, barracks and gun emplacements bear silent witness to its military history. For centuries Scapa Flow had been a safe, sheltered and heavily defended anchorage for the Royal Navy. Great warships and dramatic deeds are an integral part of that past.

In the First and Second World Wars, the main Atlantic Operations HQ was set up at the naval base of Lyness on Hoy. Today the naval presence is long gone and modern tankers and oil-supply vessels mix with small and large fishing boats in the crowded harbours. But it is what lies beneath the waves of Scapa Flow that makes Orkney a magnet for today's sports divers.

For seven long months from November 1918 the German Imperial Navy's High Seas Fleet, consisting of some 74 warships, had been interned at Scapa Flow as a condition of the Armistice, which had halted the fighting that November. The interned fleet of powerful dreadnoughts was made up of five battlecruisers, eleven battleships, eight cruisers and fifty destroyers. Built up over the preceding 20 years in a naval arms race with Britain, the High Seas Fleet had been created at huge cost to the German nation to challenge the traditional naval supremacy of Britain.

The mighty force of the High Seas Fleet had not been surrendered to the British, nor had it been crushed in any sea battle. The German land forces were facing defeat, and their leaders had pressed for surrender terms with the Allies. The High Seas Fleet, which had not fought against the Royal Navy in any significant fleet action since the Battle of Jutland in 1916, was a pawn in those negotiations. It had survived the war relatively intact and could still pose a significant and potent threat if the Armistice broke down and fighting recommenced. Therefore, as a condition of the Armistice, the Fleet was to be taken into internment and be heavily guarded at Scapa Flow until the Treaty of Versailles determined its fate.

Once the Armistice was called, arrangements were made by the Allies to receive the High Seas Fleet into internment. The entire British Grand Fleet had rendezvoused with the High Seas Fleet in the North Sea to escort it into Scapa Flow, where it was thought the German Fleet could be kept safely under guard. No such sea force had ever been gathered before – a staggering 90,000 men were afloat, on a total of 370 warships.

The British were taking no chances on any German treachery. Their guns were loaded and all crews were at action stations, alertly looking out for any signs of trouble. The British Grand Fleet split into two long lines of battleships, six miles apart and stretching beyond sight into the distance.

The German High Seas Fleet sailed through the passage thus created in single file and was escorted by the British Grand Fleet up to Scapa Flow and into internment. Once in Scapa Flow, the German ships were lined up in neat compact rows, sometimes with up to three or four of the smaller vessels moored to the one buoy.

The warships, although under Allied guard, remained German property. By June 1919, they were manned only by skeleton crews of up to 200 on the larger vessels. The bulk of the 20,000 German sailors who had brought the ships to British waters had been repatriated. There were no British guards aboard the German ships, which were prohibited from flying the German Imperial Navy ensign with its black cross and eagle.

The German sailors had to endure the savage cold of a long Orcadian winter as their ships swung at their moorings. They were not allowed ashore and all their provisions, other than water and coal, had to be sent to them from Germany. The peace negotiations dragged on as the Germans and the Allies made demand and counter-demand. The snows and cold of winter gave way to spring and then in turn to summer. And still the ships swung at their moorings.

Rear Admiral Ludwig von Reuter, in charge of the High Seas Fleet, learned from a four-day-old newspaper given to him by the British that the Armistice was due to end on 21 June 1919. He read that the peace negotiations were in trouble and the newspaper reports indicated that no agreement was likely to be reached. If the peace negotiations broke down then the fighting would start again. Manned by a skeleton crew and with his guns disarmed, his fleet could not defend itself if the British tried to seize it when the Armistice ended.

At 9 a.m. on 21 June, the British battleships of the Grand Fleet sailed out of the Flow with their supporting cruisers and destroyers, leaving only two serviceable destroyers on guard duty. The Armistice had been extended by two days and they were under instructions to be back in the Flow by then to deal with any trouble that might arise should the Armistice not be further extended.

At 10 a.m. von Reuter appeared in full dress uniform on the quarterdeck of his flagship, the cruiser *Emden*. He proudly bore the insignia of his highest decorations around his neck. The Iron Cross and his other medals were pinned to the breast of his frock coat. He studied his ships through a telescope and was advised by one of his staff that the British Fleet had left on exercise earlier that morning. He could hardly believe his luck. He issued an order that the international code flags 'DG' be raised on *Emden*. This alerted officers on the other ships that they should be alert and watch for other orders.

At 10.30 a.m. Rear Admiral von Reuter addressed an attendant signaller, and shortly afterwards a string of command flags appeared over his ship, even although this was well outwith the permitted times for issuing signals. The order read 'PARAGRAPH 11. BESTÄTIGEN.' (Paragraph 11. Confirm.) The prearranged coded order to the commanders of the other ships in the fleet to scuttle had just been given.

The details of the plan to scuttle the fleet had been finalised four days earlier on 17 June with a view to preventing the Allies from seizing the powerful warships. (Unbeknown to Reuter, the Allies had plotted to do just that, as part of their contingency planning months before.)

The signal to scuttle was passed from ship to ship by semaphore and Morse code on signal lamps, and travelled slowly around the fleet. The southernmost ships of the long lines of destroyers were not visible from the

Emden. They had to wait for a full hour until the order reached them. The prearranged formal responses came back, slowly to begin with. The first signal reached *Emden* at about 11.30 a.m., just as the original signal reached the last of the destroyers: 'Paragraph 11 is confirmed.'

In a patriotic gesture of defiance, many of the German ships ran up the Imperial Navy ensign at their sterns. The prohibited white flags with their bold black cross and eagle had not been seen at Scapa Flow before. Others ran up the red flag, the letter 'Z' which in international code signalled: 'Advance on the enemy.'

At 12 p.m. an artist, who had hitched a ride on one of the patrolling British Navy trawlers to sketch the assembled might of the interned German Fleet, noticed that small boats were being lowered down the side of some of the German ships, against British standing orders. Sixteen minutes later the first of the German ships to sink, the *Freidrich der Grosse*, turned turtle and went to the bottom.

The other ships in the Fleet also began to list as the water rushing into their hulls altered their buoyancy. For the last four days, von Reuter's trusted sailors had been opening all the doors and hatches and fixing them in the open position to allow water to flood through the hull more easily. Seacocks were set on a hair turning and lubricated very thoroughly. Large hammers had been placed beside any valves that would allow water to flood in if knocked off.

The sea valves were now opened and disconnected from the upper deck to prevent the British closing them if they boarded a ship before it went down. Sea water pipes were smashed and condensers opened. Bulkhead rivets were prised out. As soon as the valves and seacocks were open, their keys and handles were thrown overboard. They could never be closed again. Once the vessels had started to sink, they could not be saved other than by taking them in tow and beaching them.

Some of the great vessels rolled slowly on to their sides while others went down by the bow or stern first, forcing the other end of the vessel to rise high out of the water. Others sank on an even keel. Some had been moored in shallower water and settled quickly into the cold waters, coming to rest on the seabed with their upper superstructures and masts jutting proudly from the surface of the water.

Blasts of steam, oil and air roared out of the ships' vents and white clouds of vapour billowed up from the sides of the ships. Great anchor chains, run out to moor the ships, snapped with the strain and crashed into the sea or whiplashed against the decks and sides of the ships. The ships groaned and protested as they were subjected to stresses and strains for which they had never been designed.

As each vessel passed from sight a whirlpool was created. Debris swirled around in it, slowly being sucked inwards and eventually, remorselessly, being pulled under into the murky depths. Gradually, oil escaping from the submerged ships spread upwards and outwards to cover the surface of the Flow with a dark film. Scattered across the wide expanse of the Flow were boats, hammocks, lifebelts, chests, matchwood and debris. Hundreds of German sailors abandoned ship into lifeboats.

The British guard force, which had left the Flow that morning on exercise for the first time in the seven long months of internment, learned of the attempted scuttle and turned to charge back to Scapa at full speed. But the first ship would only be able to get back at around 2 p.m. By 4 p.m. when the last British ship had returned, only three German battleships, three light cruisers and a few destroyers were still afloat out of the total interned force of 74 warships. It was – and still is – the single greatest act of maritime suicide the world has ever seen.

At first, the Admiralty resolved to leave the scuttled ships to rust away in the dark depths of Scapa Flow. There was so much scrap metal about after the war that prices were low. By the 1920s, however, the price of scrap metal had picked up and the attentions of entrepreneurial salvagers started to turn to the seemingly inexhaustible supply of finest German scrap metal at the bottom of the Flow.

Over the course of the coming decades the majority of the warships were salvaged, and today, only eight of the original Fleet remain on the seabed waiting to be explored. They are the 26,000-ton battleships, *König*, *Markgraf* and *Kronprinz Wilhelm*, the 5,500-ton light cruisers *Dresden*, *Brummer*, *Cöln* and *Karlsruhe* and the 900-ton destroyer *V 83*.

Over the years many other vessels have also come to grief in Scapa Flow. Steamers and tugs have struck mines. Attacking U-boats have been depth charged and trawlers have succumbed to the fierce northern gales. The scale of human loss in Scapa Flow is huge. Some tragedies took hundreds of young lives together in a single instant.

The 19,560-ton British battleship *Vanguard* was destroyed in one cataclysmic magazine explosion on 9 July 1917 with the loss of more than 700 men.

A U-boat managed to slip past the British defences on 14 October 1939 in the dead of night and torpedo the 29,000-ton British battleship *Royal Oak* at anchor in Scapa Bay. The *Royal Oak* turned turtle and sank within five minutes into thirty metres of water with most of her crew trapped inside her. The torpedo explosions destroyed the power circuits and the whole of the ship below decks was pitched into darkness. Desperately the crew stumbled around in the darkness groping for a way out as the ship heeled over. Flash fires of burning cordite swept around the corridors. In all, 833 officers and men died in that one attack. (These two latter wrecks are war graves and no diving is permitted on them.)

Finally, during both the First and Second World Wars, 'blockships' were sunk in some of the channels leading into the Flow to place immovable and insurmountable barriers in the way of any enemy vessel trying to get into the Flow to attack British shipping.

Today, this concentrated profusion of wrecks in one relatively small area of sea, some 12 miles wide, draws thousands of divers annually to Scapa Flow from all over the UK, Europe and the United States. Diving has become big business in Orkney, and from April to October there are usually 10–15 charter hard boats working the Flow, taking parties of up to 12 divers per boat out to dive the wrecks each day.

The diving at Scapa Flow is relatively deep and exhilarating. The depths to the seabed on any of the main wrecks in air diving range vary from 25–45 metres. But you don't need to go down that far because as the German wrecks are such huge warships, the shallowest point on them usually comes up to between 10–20 metres from the surface.

With such a powerful collection of fabulous wrecks in Orkney, I found the attraction of going there to dive them irresistible. As a result, I found myself waking as my alarm went off at 2 a.m. on a May morning, in time for me to hitch up my boat, load my dive gear and pick up some diver friends in Aberdeen for what I guessed would be a five- or six-hour drive. We would motor across to Inverness then cross the Kessock Bridge and continue right up the north-easternmost coast of Scotland to the ferry port of Scrabster, just a couple of miles to the east of Thurso. I had booked my car and boat on the 12 noon sailing.

The journey was fairly uneventful and after crossing the Kessock Bridge we motored north, following the coastline, sometimes almost beside the sea itself. At other times the roadway winds and climbs up steep hills, over headlands and through majestic Highland scenery of open heather landscapes intermixed with areas of dense forest. As dawn broke we were driving level with the sea. The engine of my beat-up Renault was running sweetly and my boat trailer was towing well. Just as the first rays of the early dawn preceded the orange blaze of sunrise I had Pink Floyd's *Wish You Were Here* as loud as it could go on the stereo. The first slow yet powerful chords of the opening introduction, which seems to last for eternity, hauntingly paralleled the slow arrival of the sun's glowing orb.

The two-hour ferry crossing was amazing. I watched spellbound as the towering cliffs of Hoy passed by on our starboard side, and scrambled for my camera at the first glimpse of the fabled rocky pinnacle of the Old Man of Hoy. Soon the ferry was passing by Burra Sound, a small channel that leads into the Flow itself. As I looked up the channel I was staggered to see the forward section of a wrecked oil tanker from the Second World War jutting out of the sea, its bows sharp and powerful but black with rust, mussels and seaweed.

All too soon, this fleeting glimpse of something special was past and we turned to our starboard side, into the turbulent waters of Hoy Sound before swinging to the north for the run into Stromness. I started to see the first scattered houses lining the shore. The houses here were nearly all constructed of a unique flat stone and all the houses fronting the sheltered water had small slips called *nousts* which ran down to the sea. This was obviously a town steeped in the sea. I overheard a local aboard telling a tourist that the Hudson Bay Whaling Company used to have a base in Orkney and from here, whalers would range out over the North Sea and Atlantic.

Soon, the *St Ola* had berthed and we were on the move again. We had chosen to stay at the Scapa Flow Dive Centre on the small island of South Ronaldsay, just south of Burray on the other (easternmost) side of Orkney, so we were off on another drive of an hour or more. By the time we arrived it was 6 p.m. and I had been either on the road, driving or in the ferry since 2 a.m. that morning.

The eastern side of Orkney is a collection of small islands: Lamb Holm, Glims Holm, Burray and South Ronaldsay. During the First World War, blockships had been sunk in the small tidal channels separating these islands to protect the British Grand Fleet, which was using Scapa Flow as its North Sea and Atlantic base. The Admiralty had thought they had constructed a wall of steel through which no enemy shipping could pass. These blockships, allied with the other serious defences put in place, had earned Scapa Flow the nickname 'Impregnable Scapa Flow'.

However, that name tag was to be proved tragically flawed by the attack on HMS *Royal Oak* in September 1939, just six weeks after the start of the Second World War. Churchill resolved that such an event would never happen again in Orkney and ordered the construction of giant causeways of five-ton concrete blocks to permanently seal off the eastern channels into the Flow.

These causeways now have modern roads atop them and are an invaluable link for locals to pass freely from one island to the next. The drive down the 'Churchill Barriers', as they are now known, is a fabulous and unique drive back in time. On either side as you drive down, the rotting remains of some of the blockships sticking out of the sea. Others lie collapsed or dispersed under the water.

As we drove down the Churchill Barriers to get to South Ronaldsay we stared spellbound as these rotting hulks passed by on either side. The dive centre we were staying at had a fabulous-looking wreck, the *Pontos* sitting just 50–100 feet offshore to the eastern side of Barrier No. 4 which connected Burray to South Ronaldsay and sealed off the channel, Water Sound.

We went out for a walk along the sand dunes that now line the barrier and were able to explore the wreck of the *Carron*. Substantially intact, the

Carron sits close to the barrier itself and her superstructure has been almost engulfed by sand that has been driven against it by winter storms. The wreck now forms part of the beach to the east of the barrier. At low water, her bridge area was dry and we were able to clamber over her remains without getting wet.

At the southern end of the barrier was another blockship wreck, the *Collingdoc*, a 1,780-ton single-screw steamer which for many years saw service as a Great Lakes steamer in Canada, before being taken over by the Admiralty and sunk as a blockship in 1942. Her concrete-lined bridge – a form of inexpensive armour-plating – and her bow were firmly embedded in the sand. At low water at that time, her bows were dry and again we were able to clamber up and inspect her remains. The unrelenting sands have engulfed this wreck in recent years and now only the concrete bridge section remains above the sand.

But it was the *Pontos* that took our breath away. She was a single-screw steamer of 3,265 tons, built in Glasgow in 1891 and registered in Andros, Greece. Formerly known as the *St John City* and then the *Clan McNab*, she was sunk in her present position in 1914. She sat on an even keel with her main deck at sea level. At that time, her main mast still stood proud despite the ravages of 80 years of Atlantic storms. Sadly, the mast collapsed in 1992.

Her hull was structurally complete and we could see lifeboat davits, winches and cranes jutting out of the water. Here was a largely intact wreck sitting just 100-feet offshore, about 300 yards from our dive centre. We decided that as we were so close to such a wreck with all our kit, it would be a pity to waste the opportunity to dive it. It was a simple dive, but to add a bit of spice we decided to wait until it got dark and then do it as a night dive.

At about 9 p.m. we loaded up the Renault with our dive kit and drove up until we were level with the wreck of the *Pontos*. As we strode into the water, I immediately noticed that it was much colder than I had expected. The sun may have been shining all day but the water had still not thrown off its winter chill.

We switched on our dive torches and flopped into the water. Sweeping my torch downwards I saw that the sandy seabed shelved off steeply, down beyond the limit of my torch beam. I popped my head up, took a compass bearing on the wreck and stuck my snorkel in my mouth to save using air from my tank. We kicked our legs and started moving out towards the wreck.

The seabed disappeared almost immediately as it plunged off into the depths. Soon all we could see were the beams of our torches disappearing into nothingness. After a few minutes' finning, the hull of the *Pontos* appeared, covered in seaweed. We dropped down to the bottom at about ten metres and toured round the whole exterior of the wreck. Here and there were openings into the hull itself and before long we were squeezing through these into the wreck's innards. She had been largely gutted but was still an interesting dive in the pitch darkness that now engulfed us.

After about 45 minutes exploring this wreck we exited from her and I took a reciprocal compass bearing to take us back to shore. We were soon back in the warmth of the dive centre, our gear dripping dry in the wet room.

We had decided to dive the next day on the wreck of the 5,531-ton light cruiser *Cöln*, which lies in 35 metres in the centre of Scapa Flow not far from the small rocky island used in history by locals to hide their produce from tax inspectors, the Barrel of Butter.

During the scuttling of the Fleet, the *Cöln* had been moored not far from von Reuter's flagship *Emden*. *Cöln* was one of the first of the vessels to receive the order to scuttle. Once the scuttling had been set in motion *Cöln*'s crew abandoned ship into small boats.

The light cruiser, *Brummer*, was moored nearby. Her crew, in small boats, closed to join company with the crew of the *Cöln*. Sailors on a British drifter nearby fired small arms warning shots, spraying the water around the small boats, forcing them to part in an effort to drive the crews back to their own vessels. Kapitänleutnant Heinemann, in charge of the *Cöln*, ordered his men to take off their caps so that they could not be identified from the name ribbon on them and forcibly put back on their ship with orders to stop the vessel sinking.

A British destroyer came alongside *Cöln* in an attempt to get a boarding party onto her or to tow her into shallow water to beach her. The attempt narrowly escaped tragic consequences. The bow of the *Cöln* started to lift slowly as she settled by the stern and the water rose up to the level of her main deck. Gracefully she rolled over onto her starboard side and went down by the stern – only just missing the British destroyer alongside.

The *Cöln* finally slipped under the waves at 1.50 p.m. on 21 June 1919, some two and a half hours after the order to scuttle had been given by von Reuter. She plunged down through the dark waters of the Flow before impacting onto the seabed and settling on her starboard side. Huge clouds of fine silt were sent billowing upwards from the seabed before gently raining down on her and covering her with a fine film of silt, and the process of colonisation of her by sea life began.

On the surface far above, her crew remained in the open cutter, watching their home of the last seven months disappearing from sight and passing into history. A British drifter took the cutter in tow and the crew was placed under arrest aboard Fremantle's flagship HMS *Revenge* before being eventually repatriated to Germany.

We launched our inflatable dive boat on the slip at Burray and loaded it up with our gear before motoring west along Water Sound as it opens into the wide expanse of Scapa Flow itself. Once we had entered Scapa Flow I was immediately struck by its size and scale and by the fact that all around me was land, often far away in the distance. We were motoring across a seemingly vast expanse of water, some 12 miles across yet completely ringed by land. I could understand how it had been possible for the 74 warships of the German High Seas Fleet to be easily accommodated in this impressive natural harbour.

Nowadays in Scapa Flow, all the main German wrecks are buoyed and easy to locate. But in the 1980s the wrecks were not buoyed and we were going to have to locate the wreck of the *Cöln* the old-fashioned way, by using a sighting compass and taking a bearing from the Barrel of Butter from an Admiralty chart.

We zipped across the Flow, passing across the vast main southern entrance into the Flow, Hoxa Sound. Before long we could see the Barrel of Butter with its small stone-built tower – an unmistakable landmark in the wide expanse of the Flow.

Once we had arrived at the Barrel of Butter we motored around it, disturbing a colony of grey seals which used it as a haul-out site. Taking a bearing from the northern side of the Barrel we motored out on the bearing, slowly heading northwards at about eight knots. I watched the LCD (Liquid Crystal Display) on my echo-sounder and it showed a flat, unchanging bottom at 35 metres. Suddenly the bottom trace on the sounder jumped up to show the depth change in an instant from 35 metres to only 18 metres. We had arrived over the unmistakable 47-foot beam of the wreck of the *Cöln*.

We dropped our anchor and tied the anchor line off to the boat. The still water around the taut anchor line showed that there was absolutely no current here in the Flow. Above us the sun shone, glistening on the oily, still waters. It was a perfect day for diving – but the water still looked dark and foreboding.

We rigged up on the boat and as I got my dive gear ready my mind whipped over the few facts that I had read in anticipation of the dive. The *Cöln* was built in Hamburg in 1916, by Blohm & Voss. She was a sleek, fast and manoeuvrable vessel, 510 feet in length – that's the length of two football pitches. Her control tower, forward of the bridge, was protected by 3.9-inch thick armour-plating. She originally had eight 5.9-inch guns set in single turrets, two side by side forward of her bridge, two set one either side of the bridge superstructure itself, and the remainder towards the stern of the vessel. The depth to the seabed was 35 metres, about 110 feet with the least depth to her upward-facing port side being 18 metres.

This was my first proper dive inside Scapa Flow itself and as soon as I had rolled backwards off the tubes of my inflatable dive boat and righted myself I was able to stare downwards. I couldn't see anything much more than ten metres below me. The anchor rope went almost vertically downwards disappearing out of sight into darkness.

I swam over to the line as my buddy diver splashed into the water at the other side of the boat. We met at the line and after giving each other the usual OK hand signal he gave the thumbs down signal – it was time to dive.

Dumping air from my buoyant ABLJ, I started to sink downwards, my eyes straining into the gloom for the first sign of this leviathan of the deep, hidden from sight since the final chapter of the First World War, some 70 years earlier.

As I dropped down through the water I was amazed at how still it was. There was absolutely no current at all. It was so different from diving in the sea around the Aberdeenshire coast.

As I passed the ten-metre down mark, the dark gloominess beneath me seemed to change. The uniform blackness gave way to a brown colour and straight lines started to form, running off into the distance to either side of me. Very soon the immense, silt-covered port side of the hull of the *Cöln* just materialised out of the gloom. One minute it was outwith the limit of vision, the next the whole thing was laid out in front of me.

As I had dropped downward towards the wreck I had been in a head-down position. Now, as I neared the wreck, I dropped my feet down and slowed my descent so that I landed feet first on the hull. The hull now, far from being shrouded in darkness, appeared to be bathed in sunlight from above. I could see in excess of 50 feet in either direction and this wonderful visibility allowed me to take in large sections of the hull.

As I looked to my right towards the stern I saw rows of portholes, their glass and brass fittings missing, running off into the distance. I switched on my torch and stuck it through a porthole to light up the interior of the hull, which was cavernous, black and foreboding. Then I kicked my feet and finned to the edge of the hull where it met the now vertical main deck. Looking behind me briefly I could see how the hull sloped off into the depths towards the keel.

I dropped down onto my chest at the main deck, my hands gripping the very edge of the hull. Although the uppermost port side of the hull was bathed in sunlight from above, the hull was so big that it cast a considerable shadow. As a result the main deck, guns and superstructure were hidden by an all-consuming blackness, the sunlight being totally blocked out by the massive obstruction of the hull of the ship.

As I looked over the edge I thought I could make out some anchor chain looping down from a hawse pipe to my left-hand side. We were near the bow. With a little trepidation, I finned out from the security of the sunlit hull over the black void and let myself sink downwards. I turned round to face the hull and, as I sank, I was able to make out the wooden planking of the deck, incredibly still visible after all these years of immersion.

We moved further along towards the bow. The upper side of the hull tapered sharply and ran downwards to meet the deeper starboard side of the hull which rose out of the silty seabed. The two sides of the hull met at the seemingly razor-sharp point of the bow, designed for slicing through the water at speed. Mooring bollards and cleats were dotted along the outermost section of the main deck, some with their mooring ropes still coiled around them. The two anchor chains, each link the size of a man's hand, hung in huge loops from the hawse pipes until they rose to meet the circular steam-driven anchor capstans, before disappearing below decks to the chain locker.

As I floated in mid-water, I looked up at the bow from below. It towered above me, its narrow, pointed stem silhouetted against the light green of the clearer water all around.

After taking in the layout of the bow, anchor chains and capstans we turned here and started finning back away from the bow towards where we thought the central superstructure and fire control tower must be located.

The vertical deck passed by slowly on my right-hand side about ten feet away from me. The water was so clear that, even here on the centre line of the vessel at a depth of about 25 metres, when I looked downwards I could see the whole seabed, littered with debris that had rusted and fallen off the wreck. Spars, struts, cable holders and sections of plating were interspersed with a myriad of countless scallop and razor shells.

We arrived at where the two forward 5.9-inch guns would have been situated just forward of the bridge but they were missing, presumably salvaged at some time in the past. All that remained was the circular base of their wracking, or turning, systems.

Here and there were several large openings through the main deck itself, which allowed us to peer into the cavernous hull spaces in the deck level immediately beneath the main deck. As I finned forward I became aware of a large, black silhouette projecting out from the main deck horizontally and blocking my path. I continued my approach and a large oval or circular armoured structure, the fire control tower, appeared out of the gloom in front of me. It was from here, in the relative safety of the heavy armour, that officers in battle could direct the guns of the warship.

The fire control tower was made up of two deck levels, the uppermost level being the same oval shape as the lower one, just smaller. Lines of viewing slits ringed the top of each of the deck levels. I wondered how effective such a viewing position would be in battle, situated directly behind the two main forward 5.9-inch guns, which would have created a lot of smoke when firing rapidly.

Projecting out further, horizontally from (and originally above) the uppermost or second deck of this tower, was a curious, winged piece of equipment. It was big – wider than I am tall – and I guessed that this was the optical range finder for the main guns.

Moving further aft I entered an area which was largely unrecognisable to our untrained eyes, but I knew we must be in the region of the three funnels and the accommodation deck-houses, which ran for some way aft. We had by this stage dropped right down to the seabed and as we swam along in this confused area my buddy stopped at a large opening in the deck. I watched as he peered inside, shining his torch around. Then, he kicked off the seabed, the downdraft of his fins creating mini-explosions of silt around the opening. Without any signal to me he swam straight through the opening, turned to his right inside the hull and kept on swimming. I saw the tips of his black fins disappearing into the hull, creating further explosions of silt.

We hadn't discussed doing any penetration work on this first dive, so I wasn't expecting this. I swam over to the opening as fast as I could and as I got there I stopped just outside. There was an almighty cloud of silt billowing up around the exit point, which had reduced visibility dramatically. As I hesitated at the opening, for some reason I looked upwards – the movement must have subconsciously caught my eye. I saw a long section of 4-inch pipe, which had been hanging loosely, attached by some flimsy piece of rusted metal, shift, and then drop an inch or so. Then, with surprising speed, it came loose and fell heavily down towards me. I recoiled backwards in horror and just got out of its way as it plummeted to the seabed, before stopping finely balanced end on. Then, as if in slow motion, it fell over and slammed flat into the seabed.

I looked around where this pipe had come from but nothing else seemed to be moving so I returned my attention to the opening into the hull, which had consumed my buddy. The whole opening was now a silt-out with zero visibility and there was no sign of my buddy, who must still have been inside the wreck.

I stuck my head into the silt cloud and, holding the side of the opening with my right hand, moved as far as I could inside without letting go. I hoped the visibility might improve, but it remained at zero vis. I was not going to let go of the entranceway and risk losing my way inside the hull. I settled myself on the bottom and shone my torch along to the right in the direction my buddy had disappeared.

I don't know how long I remained still, standing on the seabed just inside the entrance to the hull shining my torch, in the hope that my buddy might see it and find his way out. It was probably only a few minutes but it seemed like an eternity. I had heard folklore of divers becoming completely lost inside these huge wrecks and running out of air, unable to find their way out. I didn't know what had happened to my buddy but it wasn't going to help the situation if I got lost inside as well.

As I remained motionless, the silt settled almost imperceptibly and the visibility improved, albeit only slightly. Suddenly I thought I saw the faintest glimpse of my buddy's torch beam, its intensity blocked out by the silt still hanging in the water. Seconds later, his head, eyes bulging wide in his mask, appeared out of the cloud of silt just inches from my face. I hadn't seen him until he was that close.

I beckoned with my torch for him to follow me out and pulled backwards with my hand on the deck. Once I had gone as far back as I could, I knew I was outside the wreck, although I was still shrouded in the blanket of silt. Once I was sure I was clear of the wreck I started to rise up and my buddy followed.

One minute we were veiled in the silt, the next, like a plane climbing out of a cloud, our heads popped out and we were in clear water again. We went on with the dive half-heartedly for another ten minutes or so, before it was time to ascend and make our way back to the safety of the boat.

Once we were back in the boat I asked, 'What happened down there, mate?'

'Yeah, it was a wild one . . .' he replied. 'I swam in through the gap in the deck and into what seemed to be a long corridor. The visibility ahead of me was perfect. I could see for miles so I just kept on finning down the corridor. After a while it opened out into a big room and I looked around in it for a while. Then I thought better of where I was and turned to go back the way I had come in. It was then that I saw a wall of silt sweeping down towards me. It just washed all over me and the vis dropped to nil. I just couldn't see where I was and couldn't find the entrance to the corridor I had come in.'

'Christ, how did you get out in the end?' I asked.

'Eventually the silt seemed to settle a wee bit and in the distance I saw your light at the end of what must have been the corridor. I made straight for it. Was I pleased to see your ugly face right beside it! We'll have to watch out for that silt-out again – the stuff seemed to follow me. You could easily get well and truly lost in there.'

We poured some coffee from a thermos flask and tried to drink it. We had been in the water for a long time and were both absolutely freezing. We shook and shivered so much from the cold that, as we tried to get some of the coffee from the cup into our mouths, most of it ended up spilled all down our fronts. This brought on fits of uncontrollable laughter which only ended up getting our numb lips burnt from the scalding coffee – and more of it down our fronts.

For the remainder of the week we dived the other monstrous leviathans of the depths of Scapa Flow.

I had my first dive on a First World War battleship, the *Kronprinz Wilhelm*. We thought we had gained a good idea of the layout of the 510-feet long, 5,500-ton light cruiser *Cöln* on our earlier dive but the *Kronprinz* was a quantum leap in scale again. She weighed in at approximately 26,000 tons, nearly four times greater than the *Cöln*.

The *Kronprinz* had turned turtle as she was scuttled, the massive 600-ton weights of her five twin 12-inch gun turrets and armoured superstructure bearing her over to one side as she started to sink and lost some of her buoyancy. Battleships were so heavily armoured that, with such great weight high up in the ship, it was common for them to quickly turn turtle as they sank, often with great loss of life as men got trapped below decks, with too little time to escape.

As we descended through the water on our first dive on the *Kronprinz* the flat seabed seemed to materialise out of the gloom. It was only the hard unyielding feel of the silt as we landed on it that revealed this was in fact the upturned, silt-covered bottom of the *Kronprinz*. Like all battleships, this was almost completely flat. Rows of rivets stretched off into the distance, marking out the dimensions of her plating. Two large bilge keels, strips of metal about three or four feet high, stretched along either side of the bottom, designed to give the flat keel a cutting edge for turning the ship through the water.

Moving to the edge of the hull, we could peer down the near-vertical side of the ship. It was a vertical wall of steel that plunged down for nearly 25 metres, almost 80 feet. Drifting out over the inky void and then finning down the side of the hull, we passed endless rows of riveting before we neared the port side bulwark rail. Here the main deck started, and now ran right under the upturned hull.

The *Kronprinz* had sunk completely upside down and landed on her massive superstructure, which was driven into the seabed and crumpled up. The ship then rolled over to her starboard bulwark rail, which came to rest on the seabed. The port-side bulwark rail was thus raised up higher than the starboard side and consequently there is now a gap, several metres high, between the seabed and the bulwark rail, a black cavernous recess. Ranged along the bulwark rail we saw rows of portholes interspersed with a number of 5.9-inch casemate gun turrets set into the side of the hull itself. Some had their barrels still *in situ* – other barrels had fallen to the seabed. This chasm under the overhanging deck was an impenetrable blackness, which never saw the light of day. Sweeping our torches around underneath I started to be able to make out large sections of the upside-down superstructure disappearing in the silty seabed.

We moved towards the stern and came across the two aftmost 12-inch gun turrets, set one behind the other, both of which still held their twin 12-

inch gun barrels. I was staggered at just how big these turrets were and how long the barrels were, each being 35 feet long at least.

The after-superimposed gun turret was half buried in the silt and its twin 12-inch gun barrels projected from it, partially covered in silt. Around the flat sides of its armour-plating were dotted viewing slits. Further aft the aftmost 12-inch gun turret was open for inspection with both of its gun barrels clear of the seabed, their ends jammed into the teak deck planking above.

Moving past the gun turrets the hull swept round to the stern and, rising upwards here, we came upon the large rudders still standing proudly erect. As we finned back along the top of the hull towards the down line from our boat, we came across a large section of the keel which had been opened up. There was a hole about 50 feet across which dropped down through many deck levels internally and allowed a glimpse into the innards of this huge vessel. We were in the vicinity of the engine room and here, aeons ago, hard hat salvage divers had used explosives to blast their way in through the hull to remove the valuable non-ferrous engine room fitments.

As the white down line hove into view, leading up to the dive boat, my mind boggled at how big a vessel this had been, the once invincible battleship *Kronprinz Wilhelm*.

The next day we went back to dive another light cruiser, the *Dresden*, 510 feet long and 5,531 tons, the same Dresden II class as *Cöln*. She lay on her port side in 35 metres of water. Once we had located her, we buoyed her and over successive days returned to dive this one vessel a number of times, becoming very familiar with her layout and spending more time exploring smaller sections of her. We managed to get hold of copies of the general arrangement drawings for the *Dresden*, and were able to decide where we were going to explore. On one of the dives we were able to work our way through the wreck just aft of the bridge and get into the galley area.

By the end of the week, I had dived two battleships, two light cruisers and a number of the smaller blockships. These huge, intact vessels lying in such still, clear water had caught my imagination. I saw them as time capsules of an era of sea power and majesty that had long since passed into the history books.

Before taking up diving, and learning of the fabled wrecks at Scapa Flow, I had never heard of the scuttling of the German High Seas Fleet at the end of the First World War. To non-divers who were aware of the scuttling, this was a momentous act but one consigned to the history books – something which they could not directly experience. It was a conflict from long ago, where the vast majority of the participants were now no longer with us.

For me, as a diver, I was able to see and touch these wrecks, to explore them, floating weightlessly wherever I wanted to go. I was able to gain an understanding of the vessels that had taken part – to see and touch history.

I read more and more about the scuttling and appreciated how much that act, committed such a long time ago, is still interwoven into the very fabric of Orkney life. Von Reuter's actions that single day in 1919 still directly affect Orkney in many ways, each and every day. The diving industry there deals daily with the legacy of his actions. Diving brings many welcome tourist pounds into the shops, hotels and dive businesses.

I had been gripped by Orkney and its sunken treasure trove of wrecks. Each year following that initial week's diving, I returned to dive the wrecks, gaining more information and a better understanding of them. However, I was always hampered by the almost complete lack of diver information on them. As a consequence, I eventually collated the information and knowledge of the wrecks that I had gained into my first book, *Dive Scapa Flow*. This book was published as a paperback version in 1990 but soon sold out and was reprinted.

Realising the demand for the book, my publishers, Mainstream of Edinburgh, put out a second edition in hardback in 1993. With my later involvement in 'technical diving', using mixed gases, this stripped away the 50-metre depth limitation associated with diving whilst breathing compressed air. I was able to expand the book for a third edition in 1997, which included a couple of deep 'technical' wrecks previously undiveable on air.

The major addition was HMS *Hampshire*, which lies just outside Scapa Flow in 70 msw (metres of seawater). This was the vessel on which Lord Kitchener perished when she struck a mine in 1916, en route to Russia. I was also able to survey the wreck of the boom defence vessel HMS *Strathgarry* which was discovered in the early 1990s lying in 58 msw in Hoxa Sound.

I retain a special fondness for Orkney, the people and the diving there. Although my interests have taken me to many other remote and far-flung places around the globe in recent years, I still love spending time diving the scuttled German Fleet at Scapa Flow. It is some of the best wreck diving in the world. Scapa Flow is justly recognised in wreck diving circles around the world as having one of the most important collections of historic wrecks around.

CHAPTER SIX

Ceilidh on Hoy

'An Imposing Spectacle; Flotta Encircled by Warships'

The Orcadian

In 1990, a year or so after the publication of *Dive Scapa Flow*, I and my then regular diving buddy, Richard Cook, joined forces with another experienced diver, Bill McIntosh, and a TV director who had just taken up diving, Rick Wood. We formed a company called Underwater Films Ltd and hatched a plan to make a commercial video about diving at Scapa Flow.

We decided upon a week to film the video at Scapa and I started writing a script for it. We recruited a group of back-up divers from the Ellon Branch of the BSAC, of which I was still a member, and selected which wrecks we were going to film and which shots we were going to try and get. We wanted to get good visual images, like gun turrets, which would enable the viewer to quickly recognise what we were diving. We thought the visibility at Scapa would be good enough to capture the sheer scale and majesty of these wrecks on film.

The normal dive boat I used at Scapa Flow, Keith and Pearl Thomson's *Evening Star*, was already booked for that week, so we were put in touch with another skipper, who was just starting up in the business. I was told he had just finished refurbishing his boat and that it was free the week we needed it. I talked to him on the phone in the weeks leading up to the expedition and he seemed pleasant and knowledgeable.

The week of filming arrived and we set off in convoy in the early hours one Saturday morning, for the long drive up to Scrabster to catch the ferry. We were carrying a mountain of dive equipment, camera equipment for both topside and underwater work, specialist underwater lights and all the paraphernalia necessary for a week's diving.

As we rolled off the *St Ola* at Stromness we saw our dive boat, the 50-foot-long ex-fishing boat, MV *Crombie* tied up at the harbour. We loaded our dive kit onto it and checked into our accommodation ashore.

The first day's diving was scheduled to be on the *Kronprinz Wilhelm*, the colossal battleship lying upside down in 35 metres of water. In advance of the dive we had a briefing in which we ran over the way the wreck was lying and the main points we wanted to film. Divers were allocated to act as models and others to provide lighting with large, very bright, underwater lights.

We boarded the dive boat eager and fresh at 9 a.m. and settled into the lounge spreading out our gear. I went for a walk around the boat. I chatted to the skipper and learned that he was an ex-joiner and had just finished refurbishing the wheelhouse. As I admired it, I realised that instead of being set back somewhat from the gunwales of the boat at either side, this wheelhouse was now actually projecting almost out beyond the gunwales. I then learned that in fact we were the skipper's first charter, but he was still confident that he would be able to do the job for us. We had a lot of time and money invested in this one week's diving and filming.

The harbour that Sunday morning was filled with dive boats, fishing boats and several very large trawlers. These trawlers were not your ordinary wooden fishing boat, they were steel vessels the length of merchant ships with high sides and towering superstructures designed for mass fishing in distant waters.

Our skipper had to manoeuvre his boat to get it into a position to pass through the ranks of vessels to the main channel out of the harbour. As he did so, he headed perilously close to a large steel trawler, whose sides flared out above us up to its deck, some 20 to 30 feet above the deck of our boat.

As we gathered on deck to watch we all stared in dumbstruck silence as our boat crept right under the flare of the trawler's steel bow. Suddenly there was a loud crack as the mast on our foredeck struck the overhanging hull. It didn't come down but some terrible damage had been done to it. Our boat scraped down the side of the steel trawler for some way before our skipper managed to get away from its side. We stared at each other perturbed at this start to our filming. This most definitely was not in the script.

Once past the trawler we headed out into the open expanse of Scapa Flow, towards the wreck of the *Kronprinz Wilhelm*. As we motored out, the skipper became very agitated and then asked me if I could take him to the wreck as he didn't have a position for it and wasn't sure where to go. I did what I could to help but it was clear that he wasn't going to be able to find it. Eventually he got on the VHF radio to another skipper who was able to work out from his radar where exactly our boat was and guide him to the site. It was with relief that we eventually arrived over the wreck of the *Kronprinz*.

The filming down on the wreck didn't go as planned either. It very soon became apparent that it was very hard to direct divers underwater and, in such deep, dark water, to film to a predetermined script and storyboard. The quality of the footage we got was not at all what we had hoped for.

After filming on the *Kronprinz* we moved over to the Barrel of Butter to see if any seals were about on this favoured haul-out site. There were many seals around today and as we approached they all shuffled off the rocky crag into the water. We got the hard boat to go as close inshore as the skipper dared before we quietly slipped into the water with our lights and cameras.

Seals are the underwater equivalent of inquisitive dogs and very soon they were swimming up to us to have a good look at the unusual visitors. We filmed as they zipped their way through our group of divers, sometimes having a playful nibble at our fins. Their sleek, speedy and agile movements through the water made us look slow and ungainly. We spent about 30 minutes filming here and got some unexpectedly good footage which made up for the disappointing footage from the *Kronprinz* in the morning. But things were really not going to plan.

After this interval it was time to head across to one of the western channels into the Flow, Burra Sound, where we were going to film on the half-exposed tanker sunk as a blockship in the Second World War, the *Inverlane*.

The *Inverlane* was an 8,900-ton tanker built in West Germany in 1938. She was damaged by a mine off South Shields in 1939, and split into two sections. The stern section sank off South Shields, but the bow to midships section was rescued and made watertight, before being towed to Scapa Flow to be sunk as a blockship across the Sound.

Burra Sound is famous for being an extremely tidal stretch of water. It is about half a mile wide and the western end, where the *Inverlane* was sunk, opens out onto the Atlantic; there is nothing between this and America. As a result, the awesome oceanic tidal forces of the Atlantic try to push water through the small channel, creating extreme currents.

The *Inverlane* sat broadside onto these currents across the channel resting in just nine metres of water. Her bows are in the shallowest water near the north side of the Sound, her midships out into the deeper water of mid-channel. Some 100 feet of her bows and hull from the bridge forward jutted out of the water and her 100-foot-high foremast still stood proudly in place. I found it remarkable that she had survived the daily ebb and flow of the huge Atlantic currents for more than 60 years and still rested intact in her long-spent defensive position. (Sadly, winter storms would eventually break up the wreck in the late '90s.)

We moored to the leeward side of the wreck, sheltered from the current so we could then climb from the dive boat onto the wreck and ferry our heavy tanks and weights onto her rusted deck, which angle upwards at about 25 degrees. If you stopped on the deck for a second you could sense the whole hull, several thousand tons of steel, swaying slightly in the current. The wreck felt like a ghost ship and eerie sounds came from within it, caused by the rushing of water through its cavities. The cries of seabirds were the only living sound. Once we had all our kit aboard we did some topside filming around the wreck to capture the essential eerieness of this silent sentinel of Scapa Flow.

There was a small pump room in front of the bridge, in which a staircase had originally led down to the decks below. The surface of the water was now conveniently about four or five feet beneath the deck of the pump room, so a simple stride entry into the water-filled stairwell was all that was needed to drop down into the water and have immediate access to the innards of this huge vessel.

Forward of the pump room were two large open oil tanks, their tops well above the water level. Visitors to the wreck could peer down several deck levels into these tanks, which had rotted ladders running down their sides, to the clear water moving slowly through the skeleton of the wreck. Because it is scoured daily by the might of the Atlantic, Burra Sound has not a single atom of silt in it to cloud underwater visibility. It is famous throughout diving circles for gin-clear visibility of 30 metres and abundant sea life living in the strong currents. We planned to film inside the wreck in the crystal-clear water, as we thought it would give us the crisp, exciting images of large parts of the wreck that we wanted.

Topside, ladders led up from the main deck to the fo'c'stle deck at the very bow, complete with anchor winches. The bridge superstructure, aft of the open oil tanks and pump room, was well rotted and somewhat unsafe.

Behind the bridge, more tank hatches lay open for inspection before the slanting main deck disappeared beneath the water. When the current was running it collided with the submerged section of the wreck, causing the water to churn and boil as it fought its way over the wreck.

Once I had leapt into the water I righted myself and looked down. It was as if there was no water beneath me as I could clearly see every detail of the bottom of the ship nine metres below.

The rotted handrail of the stairway in the pump room snaked downwards beside me and I followed it to the bottom of the wreck. One by one all of our divers arrived down beside me and together we moved aft, passing through connecting doorways in bulkheads that had, in her days afloat, allowed her crew to pass the same way between oil tanks. As we passed the last bulkhead, we exited from the doorway into a large open area where piles of towing hawsers were coiled.

Looking astern there was a blinding blue wall of light where the hull had been sheared off. The whole width of the hull was open to the sea. From the shadowy darkness of the confines of the wreck we were able to look beyond the protective safety of the hull out into the open water of the Sound. Long strands of kelp flapped and waved in the underwater breeze – even though the current had seemed weak topside there was still a lot of motion in the water here as it funnelled around the obstruction of the wreck.

We filmed divers as they swam out of the hull into open water, but it was clear that as soon as we moved out from the shield of the hull into open water, the current tried to ensnare us and carry us away.

We then swam back inside the hull to continue filming. Once I had been underwater for about 45 minutes my buddy and I decided to call it a day and ascend. Some of the divers stayed behind with the cameramen to film some more general shots, as the wreck was hugely photogenic. Fish abounded and the whole skeleton of the wreck was festooned in white and orange anemones, filter-feeders living off the rich nutrients brought by the strong currents.

I found my way back to the the pump room and ascended the stairway slowly, hand over hand. As soon as I popped my head out of the water, I found our skipper in an extremely agitated state.

'The tide has turned, Rod. The current's picking up in the other direction and if we don't get off the side of this wreck right now, we'll be pinned against it.'

'We've been in the water for so long that slack water has come and gone,' I said. 'Can you move your boat to the other side of the wreck?'

'No, just get your gear aboard as fast as you can and we'll cast off.'

But this task could only be performed so fast, given the number of divers and the amount of equipment we had. One by one the other divers were surfacing in the pump room and being helped out of the water. We then had to get the camera equipment and lights out of the water and then transfer it across the deck of the *Inverlane* and pass it onto the *Crombie*. As we were doing this, the current was picking up all the time and was now pressing the *Crombie* hard against the corroded hull of the *Inverlane*. With each passing minute our skipper was becoming more and more agitated and was almost hopping up and down as we finally got the last of the kit aboard.

Anxiously we cast off the bow and stern ropes holding us to the wreck. We could see the surge of the current hitting our boat and pressing us against the tanker and no matter how hard our skipper tried he couldn't prise the bow or the stern of his boat off the flat hull of the *Inverlane*.

Abandoning his attempts to get us off the side of the *Inverlane* the usual way he then put his engines ahead and motored forward. As he did so, because it projected over the gunwales, his newly constructed wheelhouse came in contact with the side of the wreck. There was a grating sound and then a shower of large splinters of his wheelhouse, intermingled with large rotted shards of rusted ship's plating, clattered down on the deck. We all moved to the other side of the boat away from the contact area.

The skipper motored forward grimly along the remaining length of the hull, further damaging his wheelhouse and bringing more rotted metal cascading down onto his deck. As we reached the end of the wreck, the *Crombie* was picked up by the surge of the current. She whipped round the end of the wreck and we were free of the *Inverlane*.

In easier water we motored slowly back to Stromness. The skipper had had a hard introduction to skippering on the wrecks of Scapa Flow that day, and his boat had suffered a fair degree of damage. He had also lost face. He was a very unhappy man on the way back.

The straw that broke the camel's back came when he tried to moor up against the harbour wall back in Stromness. He came in at the wall bow on, at a speed of a few knots. We stared ahead at the approaching wall, wondering when he was going to kick the *Crombie* side on to moor flush up against the wall. But the *Crombie* never wavered and her bow ran straight onto the wall. There was another cracking sound before she moved backwards and he repeated the manoeuvre, this time successfully.

Once we were tied up and the engine switched off we went to talk to the skipper. We were unhappy at the position we had been put in through his inexperience and equally, it had been a tough first day for him out in the Flow. In fact it had been simply too much for him. He told us there and then that the rest of the trip was cancelled and we had to get our kit off his boat. We had been thrown off the dive boat at the end of day one of our shoot!

There was no point arguing about it – it was his boat and he just wasn't going to go to sea with us the next day. Dejectedly, we offloaded all our gear onto the quayside, not knowing what our next move was. Without a boat, the whole trip and the making of the video were in jeopardy.

I telephoned Pearl Thomson in South Ronaldsay who, with Keith, owned the boat I normally chartered, to see if she had any other ideas. Pearl, bless her, agreed to see what she could do to help. Before long, she was in touch again to say that she had sorted something out for us. Terry Todd, himself one of the legends of Scapa Flow, who ran the dive boat *Girl Mina*, didn't have a charter that week and was willing to take us on. We talked on the phone and agreed to meet down at the boat at 9 a.m. the next day.

The *Girl Mina* is a boat with a history. She was once a 50-foot fishing boat that sank in an Orkney harbour in the 1960s. She was later refloated and refurbished and became one of the first charter hard boats at Scapa Flow taking divers out to the wrecks of the German Fleet.

There was no fo'c'stle, just a flat forward deck and hold. The wheelhouse was large and extended backwards with a galley and fixed table and seating. It was a good dive boat to be on, particularly in Terry's hands, as he handled it precisely and effortlessly. Terry, a one-time commercial diver, is a large man, both in stature and character. Stories abound of the antics that her previous skipper and owner used to get up to with divers and Terry was following in those footsteps. Legend has it that when a party of divers from England arrived at the pier one day at the appointed time to start a week's diving they found the boat empty – no skipper. Terry was on the other side of the small harbour. Stripping down to vest and trousers, he dived into the water, swam across the harbour and climbed out of the water, arriving soaking in front of the bemused and stunned group of fresh divers. He then introduced himself and shook their hands.

That week, he was our saviour. We started diving that day, and Terry dropped us with precision on wreck after wreck. Our footage started to accumulate.

In between dives we visited the Naval Cemetery at Lyness on the island of Hoy, where British sailors of both world wars are buried alongside German sailors shot by the British on that fateful day of the scuttling, 21 June 1919.

Towards the end of the week we decided to film on the wreck of the SS *Gobernador Bories*, another blockship in Burra Sound just a few hundred metres away from the wreck of the *Inverlane*. Although it is possible to dive the *Inverlane* at any state of the tide, as divers are sheltered inside the steel hull, this is not possible on the wreck of the *Gobernador Bories*. She sits in mid-channel and is a far smaller wreck of 2,332 tons, offering less protection from the current. She is well corroded and collapsed. Although once you get down among the wreckage you are to an extent sheltered, for the dive down to the wreck, and the ascent, divers are completely at the mercy of fierce currents of up to five knots that sweep through Burra Sound. Those same currents produce fantastic underwater visibility of 20 to 30 metres but mean that, to successfully dive down on the wreck, you have to dive it at the precise time when the current stops moving in one direction and pauses before starting to move in the opposite direction. This is the hallowed period divers call 'slack water'.

The *Gobernador Bories* was built in West Hartlepool in 1882 and was registered in Punta Arenas, Chile. She was sunk in the Sound as a blockship in 1915, during the First World War, long before her close neighbour the *Inverlane* was even designed or built. She lies in relatively shallow water of about 16 metres, sitting on an even keel. Her upper works are long gone and the main decking has largely collapsed down into the hull itself. With the fantastic visibility divers can see a lot of her at once. They can look out from inside the hull down to the seabed below which is a scatter of small boulders set in fine white sand. The bow and starboard side of her hull are largely intact. Amidships, the collapsing has exposed her two large boilers. Aft of the engine room she regains her intact form at the stern.

I was to be diving this day with Ewan Rowell, whom I had met quite recently on a night out in Aberdeen through a mutual acquaintance, now his wife. Ewan had found out that night that I had just published *Dive Scapa Flow* and had immediately launched into an animated conversation with me. He had lived in Orkney for many years, earlier in his life, and although he now worked in the offshore oil industry, he had been a commercial diver for several years. Standing just over 6 ft tall with fair hair, he was as strong as an ox and had a sharp, zany wit. Lapses in conversation were never an issue when Ewan was around and his sparkling humour endeared him to all who met him. When he had heard of our trip to film in Orkney he had immediately volunteered to join in.

As Ewan and I, and our group of divers, dived down to the wreck to film, the tide was just dropping off towards slack water so we had no difficulty getting down. Once we were among its rusted and fallen side-plating, we found that the whole wreck was covered with a white carpet of anemones and dead man's fingers, and it was absolutely teeming with fish life. Fed by the current, filter-feeders abounded everywhere, covering the whole wreck with a blaze of colour. The fish life had become accustomed to the sight of divers over the years. Humans were no longer seen as a threat and large wrasse constantly swam up to us, looking to be fed by hand. When it was clear we had no food for them, the wrasse followed us around the wreck looking for a tasty morsel dislodged by a fin stroke. I reached out my hand and was able to stroke one or two of them. All this made for great footage.

After about 45 minutes down on the wreck, we decided we had enough footage and agreed that we would all ascend. We gathered at the shot line and started up. As soon as we left the shelter of the wreck we realised the tide had turned, for the force of the current on us was intense. Anxious not to be separated from the buoy line and boat above, we went hand over hand as we slowly ascended the line. The effect of the current driving on six large divers' bodies very quickly pulled the small buoy under and, as we made our way along the line, I became aware that we had stopped going up. The end of the rope arrived and then the buoy itself, even though we were still ten metres from the surface. There was nothing for it but to let go of the buoy and let the current take us off towards the *Inverlane* and America beyond.

The current separated our large group into smaller groups as each of us tried to stay in contact with our allocated buddies for the dive. We had two divers carrying cumbersome underwater video cameras in housings with lights attached, and the others were carrying the specialist underwater lamps.

I stayed close to Ewan and we broke the surface together. I turned round and saw the looming hull of the wreck of the *Inverlane* as we steadily moved towards it, borne along with the current flooding out of the Scapa

Flow. I wondered what was going to happen when we hit the *Inverlane's* massive bows. There was no way we could fight the five-knot current.

I looked around and was extremely relieved to see the *Girl Mina* charging over towards us at full speed. Deftly Terry slowed the boat to a halt beside me.

We continued to advance towards the *Inverlane* at speed and were perhaps only 100 metres from it now. I was about to climb up the ladder into the *Girl Mina* when Terry called down: 'Just grab hold of the ladder and hold on! There's no time for you to get out.'

I took a good hold of the thick steel rungs of the stepped ladder and Ewan came in beside me and grabbed hold of the other side.

Terry kicked the *Girl Mina* into gear and throttled forward against the rush of the current and away from the looming hulk of the *Inverlane*. The *Girl Mina* was soon flat out against the five-knot rush of the current, and the combined speed of water started to make my regulator free flow, forcing air endlessly into my mouth. The rush of water was surging against my mouthpiece and depressing the rubber mushroom valve that controls air being bled into your mouth during normal diving. It wasn't designed to cope with this sort of scenario.

I tried moving my head into another direction to get the regulator out of the rush of water. This resulted in water being forced in the exhaust valve of the regulator and flooding into my mouth. Either way, it wasn't good news and I was struggling to breathe while being towed through the surging water.

I moved the position of my head again, creating an eddy where my body was screening the water from my face. This area of slacker water allowed my regulator to start functioning properly again and I gasped for breath.

I had hooked my right arm round one of the ladder rungs, and my arm felt as though it was getting longer by the second. I looked at Ewan who was stoically hanging on for dear life as well. I looked back down into the water below me. It was so clear that I could see the fronds of kelp bent double on the bottom of the Sound by the current.

As I looked back under the boat I saw it was fitted with a protective steel keel strip running the length of the boat. I was also relieved to see a large cage framework around the propeller, a prop guard to protect divers from getting chopped to bits by the prop in unfortunate circumstances.

Terry managed to drag us back up the Sound, gaining enough distance between the *Girl Mina* and the *Inverlane* to allow us to climb up the ladder to safety.

As I slowly and heavily lumbered up the ladder I looked down the Sound to see if there was any sign of the other divers in our group. I picked out two divers, one holding a video camera, being swept the last few metres up to the *Inverlane* and then impacting onto its sheer steel side.

As soon as Ewan and I were aboard, Terry throttled up the engines and we turned and headed back towards the *Inverlane* at full speed. As we approached, we saw the two divers get swept by the wash, down the side of the wreck to where it disappeared under the water. There they managed somehow to grab hold of some part of the rusted gunwale of the *Inverlane* just where its decks slanted off underwater, arrest their charge towards America and clamber out onto the wreck and up its decks to safety.

I then looked for the remaining diver, Richard Cook, who was holding the other video camera by its two large side handles. I saw him to the south of the others, towards mid-channel and heading towards the aftmost submerged section of the wreck. As I watched, he was swept towards the area of churning, foaming white water where the current fought its way over the submerged part of the *Inverlane*. The water frothed and boiled for a lateral distance of perhaps 100 feet back from where the wreck disappeared under the water. Richard's red-suited figure swept through this white water as he manfully clung to the video camera. He was pummelled by powerful thrusts of white water and waves broke over his head. Very quickly he was through the white water and then moving at speed out towards the open Atlantic.

Terry had the *Girl Mina* flat out and with the five-knot current now working for us, we charged out towards Richard, who was fast becoming a small speck of humanity in the distance. But gradually we closed in on him. As we left Burra Sound, the current dissipated in the open expanse of the sea and Richard was soon safely on board.

We then headed back and briefly moored up alongside the *Inverlane*, where the two remaining divers were able to clamber aboard. Another exciting and unplanned day, but we had the footage we needed.

The week progressed without further incident and we managed to shoot sufficient underwater and topside footage. By the last day of diving we were reasonably confident that we had enough to put a good diving video together. We were booked on the 8.45 a.m. ferry from Stromness the next morning, which was Saturday. Terry suggested that he take us across to the island of Hoy that night, as there was a ceilidh being held that would be a good craic.

'How long is the journey across by boat going to take, Terry?' I asked.

'About four tins of export, Rod,' came his reply.

After packing up all our kit and getting the boat cleared for the early departure the next morning we trooped off and got ourselves a carryout. By 7 p.m. we were all on the *Girl Mina* again, for the first time clad in ordinary clothes instead of our customary dry suits and thermal undersuits.

We had a very convivial passage out from Stromness harbour in the direction of the *Inverlane*, which stood dark and foreboding in the evening twilight. Sure enough, four tins of export later, Terry was taking the *Girl*

Mina up to the small pier of Graemsay on the southernmost side of Burra Sound. The pier was set in almost total isolation with only a few small houses scattered in the distance.

The tide was fairly well out so we clambered up the iron ladder rungs set into the concrete blocks of the pier wondering where the ceilidh was going to be held. Terry pointed up towards the dark looming hills of Hoy.

'The ceilidh is up there in the village hall,' he said pointing upwards at some indistinct buildings high up in the distance. I was just wondering how we were all going to get from this remote pier when he added: 'I've arranged some transport from my mate Terry for you. We'll go to the pub first though.'

At this, a small white van came over the nearby summit of the narrow road leading away from the pier. There were ten of us but only the one van on its way.

As the white van pulled in beside us, our driver for the night jumped out and introduced himself. His name was Terry Thomson and he had been in charge of diving operations in the 1970s, working for Dougall Campbell who had bought the salvage rights to some of the German wrecks in the days before their historical worth was really understood.

Salvaging of the German wrecks had gone on since Cox and Dank's legendary feats in the 1920s and '30s when the majority of the 74 sunken warships were raised intact. Throughout the post-war years, other small-scale salvage works had been carried out on the remainder of the sunken fleet by firms like Metal Industries. Holes had been blown in the ships in the vicinity of their engine rooms to allow hard-hat divers inside to remove the valuable non-ferrous engine fittings like condensers.

In the 1970s, Dougall Campbell was simply continuing that long line of salvage work as he removed the armour plating from the battleships *Kronprinz Wilhelm* and *Markgraf* and salvaged other valuable parts of the light cruisers, such as the submerged torpedo tubes, which were made of pure bronze.

Terry Thomson opened the back door of his van and ushered us all inside. Once we were all squashed in, he drove us for a mile or so to the local pub. When he opened the back door, we all tumbled out like corks from a bottle.

Once inside, Terry Thomson was soon talking to us about his days in the 1970s in charge of the salvage divers. He was pleased to have an audience of divers to talk to and as divers we were all fascinated with his stories. Slowly we all seemed to congregate around him and very soon we found ourselves in a quiet part of the pub gathered round him like attentive schoolboys, listening to his tales.

Terry Thomson recounted using explosives on the light cruiser *Karlsruhe* to free the copper portside bow torpedo tube. The quantity of explosives used had blown through to a candle locker and released hundreds of candles that had floated up to the surface. They all bore the legend of the German High Seas Fleet, '*Kaiserliche Marine*'.

On another occasion, he told us, Dougall Campbell himself had set an underwater charge. The detonating cord ran from the wreck up to the surface where it had been connected to the detonating unit itself in a small rowing boat. The main salvage vessel itself, for safety reasons, stood well clear of the site of the proposed underwater explosion. The rule was that the person who set the underwater charge would detonate it from the rowing boat.

As the large vessel stood off the scene, the crew realised that Dougall, in the rowing boat, was unknowingly drifting over the site of the intended explosion. They tried to attract his attention to warn him, but it was too late, the charge was fired.

There was a loud 'Crump!' from deep underwater as the charge went off. About a second later, the sea around the rowing boat, with Dougall in it, frothed and boiled white as the blast threw the water into the air, and Dougall disappeared. When the water and spray subsided they found him safe and well – but very wet.

We listened awe-struck to Terry Thomson's tales of salvage. He told us about how the entire bridge superstructure of the *Karlsruhe* had been made of non-ferrous, and very valuable, best German brass. They had blown the bridge superstructure off the wreck in one piece and floated it to the surface. Righting it to its correct attitude, the bridge was towed under a five-ton lifting bag to Rinnigil for scrapping.

By the time we had had about an hour of such tales it was time to get going up to the ceilidh. We had all had a fair skelp of beer inside us by now and were feeling pretty boisterous. We were up for what we pictured would be a rip-roaring west-coast ceilidh. We all piled into the back of the van again and Terry Thomson drove us up the looming hillside towards the hall.

Once there, we all jumped out of the van and Terry Todd led us up some steps and into the hall. I had expected the ceilidh to be in full flight, but as we all rather nosily stumbled into the public hall, we saw rows of tables lined with very silent people who turned to stare at our intrusion.

At the far end of the hall was a small stage upon which a single guitarist was seated strumming and singing a song I didn't recognise. We shuffled into the hall self-consciously and stood around at the back waiting to see what would happen. It was going to be a long night if this was the way it was going to go.

As the solo singer/guitarist finished, there was a round of polite applause before an MC got up, and in a lilting west-coast accent announced, succinctly: 'And now we'll have the dancing – can we clear the tables?'

With one accord the entire mass of the audience got up and started noisily pulling large wooden tables to the side of the hall to create a dancing space. Within 20 minutes the hall had been transformed – the audience were now all on their feet, a ceilidh band was on the stage and the first lilting strains of a Strip the Willow were starting to resound around the hall.

The locals, despite their initial stony silence at our arrival, proved to be very friendly and came up to speak to us to find out about us and why we had turned up at their ceilidh. A great number of the people at the ceilidh turned out not to be local islanders at all, but people drawn to work on the islands by the salmon farms and other cottage industries. Everyone seemed to know our skipper, Terry Todd, who was treated like royalty. The fact that we were with him seemed to be enough – we were immediately accepted and got on with the serious business of drinking and dancing.

At about 1.30 a.m. we noticed Terry Todd quietly slipping out of the hall. We were all having such a good time and he'd not put any pressure on us to leave, so we all stayed on. By about 3 a.m., we had had our fill and Terry Thomson, in full evening dress, appeared out of the darkness from another function to drive us back down to the boat.

When we got to the pier we clambered down the ladder onto the boat. All was silent and we jumped into the wheelhouse with its lounge and galley behind and found Terry Todd fast asleep. He'd obviously given up on us.

We tried to rouse him but he was in a deep slumber and was not for being disturbed. I went back outside and told Terry Thomson that we couldn't rouse Terry Todd. He offered to drive the boat across to Stromness but we declined. It wasn't our boat after all.

After some strenuous efforts we finally managed to wake Terry up. We couldn't afford to be stuck in Hoy overnight: we were to be catching the early ferry from Stromness back to the mainland the next morning and still had all our kit to get aboard.

Soon, coffee mug in one hand, Terry had the *Girl Mina*'s engines roaring into life. As we moved away, heading westwards out towards the Atlantic, we left the glare of the pier lighting, and I realised just how dark it was. We were well away from any lights of habitation and it was quite simply pitch black.

As I looked forward through the wheelhouse window I saw that the glow of the fluorescent strip lights of the lounge immediately behind us rendered the wheelhouse window almost opaque. As I stared out, trying to make out where we were, Terry stuck his head out of the side window and said, 'We should be passing the *Inverlane* any minute now.'

As we all peered forward, the huge rotted mass of the tanker suddenly moved past us at a speed of about ten knots just feet away, a black silhouette that blocked out the small island to the north and the stars of the night sky.

We had passed to the south of the *Inverlane* and as soon as we were past it, Terry announced, 'It'll be the Hoy Skerries next . . .'

I remembered from our dives on the *Inverlane* and *Gobernador Bories* earlier in the week that there was a large shoal of rocks that ran out from the southern shore of Burra Sound and broke the surface just beyond the *Inverlane* at low water. Even at high water they would be very dangerous if you went near them.

Ewan, Dave Hadden and I clustered around the echo-sounder and watched the scrolling bottom line trace getting shallower and shallower. The digital read out on the echo-sounder gave the depth beneath the keel.

At first it was reading about ten metres as we passed the *Inverlane*. Then, steadily, the depth decreased. Nine metres, eight, seven, six, five, four, three . . .

Ewan and I looked at each other. There wasn't a lot of water at all beneath the keel. The sounder just kept going – two metres, one metre . . . Then it showed a depth of zero metres beneath us.

Ewan and I looked at each other again for a split-second wondering what was going to happen next. Suddenly we hit something submerged and the whole boat seemed to rise up slightly as we rode up and over the obstruction, part of the Hoy Skerries. I remembered thankfully the large steel keel strip that ran the full length of the hull, which had probably just saved a lot of damage being done to the boat.

After we rode the Hoy Skerries we entered calmer, deeper water. I worried that the boat had been damaged by the impact and as we motored along towards to the end of Burra Sound my mind conjured up images of the *Girl Mina* sinking and the whole team being cast into the water in the pitch blackness of our surroundings. Clad only in jeans and fleeces, we wouldn't last long in the freezing waters beneath us. The tales of the sailors from HMS *Royal Oak* after her 1939 torpedoing, succumbing to hypothermia and dying in the shockingly cold waters of Scapa Bay raced through my mind. They didn't last long – and neither would we.

But we made it. Terry got his then partner Mo, who had been at the ceilidh with us, to get right up to the bow and give warnings of any obstructions like buoys in the water. Eventually, we got back to the safe confines of Stromness harbour, where Terry slung one bow rope over a bollard.

We all scrambled back to our hotel for a few hours' sleep. At 8 a.m. the following morning we wearily made our way down towards the *St Ola*. The tide was fully in and we saw the *Girl Mina* floating well out from the side of the harbour tethered only by that one bow rope.

We boarded the *St Ola* for the short two-hour return voyage to the mainland – and the longest-ever five-hour drive, back down to Aberdeen.

CHAPTER SEVEN

Chuuk Lagoon, Micronesia, Pacific

'No more shall you behold the evils I have suffered and
done'

Sophocles I, *Oedipus Rex*

After our return from the tumultuous Scapa Flow video shoot we began the
laborious task of putting the video together. I'd never been involved in
video production before, and I was able to glimpse just how much work
goes into producing even a short video. I had written the script prior to
going to Scapa, but the footage we eventually came back with differed
hugely from what we had intended to get. Some of the shots we had
planned for simply didn't work because of diving conditions. It had proved
near impossible to direct and co-ordinate divers underwater, where no
communications other than rudimentary hand and light signals were
possible.

We had, on the other hand, been lucky to get lots of good atmospheric
footage of the *Inverlane* and the Churchill Barrier wrecks, which we hadn't
really planned for. In the end these turned out to be the most visually
haunting images from the shoot.

The deeper German wrecks proved very dark and gloomy with only
small sections of them being lit up by the camera lights at any one time.
The *Inverlane* and *Gobernador Bories* were much shallower and set in the
fantastic visibility of Burra Sound which filled the camera lens with
brightness and panoramic seascapes. The topside film we shot on the decks
of the *Inverlane* gave non-divers an idea of what a wreck really is like.

Rick Wood and the rest of the team spent countless hours painstakingly
cutting the footage and mashing it into a production. We hired a musician
who reviewed the footage and created a catchy soundtrack for the images.
The script was finalised and passed to the well-known actor Patrick Allen

for him to narrate. The skill he used and the depth of feeling he brought to the simple words of our script let me glimpse how much of an art there is even to reading simple lines for a voice-over.

Once the master video was finalised it was sent for copying whilst the cover was designed and printed off. For the cover we used a topside shot of the *Inverlane*. The background was coloured to give the impression of the bows of a wreck underwater. We then took images of two divers and added that to the picture to complete the effect. Once the video prints were ready, labels were added and they were all boxed up.

When we started advertising the video in national diver magazines we were pleased by the response. The orders came in steadily and we started despatching the videos. As the funds built up from sales we recouped our outlays and then started making a small but tidy profit.

The underwater images in *Dive Scapa Flow* were shot in simple standard video 8 format whilst the topside images were shot using Rick Wood's professional camera gear on Betacam SP. As funds accrued we agreed that we should consider doing a few more video productions, and with this in mind, we invested in new Amphibico housings for Hi 8 video, which had a far higher clarity. Each time we copied original footage onto another medium, such as VHS format for the tapes themselves, we were losing a degree of sharpness. Hi 8 would give sharper images, which would reproduce with a corresponding higher quality.

As we discussed what our next project would be I came up with the idea of Chuuk (or Truk, as it was then known) Lagoon, perhaps the most famous wreck dive site in the world. It was far away, stuck out in a remote part of the Pacific, but was international in its appeal and we thought there would be a market for a good diving video in America and Japan as well as in the UK.

Chuuk Lagoon is part of Micronesia, a collection of hundreds of tropical islands scattered across the Pacific Ocean between Hawaii and the Philippines. Its coral islands are bursts of colour amidst the deep blue of the ocean. Chuuk Lagoon itself was once a large volcanic island, which sank over millennia. The 15 high lagoon islands, mountainous and wooded, are the tallest peaks of that original island, the rim of the volcanic island itself.

The 15 islands form a lagoon 40 miles across and surrounded by 140 miles of barrier reef creating a natural, deep anchorage, protected from the might of the Pacific. There are five main entrances into the lagoon and in the twentieth century it became a defendable strategic base for the Japanese military expansion.

Legend has it that the first native settlers arrived at Chuuk Lagoon by canoe in the fourteenth century from the island of Kosrae. The first Europeans to arrive were the Spanish in the *San Lucus*, captained by Alonso de Arellano in 1565. The natives, fierce warriors, set after the *San Lucus* in hundreds of canoes forcing the Spanish to take flight. No European dared to return for the next 250 years.

The Germans took possession of Chuuk in 1899 and developed a copra trade. Germany's ability to protect this far-flung outpost was latterly weakened by the Great War in Europe. The Japanese took advantage of this and occupied the Chuuk islands in 1914 and began to fortify them.

Japan believed that the islands, once fortified, were impregnable and the Lagoon earned the title the 'Gibraltar of the Pacific'. Chuuk became the Japanese Imperial Fleet's most important central Pacific base. Its huge sheltered lagoon, with only a few entrances, created a perfect, calm anchorage. Five airstrips and seaplane bases were constructed. Heavy minefields were sown in all the passes into the lagoon except the north and south passes, which were used by the Japanese. These, allied to small beach defensive mines, were considered to be the main deterrents against invasion.

Controlled mines were placed in the north pass in two rows, spaced about 160 metres apart. In between the two rows were underwater detector coils, which could detect the passage of ships over them. Listening stations ashore could remotely detonate the mines via underwater cables.

Chuuk was indeed heavily defended. But there was a flaw in the Japanese thinking which would be tragically exposed in the Second World War. With only a few entrances into the lagoon, it would be too easy to seal a fleet inside.

On 17 February 1944, American naval forces launched an air attack on the Japanese Fourth Fleet at anchor in the lagoon, codenamed 'Operation Hailstorm'. The attack took the Japanese completely by surprise although, unknown to the Americans, most of the Japanese capital ships and an aircraft carrier had slipped anchor and left the lagoon a few days before the attack, after a single American reconnaissance plane was spotted.

American F6F fighters attacked in the first wave, making a circular run encompassing nearly the whole lagoon before encountering enemy fighters. The F6F fighters swooped in over this tropical paradise, knocking Zeros out of the skies, and catching many on the ground or in the process of lifting off, as they dashed to get airborne to repulse the surprise invaders. Zeros fell from the skies trailing smoke, some crash landing in dense forests and others splashing into the clear waters of the lagoon.

Once the Japanese air cover was destroyed, the large slow merchant ships of the fleet were sitting ducks in their lagoon prison. Continuous waves of American Helldiver bombers and Avenger torpedo bombers attacked non-stop for two days.

Finally Douglas Dauntless bombers joined the attack, dropping fragmentation clusters and incendiary bombs. The bombing was unrelenting and few Japanese vessels managed to escape from the confines of the lagoon, which fast became the graveyard of the fleet.

By the end of the second day of the American attack, Japan had lost over 40 ships and 270 aircraft. Fuel depots, vital to Japan's war effort in the Pacific, had been destroyed, crippling her operations and marking the beginning of the end of Japan's grip on the Pacific islands.

Once the war was over, calm and serenity returned to the lagoon. On land, the thick jungle soon consumed the scars of the American attack. The lagoon closed over the sunken fleet and the world forgot about the ghost ships lying deep in the clear warm waters.

The Japanese fleet lay undisturbed for 20 years, quickly becoming a welcome shelter for a myriad of corals and sea life. Each wreck became an underwater island, a place of refuge and food, each one a delicately poised marine eco-system. The wrecks themselves were time capsules, each one frozen in time at the moment of its sinking.

By the 1960s, the sunken fleet had passed completely from human memory. But then, however, a plague of coral-eating Crown of Thorns starfish caused a flurry of activity in the lagoon's waters, and the intact, unsalvaged wrecks were rediscovered.

News of such a fabulous discovery flashed round the diving world. The perfectly preserved wrecks, with all their contents *in situ*, lying in crystal clear, warm water and beautifully colonised by corals and abundant sea life, began to draw divers. Over 100 wrecks have so far been charted in and around the lagoon: oil tankers, submarines, tugs, cargo and passenger ships and a German First World War battleship. Scores of Japanese and American warplanes litter the seabed.

The wrecks have not been salvaged or pilfered in any way, as most of the shallow-water wrecks around the British coast have been. Every porthole, every telegraph, every helm and every compass binnacle still stands in position.

This was a war fleet, and cargo holds are still full with the machinery of war: crammed full of trucks, artillery, fighter planes, ammunition and even small Japanese two-man tanks. In all, some 250,000 tons of supplies and munitions were sent to the bottom of the lagoon in the attack.

Dining areas and galleys are littered with dishes and silverware. Sake bottles, typewriters and all sorts of personal effects are stacked or strewn about. Portholes hang open, as they were when afloat, to allow the sea breeze to cool the tropical heat. The water is as warm as a bath, about 85°F.

The lagoon has been declared an underwater museum by the Philippine government to prevent pilfering of the wrecks' contents. All diving has to be carried out under the watchful eye of a local guide.

Truk Lagoon, as it was then known, became even better known among divers when Jacques Cousteau filmed one of his series of underwater diving programmes there. Haunting images of sunken ships, artillery and fantastic sea life drifted across TV screens, imprinting themselves in my childhood mind.

Chuuk would be the pinnacle for our fledgling underwater film company. If the lure of these fabulous sunken ships, with the fantastic pictures we knew we would get, wasn't going to sell videos then nothing would.

As we planned the trip we decided to try to produce three videos to maximise our return from our time out in the Pacific. First we would stop for a week in Guam. It was the fulcrum for all internal flights around Micronesia and we would shoot a video there. After moving on to Chuuk for a week or so we would then move over to another Micronesian island, Palau. Palau was far less well known but had an equal number of sunken wrecks and offered more varied diving, with better coral dropoffs, the legendary 1,000-foot vertical Ngemilis Wall and more sharks. I set to researching the wrecks and roughing out draft scripts.

The flight out to Guam was hard going. We flew out of Aberdeen to London. From there we had to fly to Tokyo, then transit to Osaka from where we hopped down to Guam. In total it was some 36 hours of travelling.

After filming in Guam we flew out to Chuuk, landing at the tiny strip and cluster of buildings set amid the tropical green of the jungle. From there we were whisked out to the rather grand-sounding Chuuk Continental Hotel on Moen Island, the largest of the islands. This hotel was a low collection of apartment buildings, which lined the coral sand of the lagoon itself.

Palm trees fringed the grounds of the hotel hanging out over the beach. Sunsets were magnificent, the glowing red orb of the sun slowly sinking below the horizon in a blaze of brilliant colour across the open waters of the lagoon, and were followed by the intense blackness of a tropical night.

After sorting out our kit at the Blue Lagoon dive shop we arrived at the small pier just outside the hotel where we loaded up into two small local boats. These 20-foot-long vessels had two small outboard tiller engines. One was fixed dead ahead, the other was tiller driven and used for controlling our direction.

Both engines were fired up and we sped across the open expanses of the lagoon. The boats had no electronic position finding equipment; GPS systems hadn't yet become available at this time. We were guided to the wrecks by nothing other than the expert knowledge of the local boat crew.

The wrecks were located well out in the 40-mile-wide lagoon. The crew navigated by using land transits from the surrounding islands, lining up fixed points on the distant land masses. One transit would give a track to run along until a second transit lined up. When both transits were lined up the resulting intersecting point marked the location of the wreck. Throughout the week the crew would regularly motor the dive boat right up to these distant wrecks with pinpoint accuracy using these simple transits. It was clear that they were expert seamen.

Our first dive was to be on the aircraft ferry *Fujikawa Maru*: 435 feet in length, she sits on an even keel in 34 metres of water, sunk by a single torpedo striking her starboard side just aft of the superstructure. Even though she lies in over 100 feet of water her two masts rise up and still just break the surface, providing a ready guide down to the main parts of the wreck below.

One by one, our group of divers kitted up and rolled backwards off the gunwales of our dive boat to disappear in an explosion of bubbles. As the bubbles from my entry disappeared the underwater visibility stunned me with its clarity. I could see for about 100 metres laterally in every direction.

I looked over to the mast and saw a wild profusion of brilliantly coloured corals encrusting it. I let my eyes follow the mast down into the depths and was staggered to be able to see at least one half of this great ship far down beneath me on the seabed. I could look forward to the bow itself and then follow the ship back past huge open-topped holds, seemingly black inside, to a large and atmospheric bridge superstructure which ran off into the distance.

As a group we all descended down beside the mast in the warm, clear water, falling and falling down towards the wreck. As we arrived at the wreck the two cameramen that day started filming and we finned forward in the perfect slack water of the lagoon. At the bow, a large naval gun still stood, its bearing telling us that this gun had been in action just before the sinking. Even though the steel parts of the gun were covered in coral we located a bronze maker's plate to which no coral had attached itself, which gave a date for the gun of 1899. This gun was an antique at the time of the battle, more than 40 years old, and would scarcely have been able to provide much defence for this huge but slow-moving giant ship.

As we moved back aft from the tip of the bow, we came across the huge hatch for Hold No. 1 which was easily 30 feet wide by about 40 feet in length. Cautiously, we finned over the edge of the hold and hung in mid-water, shining our torches down into the darkness. I could see that large girders ran across the hold and that it dropped down through a number of deck levels.

Gently we dumped some air from our buoyancy wings and dropped down into the hold, passing the 'tween-deck level and heading on down to the bottom of the hold. Here we found her cargo, so carefully worked into position all those years ago. Stacked or scattered all around were spare wings, engine cowlings, propellers, wheels, heavy aircraft machine guns and cartridges for Zeros, along with 6-inch shells and innumerable stacks of oil drums. In a darker part of Hold No. 2, we found complete Zero fuselages.

After spending some time down at the bottom of the foredeck holds we finned slowly upwards, towards the distant rectangle of blue light that marked our escape point from the hold.

Once back on the main deck we moved back to the bridge superstructure. Passing through clouds of small Pacific baitfish I moved into the bridge through gaping window openings and then passed beyond, into the midships accommodation. Although this was wreck penetration, it didn't feel like it at all. Around me were blue shafts of light streaming in from open doors, windows and rotted holes in the steel walls of the deck-house. Electric cables hung, partially suspended from the roofs and encrusted by coral, like a marine spider's web. Everywhere I looked, doors led off into different parts of the superstructure and the temptation to forget your dive discipline and explore indefinitely was seductive and disarming.

I found a door leading into the engine room and moved forward into a huge black space, and hung in mid-water near the roof. There were no bright openings here to allow ambient light in to lift the veil of darkness. It was black, the pitch black of eternal darkness.

All around the sides of the engine room, catwalks snaked off into the distance. I shone my torch directly down to try and light up the engine itself, which would be located at the very bottom of this room. But there was no trace of the engine or, indeed, the bottom of the engine room. It was out of range of my powerful torch, well beneath the level of the seabed around. With time for the dive fast running out, it wasn't the moment to drop back down to the deepest part of the wreck. Exploration down there would have to wait for another day.

I made my way back to the entrance doorway and left the superstructure. As I moved out of the rotted deck-housing back into free water I was dwarfed by massive RAS masts (short for Refuelling At Sea) – huge H-shaped masts from which fuel pipes could connect to other vessels.

When all our divers were out of the water at the end of the dive, it was clear that we were all blown away by the experience. Such a fantastic wreck, so intact and so full of artefacts, in such clear water, was amazing.

The dive boat headed over to Eten Island where we were able to tie up at a small pier and go ashore for a light lunch and a surface decompression interval before the afternoon dive. The local guide demonstrated how he could climb easily up a 40-foot-high palm tree to chop down coconuts for us. Deftly, with a large diving knife, he stripped off the outermost coarse layers and then cracked open the tough brown shell, without spilling a drop. Sadly, later that week, the guide's brother would be killed elsewhere after falling from a palm tree while recovering coconuts.

The afternoon dive was a shallow one, onto the near-intact remains of a Japanese 'Betty Bomber', in just nine metres of water not far offshore. This bomber had been returning to base to refuel when it was shot down by American fighters.

Betty Bombers were long-range tactical bombers fitted with huge unprotected fuel tanks, which became notorious for bursting into flames when hit. The Americans christened the Betty the 'Flying Cigar', partly because of its shape and partly because of this serious shortcoming.

As we splashed into the water from the dive boat and looked down, we could see immediately the whole of the bomber lying on a clean white sandy seabed. Corals love steel but hate the taste of aluminium, from which these bombers were constructed. The fuselage of the plane was completely clear of coral – it was as though the plane had just gone down yesterday.

We could see that the plane must have been travelling at some speed when it hit the water, as the force of the impact had broken off a large section of the nose cone and cockpit and pushed it to its port side. Each of the two wing-mounted engines had been ripped from their wing mounts, and were sitting in the seabed about 100 metres ahead of the wreck of the plane itself. The blades of the propellers were curved backwards from the impact.

The waist gun positions midships on either side were open and allowed entry into the plane itself. Inside, it was as though the crew had left the plane only the day before. All around were internal fittings like fire extinguishers and heavy machine guns. Although the coral had generally left the aluminium of the bomber clean from any growth, we found that the two engines, which were filled with steel parts, had become overgrown with brain coral, leather coral and twigs of multiplex coral.

The next day we dived the *Yamagiri Maru*, one of the largest vessels in the lagoon, a lightly armed freighter lying on her port side in just over 30 metres of water. We soon found that she was guarded by large numbers of gently pulsating, giant jellyfish.

In Hold No. 5 we found a huge mound of hundreds of giant, 1–2-metre-long shells for the most powerful guns of the Second World War, the 18.1-inch guns of the super-battleships *Yamato* and *Musashi*. These huge shells had a range of over 30 miles and could pierce through the thickest armour plating. It was a sobering thought to be cocooned in that dark 'on its side' hold, with such a huge amount of high explosive around. Just one of these shells going off in action would have completely devastated the entire ship.

As we left the hold, our ever-present local guide beckoned us into the rear of the midships superstructure and led us through into a deeply recessed room. There, he put his hand behind a sheet of rotted steel and pulled out a human skull. I think that both my dive buddy that day and I were saddened by this. The guide obviously thought he was doing something which would look good for the camera but I was sickened to think that some poor Japanese sailor's skull was being used as a curio for underwater tourists. We had been told at the outset that Japanese divers had recovered all the human remains from the wrecks for cremation some considerable time ago. This one had obviously escaped.

After dutifully filming the skull, it was hidden again by the guide, presumably for the next party of underwater tourists, and our group moved on to explore another part of the wreck. Although this wreck too was stunning, with clouds of baitfish swimming among the brilliant-coloured corals, my thoughts remained with the ethics of what we had just witnessed.

That afternoon, we dived on the upside-down remains of a Japanese Zero fighter. Again the corals had found its aluminium unpalatable and the plane was clean. We could see all the workings of the plane and also a line of machine gun bullet holes, which had raked across its underbelly. The soft aluminium had been peeled back and ripped open like cardboard, sending this fighter plunging down into the sea.

The following day we had our deepest dive, onto the freighter *Nippo Maru*, an army supply vessel which sat almost upright in just over 40 metres of water. American aircraft had dropped a time bomb that blew the keel out of the ship from below.

As we dropped down through the clear water I felt the rush of nitrogen narcosis as I passed the 30-metre mark. The water seemed darker down at this depth and gave the *Nippo Maru* a haunting, ghost-like feeling. As I arrived down on the main deck of the ship at about 40 metres, I knew I was well affected by the wash of narcosis, but the wreck was still spellbinding. Parked on the main deck were small Japanese two-man tanks, covered from tracks to turret top in marine life. Heading past the tanks we came across the huge bridge. Moving inside through gaping doorways, I saw traces of the wooden decking, the wood itself overlaid on a steel floor. Wood-eating micro-organisms had attacked the wood and consumed it. Where the deck planking was screwed to the steel deck beneath, metallic salts had leached out into the surrounding wood forcing the woodborers to stop their destructive work. If there is one thing that leaves a bad taste in a woodborer's mouth, it's anything metallic.

The telegraph still stood upright fixed to the floor and in the ten o'clock position and the helm still looked as though it could steer the ship. With such a deep dive, our bottom time on the wreck was sadly limited and after the briefest of explorations of the bridge it was time to raise our heads and strike out for the long slow ascent to the surface. As I rose up from the wreck and looked down, I could see that the whole hull of the ship was covered in a blaze of coral.

The following day I awoke in my room to another beautiful tropical morning. The azure seas of the lagoon lapped at the coral beach only a stone's throw from our rooms. Already the din of the jungle night creatures had been replaced by the buzz of its day inhabitants. After a breakfast of cereals and tropical fruits, in swim shorts and T-shirts we made our way down to the pier, carrying all our diving equipment. Already, even though it was barely 8 a.m., the sun was oppressively hot and burning off any moisture left from the long tropical night.

Once down at the shore, we loaded our gear onto the dive boats and were soon underway. Immediately, the cooling sea air was a pleasant relief from the heat ashore. We were all starting to get wetsuit tans: brown on those parts of our legs and arms that were exposed whilst retaining a Scottish tan – pure white – on those body parts that were covered up all day under T-shirts and wetsuits. At sea you get double the direct sunlight you get when ashore. Sunlight hits you directly from above, as on land, but in addition you get sunlight reflected from the sea. At sea, you can get sunburnt more easily than ashore and whilst out at sea in these small boats with no cover we were very exposed. We tried to keep covered up as best we could.

This morning's dive was to be on the *Sankisan Maru*, a medium-sized freighter lying in 24 metres, shallow enough that the top of her foremast broke the surface at low tide.

We headed out into the lagoon and soon I could see the top few inches of a rusted cylindrical top of a huge foremast just breaking through the surface. Short waves lapped over it.

The boat slowed as we approached the foremast and as we came alongside, our guide on the bow deftly picked up the small anchor and chain from the foredeck and plonked it down unceremoniously on the top of the foremast itself. The engine was switched off and we rocked gently in the almost glassy waves anchored to the top of the foremast.

The *Sankisan Maru* is in fact only half a ship. During Operation Hailstone she took a direct hit from American planes, in a stern hold containing munitions. This set off the ammunition in a cataclysmic explosion, which totally destroyed the aft section of the ship and caused the bow section to sink like a stone.

We all rolled into the water and its warm embrace flooded into my wetsuit. I was instantly immersed in the seascape. I moved over to the foremast and found that every inch of it was crowded with corals, sponges and large clams with their zigzag openings which snapped closed as they sensed a diver's approach.

I started to descend, following the mast downwards. There was no need to stay close to it, as there was no discernible current here to worry about. As I looked down I could see the whole forward section of the wreck below me, from the bridge superstructure to the very tip of the bow. In the foredeck, two large hatches, probably 30 feet wide by 40 feet in length, beckoned me into the innards of this vessel.

I landed on the foredeck between the gunwale and hatch rim, which projected upwards a few feet. I looked down into the hold, but the bottom was a long way down and shrouded in darkness. Checking my depth, I gingerly finned out into the open water above the void of the hold. Breathing out, to lose a little buoyancy from my lung spaces, I let myself float gently downwards. As I moved into the shadow of the hold and my eyes adjusted, the veil of darkness was lifted. Sunlight streaming down from above lit up its innards.

As I neared the bottom of the hold I saw that it was absolutely covered in a mass of small-arms ammunition. Thousands of bullets, single rounds and clips were piled up everywhere. This was my first encounter with ammunition on this scale and I didn't want to land heavily in amongst this dangerous cargo. I kicked my fins and adjusted my position as I fell, so that when I reached the bottom of the hold I would land on a large girder that ran across the bottom, projecting up from the mass of ammunition.

As I moved out to explore the hold, I came across a vast area littered with wooden small-arms ammunition boxes, some three feet in length by two feet wide. I was puzzled why the wooden boxes here had survived intact, as normally the woodborers would have turned these to dust long ago. I learned later that the high level of copper in the water from the huge piles of cartridges killed them off.

As I moved across the hold, being filmed by the ever-present cameraman, I came across engine cowlings for Mitsubishi Zeros. Nearby were a number of Toyota trucks, recognisable from their engines, tyres and chassis. The bodies of the trucks had long ago been turned to silt by the sea.

After exploring and filming in this hold for about 15 minutes we moved back up towards the bright sunlight and the shallower main deck. As I exited the hold, I saw a small deck-house with an aft-facing doorway. Swimming up to it I shone my torch inside. Stacks of canned food gleamed in my light, the labels and contents lost aeons ago. In another part of this deck-house, rows of bottle tops, most probably sake, poked out from the silt.

Once out again on deck I found the remains of yet more vehicles stowed for carriage. I ventured up to the very bow itself and finned out over the stem. Moving about 25 feet out from the tip of the bow I turned around and got a fantastic perspective of the massive bow itself with both anchors either side still held snugly in their hawse pipes, evidence that the ship had been underway and trying to manoeuvre during the attack.

All too soon our permitted bottom time on this wreck had been used up and it was time to ascend. As I rose slowly up, I finned over towards the giant foremast, which led the way up to our boat. Above me I could see the rest of our party making their way up the mast. I could easily see the underside of our dive boat and even from this distance – and depth – I could pick out the anchor, still perched on top of the foremast with its loop of chain and rope that led to our boat.

I awoke early the next day to yet another clamouring tropical morning. Breakfast was finished by 7.30, and we were loading the dive boats by 8 a.m. Soon we were being whisked out to the morning dive, the freighter *Kansho Maru*, which lies upright in more than 40 metres of water.

By now, because of the fantastic underwater visibility, we were accustomed to seeing the wrecks below us immediately on entry to the water. However, this wreck was so deep that, unusually, I couldn't glimpse any sight of it once I had rolled backwards off the dive boat into the water.

In a skydiver's prone position, I dropped down through the still waters into the darkness beneath me. Slowly the gloom materialised into the form of a massive shipwreck. Our cameraman and I were coming down just aft of the bridge superstructure and I recognised the pitched roof of an engine room. Set in the roof were open ventilator skylights, each having two portholes set in it. The porthole glass was still intact despite the trauma of the explosions that sank her. All the roof skylights were still propped open, just as they had been left on that fateful day of the attack in 1944, to let the incredible heat of the engine room escape.

I shone my torch into the black interior and let its beam trace along catwalk gratings that snaked around the outside of the room. The *Kansho Maru* had been at anchor, having previous American bomb damage repaired, when she was attacked again. With no engine power to manoeuvre she was a sitting duck when US warplanes swooped mercilessly once again out of the skies.

Realising their hopeless position, the crew took to the lifeboats at the first sign of the attack, leaving all their personal possessions behind. The entire crew had safely got away in lifeboats by the time an American torpedo had struck the freighter, sending her to the bottom. As I moved forward into the bridge section I came across the telegraph which, because of the repairs, was still at 'All Stop'.

Moving out of the bridge, I moved aft along a walkway at the side of the midships accommodation superstructure. Swathes of corals hung down over the side of the ship like a veil of curtains. As I moved along the partially covered walkway, portholes lined the inboard side of the deck-house, the glass covered in a light film of silt.

Aft of this superstructure, I moved inside a beckoning doorway and moved up a corridor from which another doorway led off to my right. Entering through this doorway I found I had stumbled into the galley. Pots still stood on stoves, just as they had been left, all those years ago, by the Japanese cooks. Crockery and cooking utensils were exactly where the crew had left them.

Leaving the galley through the same doorway, I continued my exploration of this corridor and soon moved into a large open area which had once been the senior officers' quarters. I realised that there had been a row of cabins here, each with its own porthole and sink. The thin steel walls that had divided up the cabins had rotted away to leave one large common space, punctuated by regularly spaced wash hand basins and portholes above. Electric cables hung uniformly down from the roof of each cabin from where they had fallen.

Personal effects were scattered everywhere in the layer of silt that lined the bottom of these rooms. Because the crew had abandoned ship so quickly, they had left everything as it was at the moment of their departure, as a Japanese underwater version of the *Marie Celeste*. Typewriters, drinks bottles, tin boxes holding combs, scissors and the like lay half buried by the silt amid the remains of tables, chairs and heaters. This wreck had far more personal effects than any of the other wrecks we had dived.

As the end of the week neared, we planned a dive down to the 500-foot long tanker, *Shinkoku Maru*, one of the biggest tankers in the Pacific in the Second World War. She was sunk by a single torpedo and lay upright in 38 metres.

As we descended to this wreck, we arrived at the superstructure which had swathes of corals of every description covering it. I entered the decaying deck-housing through a curtain of coral and once inside found the largest spaces or rooms of all the wrecks we had dived that week. Lounges, with the fixings and remnants of tables still present, gave way to a honeycomb of dark galleries. Everywhere I looked corridors led off to other areas and shafts of light blazed in from open windows, doorways and rotted sections of the wreck. My eyes got used to the darkness and I kept a wary eye on my exit point at all times. After finning slowly through this superstructure for some time, I was relieved to squeeze through a rotted window and get back out into the sunlight of open water.

The last dive of the week was the afternoon dive on a shallow military vessel, the *Hino Maru*. After that, it was time to pack up and head off on the next leg of our trip to the island of Palau. The week's diving in Chuuk Lagoon had proved to be one of the diving highlights of my career to that date. Each day we were diving on spellbinding, intact shipwrecks, filled with the legacy of war and set in stunningly clear water. Chuuk had far surpassed my expectations, and to this day I hanker to return, to drift amongst its amazing treasure trove of Japanese wrecks, a time capsule preserved forever in February 1944.

CHAPTER EIGHT

Republic of Palau, Micronesia

'The many men, so beautiful!
And they all dead did lie'
　　　　　S.T. Coleridge, *The Rime of the Ancient Mariner*

After our successful week's diving and filming in Chuuk Lagoon we knew we had managed to accumulate a lot of visually stunning images, and we had enough to make one, if not two, striking diving videos.

It was with some reluctance therefore, that we packed up all our dive and camera gear and made our way back to the tiny runway and one-storey airport buildings. We were moving on, to the Palau archipelago. Our research told us that there were as many Second World War Japanese wrecks there as in the fabled Chuuk Lagoon, along with a far greater variety of diving. This week wouldn't be all wrecks.

The Palau islands are a collection of some 200 limestone islands, located 400 miles north of the Equator, 800 miles south-west of Guam and 700 miles east of Mindanao in the Philippines. They are the remains of an undersea ridge of volcanic islands, which loop away across the globe in a 400-mile-long necklace. The ridge is part of the Pacific Ring of Fire, an area known for its volcanic and undersea activity.

Over millions of years, oceanic volcanoes had pushed their increasing masses up from the seabed, some erupting above sea level. Islands were formed where these undersea mountains, already covered in coral, pushed out of the sea. Once out of the sea, the corals died off and formed limestone mountains. The soft limestone of the smaller outcrops was eroded by wave action and sea life, both of which ate away at the bases of these islands to make the bases at sea level thinner than the top, giving them a mushroom-like appearance.

As we flew in towards the main island of the Republic of Palau, Koror, we could see straight away that this was a very special place we were going to dive and film. We had booked into the Palau Pacific Resort, a tropical paradise of a resort complex, where a string of low-level apartments led off a main central, ethnic-style wooden reception area. In specially constructed pools dotted around the main central buildings, black tip reef sharks cruised around and mingled with stingrays.

We immediately got to work, shooting some arrival scenes and the apartments themselves for the video and busied ourselves getting ready for the next day's dive, the first of the week here. The following morning, we were up early and were soon down at the small pier loading our dive kit aboard a large, gleaming-white dive boat. This was a 75-foot-long luxury craft powered by a water jet, which could drive the large, heavy boat at speeds of about 30 knots.

As we left the pier the dive boat powered up and we were soon up on the plane and screaming through an overwhelming collection of clustered, limestone islands as we made our way out to the fabled Ngemelis Wall area. We had two dives planned for today in this area. The first dive would be in the Blue Hole with the second dive being on the famous wall itself, an undersea cliff face that plunges vertically down from just a few feet from the surface to a depth of over 1,000 feet.

We moved at speed through the islands, our boat's captain clearly enjoying twisting and turning the boat to slip through narrow passages between the islands at speed. Suddenly, we passed beyond a small island and were in an open stretch of water moving out towards the coral reef that ringed around the limestone islands. Passing through a break in the barrier reef we moved to the seaward side of the reef, over the oceanic depths that ring the islands beyond the reef. We moved at speed along the outside of the reef, the warm tropical air buffeting us and keeping us cool.

After a short while I felt the boat start to slow – we were approaching the dive site. Our group of seven divers and cameramen started to get kitted up whilst the few other paying guests aboard the large boat also got ready. Once we were all rigged up, the skipper backed the boat up as close to the reef as he dared and one by one we all stepped off the aluminium dive platform at the stern into the welcoming and warm embrace of the Pacific.

The underwater visibility was staggering. Beneath me was open water dropping off to an incredible depth. The lighter waters near the surface gave way to a beautiful oceanic blue of mid-water, before merging with the seemingly bottomless voids beneath.

I looked across to the reef wall itself nearby and saw a wild profusion of corals in a beautiful explosion of colour around the top of the reef. As I looked down the vertical reef wall the colours seemed to lose their brilliance the deeper I looked – water progressively filters out all the red colours underwater. The deeper I looked on this sheer wall, the more the corals took on a uniform blue colour, darkening as the wall plunged away into the abyss, before the wall lost itself as it finally seemed to merge with the darkness below.

Once we were all in the water we kicked our legs and finned over to the edge of the reef. The top of the reef came to about four metres beneath the surface and on top of the barrier reef itself a plateau had been formed.

Keeping just off the bottom, out of the surge of waves breaking on the reef itself, we finned over towards the target for the morning's dive, the Blue Hole. The entire barrier reef is heavily fissured and quite hollow. A number of these circular openings in the reef top were dotted around, gaining their name because the dark blue of their deep water contrasts so much against the beautiful bright colours of the reef table top. The blue holes allow entry into this vast interconnecting series of caves and caverns.

We left the shallow waters of the reef top and swam out into the middle of the Blue Hole, which was some 75 feet across. We all dumped air from our BCDs and started to sink slowly into the hole, filming as we descended into the darkness below.

Once we were about ten metres down, the hole itself opened up into a cathedral-like large chamber with a number of cave-like passages snaking off in various directions. I turned my head to look up to our entry point and could see the complete circle of the Blue Hole above, and in the distance, at the ends of the passages leading off, could make out other blue holes which I hadn't seen from the surface.

We dropped down and down into the bowels of the hole and the sunlight from above got progressively more obstructed. Eventually, at a depth of 37 metres, we found the passageway we had been looking for. Entering this, we swam along its length as it led us horizontally through the reef wall, until we popped out through the wall itself, via a small hole fringed with giant stick corals.

One minute we were inside the honeycombed reef, becoming used to the seeming security of having the reef around. The next we were outside the reef wall looking down the fabled Ngemelis Wall proper into colossal depths. The visibility that day was in the region of 100 metres. That meant that I could see probably down to a depth of about 150 metres in total. As my eyes followed the wall down, it became a solid blue-black. There was no sign of the bottom beyond the 150-metre visible depth. The bottom was still a staggering 200 or more metres beyond the limit of our visibility.

After exploring the wall around the 40-metre mark we started to make our way slowly up the outside towards the distant surface. The wall towered over me and, as I looked upwards towards the boat, the unmistakable shadow of a large shark passed over me, silhouetted in the sunlight from above, its dorsal fins projecting from either side like the wings of a sleek jet plane. We had been told that this reef, because of the strong currents that sweep along it, is regularly visited by large sharks.

We continued our ascent and soon found ourselves nearing our nine-metre and six-metre decompression stops. We hung just off the wall, waiting as the bubbles of nitrogen flushed from our bodies. As we did so, we started to see a number of large grey reef sharks passing along the reef, working gently into the current. The sharks seemed to be all around us, some below us and some out to seaward from us. These were big sharks, some nine feet long, but they seemed to have little interest in us. They were just cruising and obviously did not think we were suitable prey. They came so close to us that I felt I could almost reach out and touch them. When a large shark came past I saw that it had a length of fisherman's rope or netting caught around its upper body. I had become so inured to seeing these large sharks, apparently so benign and at such close range, that in a brief moment of madness I thought about reaching out with my knife to cut the rope off the shark.

As I hung at the top of this vertical wall, above more than 1,000 feet of open ocean, I saw, some distance beneath me, a large section of the ever-present shoals of fish become frenzied. Thousands of fish started darting and twisting, as though controlled by a single mind, their silvered sides flashing and glinting in the sunlight cascading down from above.

Suddenly, from the depths below there was a flash of smooth, grey skin and muscle, almost too fast for my eye to discern, as a grey reef shark whipped into the seething mass of fish at terrific speed. The shoal parted like a pair of curtains being pulled back to allow the hunter to pass right through.

The kill was successful and the shark disappeared with its food into the distance. The shoal of fish closed over, the fish indifferently returning to their normal, slowly revolving mass once the panic was over. One of their kin had been snatched, but it had been sacrificed for the sake of the group. The moment was gone in a flash as if it had never happened. The lack of caring, the indifference to the kill, indeed to any kill in the undersea world, highlights one of the differences between us and the animal world: the lack of compassion.

I had been awed by the speed of the shark's movement and the kill itself. Although I felt relatively safe with my group of other divers I didn't kid myself that the sharks were afraid of us in any way. They simply did not recognise us as their natural prey. Had they decided to go for us, they would very quickly have torn us to pieces. As I hung there reflecting on the kill, I saw a shoal of barracuda drifting along the reef face towards me — another set of predators in this undersea world. A wariness of these six-foot-long sleek predators snapped me out of my reverie. We had been in the water long enough and it was time to strike out for the surface.

The following day we were scheduled to dive on our first Japanese wreck in Palau. Like Chuuk Lagoon, Palau had been in Japanese control until a fierce onslaught by American forces in 1944. There was a huge merchant fleet at anchor in amongst the protective limestone islands and over the course of the two days of the attack, every single ship was sent to the bottom.

The target wreck for us was a mystery one called, for want of the true name the 'Helmet Wreck'. It had lain undetected since 1944 in about 35 metres, until it had been found by chance in 1990. To get to the wreck site we had to load into a 25-foot-long Dory-type speedboat powered by two massive 175hp outboard engines. With such raw horsepower on tap, this long, sleek boat sped along on the calm sheltered sea, twisting and turning around the small limestone mushroom topped islands at speeds in excess of 40 knots.

We eventually sped out of the mushroom islands into the open waters of a natural anchorage. Some miles in the distance a ring of white water marked the edge of the barrier reef. I tried to cast my mind back through the years to 1944 and tried to picture a large Japanese merchant vessel afloat in this anchorage. I imagined American Hellcats plunging out of the skies, dark, vengeful dots getting larger as they spat out columns of fire at the large sitting duck of a target. Lightly armed and with no significant anti-aircraft batteries in the immediate vicinity the freighter would have been barely able to return any fire or defend itself. It was an uneven fight with only one possible outcome.

Kitted up, I rolled backwards off the gunwales of the dive boat and quickly righted myself into an upright position. I gave an OK signal to the boat and then looked down. I could easily see the top of the foremast, which rose to a depth of about ten metres. Holding up the corrugated dump tube from my buoyancy wings, I let the air out of it and started to sink down.

Once fully underwater, I slowly finned down to the top of the mast. As I approached, the unmistakable outline of a large freighter sitting on the bottom materialised out of the gloom. Reaching the mast, I descended further down towards the wreck and could see two foredeck holds with the foremast standing in the gap between them. I looked aft and could make out the square mass of the bridge superstructure silhouetted against the surrounding open water. The visibility was murkier down here and the superstructure behind the bridge disappeared into the distance.

Once down on the main deck I could see where the oak decking had rotted away to leave only the fixing points still visible. I moved out over the foremost hold and into its black interior, dropping down until the bottom of the hold came up to meet me. I turned on my dive torch and swept it around the hold, and found aircraft engines stacked for transport.

I moved back up out of the hold into the brighter water above the main deck and moved forward towards the fo'c'stle where there were two aft-facing doors open. As I shone my torch into the fo'c'stle, its beam lit up rows of oil-filled storm lanterns, stacked in a corner and half buried in silt. Thinking that this would make a good visual shot, I beckoned over the cameraman I was diving with that day and lit up the scene inside.

The cameraman and I had previously discussed how what looked like a seamless scene of a diver swimming into a room such as this had to be filmed in three distinct sections in order to make it a good piece of cinema. First of all, the cameraman would go into the room whilst the silt had not been stirred up and film the object, in this case the lanterns, in beautiful clear sediment-free visibility. Next, the cameraman would, from inside the fo'c'stle film out of the doorway as the diver – in this case, me – approached and entered the room. Then, lastly, we would both go outside and he would film from outside as I swam towards the room and entered it. It was crucial to do the whole thing back to front as, with all the movement in the fo'c'stle, there was bound to be a silt-out.

Accordingly, our plan swung into action. The cameraman gently moved into the room and filmed the lanterns in their pristine condition. Once that was done he turned around and settled himself in the silt to get a good steady position for him to film me as I entered. As he did so clouds of silt billowed up.

Once he was in position, he flashed the camera light off and on, the signal that he was rolling and ready for me to do my bit. Making sure my torch was on, to bring a bit of colour and light to the shot, I finned slowly up to the doorway and then entered the room swimming up to the pile of lanterns and examining them.

Once that shot had been done we both had to get organised and make our way out of the room. More clouds of silt billowed up and the bright rectangular blue light from the doorway turned a brown, silty colour and was almost extinguished by the silt-out.

Once outside, the cameraman got himself positioned to shoot the final section of me entering the room. At his signal, I swam forward repeating what I had just done and approached the doorway from which clouds of fine silt were now emanating. My torch couldn't penetrate through the silt but nevertheless I ploughed on and entered the room head first.

As I got into the room proper – and into the silt proper – all light was extinguished. My torch couldn't pick out anything. To ensure we got the shot however, I moved forward until I was well into the room and well out of camera shot. I then tried to turn 180 degrees to exit the room but I couldn't see anything – even the doorway with its shaft of bright light from outside had disappeared.

I found the edge of the room and then, using touch, moved along the side of the room until I found the doorway and exit point. I moved out from the room through the doorway and emerged from the silt clouds into bright open water. Once back in Scotland, we would cut the three sections to show me swimming up to the doorway, then, seen from inside looking out, I would be seen entering the doorway and sweeping my torch around and moving to examine the lanterns. The close-up of the lanterns would then be cut in as though I was looking at them.

Moving back along the foredeck we approached the bridge and then entered the engine room beyond. Catwalks ringed the engine room and gauges and valves were dotted around, on and beside massive steam pipes.

Aft of the engine room we moved along a passageway and entered the galley. Cooking pots still lay on the stoves and ranges. White crockery lay half-covered in silt, its glazed white still flashing blindingly in the glare of our dive torches. None of the crockery had any distinguishing mark which might reveal the identity of this mystery wreck, nor did any of the bridge or engine room fitments.

Everywhere, portholes hung open just as they had been left by the crew on that fateful day in 1944 when, oblivious of the murderous attack shortly to fall upon them, they had tried to allow a cooling sea breeze to slip into the innards of the ship. Bottles, cups, gas masks and clothes lay strewn about. The ship was a treasure trove, frozen in time at the moment of her sinking.

Moving aft beyond the bridge superstructure, we came to the vicinity of the single stern hold which, on one side, showed evidence of the massive explosion which had sunk her.

Passing over the hatch rim and dropping down into the hold, rows of 35 unfused depth charges gleamed menacingly in the light.

Once under the main deck, we homed in on the feature that gives this wreck its slang name, the 'Helmet Wreck'. For there, stacked one on top of another, were several mounds of Japanese army helmets, surprisingly big in the constant magnification you get in the undersea world through dive masks. The helmets had rusted and were now permanently fused together in several large lumps. It was probably this that had stopped them being pilfered by souvenir hunters. It was a unique sight.

All too soon, our allotted bottom time was used up and it was time to head back up to the surface with another good lot of footage for the planned video.

For the afternoon dive we were whisked away to do a cave dive. The entrance to the cave was at a depth of 16 metres. Once inside, we could pass through three chambers into a fourth chamber, which was air-filled and big enough to stand up in. Thinking that this would be good for the video in showing the diversity of diving in Palau, we got organised with a guide provided by the dive operator we were using.

As we slowed from our 40-knot hurtle to the dive site, we approached the limestone wall of a small mushroom-like island. Just a couple of hundred feet away from us two American Second World War landing craft swung at anchor. Whether they were still in use or had just lain there since the Second World War wasn't clear – but everywhere, both on land and below the waves, we were seeing constant reminders of the Second World War Pacific conflict.

One by one we rolled into the water backwards off the dive boat and followed our guide slowly over to the limestone wall and then started to fin down the wall towards the bottom. The water in this inland waterway was murky and full of sediment. The visibility wasn't good by the standards we had become used to – some ten metres at best.

As 16 metres clocked up on my dive computer, I saw the ominously black entrance of the cave looming up in front of me. It was perhaps 15 feet wide by about 10 feet high. Without hesitating, our guide finned into the murky blackness as we all switched on our torches, cameras and camera lights.

We swam into pitch-blackness. I shone my torch downwards and saw the bottom of the cave running off steeply downwards into deeper water out of sight. The cave was obviously opening out. Staying in sight of the roof of the cave, our guide led us forward as the light from our entry point dimmed and then disappeared. After finning for a few minutes I turned round to check on our entry point and could see it was only a speck of light in the distance behind. The walls were a rough limestone and stalactites hung down from the roof everywhere giving the cave its name: Chandelier Cave.

I became aware that our guide was now leading us upwards and we entered an area of gin-clear, fresh water. We had just passed through a halocline where the fresh water filtering down through the porous rocks from above met the seawater of the cave. Instantly, the visibility improved by a factor of ten – our torch beams seemed to go on forever.

Everywhere I looked there was a profusion of stalactites. The sheer number of them had not been appreciable in the poorer visibility of the deeper salt water. It was then that I noticed that I could only see up to the necks of the divers above and realised that their heads had now broken the surface of the fresh water and must be in an air pocket. I broke surface and found myself with the others in a small chamber filled with air that filtered through the cracks and fissures in the limestone.

Our guide removed his mouthpiece, took a large gulp of air and started telling us about how the caves had been formed. Rather gingerly, we removed our regulators and were able to speak to each other, sharing the experience of being so far inside a cave.

After a few minutes, we stuck our regulators back in our mouths and headed back down into the murkier seawater below where our guide led us into two further chambers as we worked our way deeper into the cave system.

Finally we surfaced in a fourth chamber, the largest, where we were able to partly get out of the water – we were by now some 300 feet inside the cave system. By this time however, I was starting to get a bit giddy from the constant diving, surfacing and diving again. I was pleased when the guide turned the dive and led us back through the cave system of linked chambers to the cave exit.

The night before, in our hotel, we had been put in touch with the local small plane operator. We were told we could charter him to fly us to the small island of Peleliu. There, a bloody war of attrition had been fought during the Second World War, when the Americans had tried to retake control of the island from the Japanese who were well dug in.

Some US military tacticians had worried that Japanese attacks from Peleliu and Angaur might prevent a successful retaking of the Philippines. By mid-1944 however, American air bombings had reduced Peleliu to a negligible threat. It should have then been bypassed, as were other islands held by the Japanese, but it was decided to assault the island.

US Marines staged an amphibious assault onto Orange Beach and other beaches under heavy enemy fire. The assault was successful, and once the Americans had established a beachhead they had been able to systematically push the Japanese back from the coast into the middle of this small jungle-covered island. Eventually, the Japanese retreated to the central range of hills where, some 10,000-strong, they took refuge and fought from a series of natural and man-made caves which honeycombed the jagged limestone ridges. Far away from the beaches and the threat of naval bombardment, the Japanese defended the ridges tenaciously to the death, rushing out from the caves in numbers to attack US Marines before retreating once again.

The Japanese final stand was made along a section called Bloody Nose Ridge, which the Americans assaulted on 24 November 1944. The assault stuttered and ground to a stalemate. The Japanese proved exceedingly difficult to dislodge from their fortified positions. In a handful of weeks of fighting, the Americans suffered 12,000 casualties before the Japanese were finally routed.

After the war, a conscious decision had been taken by the local government to leave the debris of the battlefield just as it was, as a testament to those who fought and died. In the late 1950s a Japanese straggler still hiding in the jungle was discovered by an old woman in her garden, his uniform torn to pieces, his hair matted and teeth blackened. He was hunted down by police who, when they captured him, bound him with rope and paraded him through the villages for everyone to see. He was the last Japanese soldier to leave Peleliu. We determined to get out to the island to film what we could there.

We turned up at the local charter pilot's small shop in the nearby town of just a few streets. After checking in and sorting out payment for the day we were led through the shop and outside where on a small, rough landing strip his plane stood – simple as that. We loaded into the small six-seater; I was seated in the front. The plane was obviously not designed for a 6 ft 2 in. Scotsman like myself and I had to force myself into the seat beside the pilot, my knees to one side up against the dashboard.

The engine started up and the plane coughed and spluttered into life. Seconds later, we were hurtling down the dusty runway and in a remarkably short distance were airborne, rushing up into the sky. The town dropped quickly away beneath us, and the encircling jungle seemed to consume it.

We were soon up to a height of a few thousand feet and below me I could see the collection of hundreds of mushroom-topped islands covered in dense undergrowth falling behind us. Soon we were approaching the barrier reef with its unmistakable white necklace of breaking waves lining along it for as far as the eye could see. On the inside of the reef, the water was shallow, azure in colour. On the outer side of the reef the water was a deep Pacific oceanic blue. As the Ngemelis Wall passed beneath our plane I knew the water plunged straight down for more than a thousand feet.

Soon we had left our small island of Koror behind and were heading south over the wide expanses of the Pacific to our destination, the island of Peleliu. The short hop by plane took less than an hour. The green dot in the ocean that is Peleliu grew steadily larger in the windscreen of the plane as we approached, its colour taken from a uniform blanket of thick jungle. Near the centre of the island there were a series of higher mountains and ridges. The unmistakable silhouette of Bloody Nose Ridge shouted its presence at us. Its sheer limestone cliffs were devoid of vegetation and stood out starkly from the uniform green of the surrounding jungle.

We flashed over the expanse of green and our pilot pointed out, with obvious relish, a small rectangular landing strip cut out from the surrounding jungle.

'This strip is a small, short strip – and the trees before it are very tall,' he said. 'So, when we go into land, as soon as we pass over the trees, I'll put the plane down very sharply. Be ready.' He looked me in the eye and his own eyes sparkled as he benignly delivered this warning.

As we made our approach to the clearing and landing strip, we dropped down and down until we were skimming the top of the tall jungle trees. The cleared landing strip flashed towards us and as our plane sped over the last of the trees we were so low that I thought we must strike the topmost branches.

As soon as the last tall trees passed inches beneath our wheels, the pilot pushed the steering column hard forward, the nose of the plane dipped heavily and we shot down to the strip. He slammed the plane down on the ground, landing heavily at speed with a thump that jarred our bones.

Just as we touched down, there was suddenly a series of short, sharp thumping staccato sounds all over the front of the plane. I didn't realise what was going on until something was shredded in our propeller and pieces of desiccated bird, blood, flesh and feathers splattered all over the windscreen.

As soon as our plane had thumped down onto the coral landing strip, our pilot put on the brakes as hard as he dared as the end of the strip charged towards us. We slowed quickly – and then it was all over and our plane was stationary.

'Many, many birds,' he said as he walked round the plane looking for any obvious signs of damage. Together we walked back up the dusty strip towards its start, where we had hit the birds. A large flock of small birds had strayed in front of us, perhaps disturbed by the noise of our approach. Their small bodies lay scattered all around the strike area. He counted them slowly. 'Thirty-three birds.'

As we came back to the plane a battered old jeep appeared out of a small road. It raced to a stop amid a cloud of dust and then the campest local Peleliuan jumped out and hands on hip, lips pouting, introduced himself. It was utterly surreal to have come out all this way to a speck of coral in the middle of the Pacific to be faced with a native islander with all the mannerisms of a Peleliuan Julian Clary.

Very quickly, he had us convinced that he was indispensable to our cause and exactly what we needed to get round the island. Sold on the idea we all piled into his jeep and headed off through the jungle in the direction of Bloody Nose Ridge. On the way there we stopped at a US Military Memorial and started to get an idea of the scale of the losses the Americans had on this small island, which in truth they could so easily have simply bypassed on their way to Tokyo. These Japanese were no significant threat and could have been left isolated on this coral speck until final victory was achieved.

Leaving the cemetery we moved further into the jungle. Suddenly, the jeep pulled over and our guide jumped out. He knew where there was a downed Zero, not far away in the undergrowth.

'You must never leave the paths and move out into the jungle,' he warned. 'So much ordnance was fired here, mines were planted all around

– and yet, after the war no attempt was made to clear it up. The paths are clear but if you stray from them you could step on something live.'

With that warning we followed him into the dense jungle. Soon we were standing beside a Zero that had been shot down and crashed here in 1944. As we pulled jungle creepers from it, we saw that the fuselage and wings were basically intact and the aluminium gleamed, seemingly still ready for flight.

Back in the jeep, we moved on to what had been a Japanese command centre which had been hit from the air by the Americans. This reinforced concrete structure had blast doors of steel six inches thick, and had been heavily defended. A huge round hole in the roof marked where a bunker-busting bomb had come straight through the reinforced concrete, the rusted brown metal strengthening rods ripped apart and peeled downwards as if made of cardboard. The bomb had then punched through the top floor, which had a similar hole in it like the roof, before exploding on the ground floor and destroying the centre.

We then drove to the foot of Bloody Nose Ridge. The jeep stopped beside a rusted American tank. The turret hatch was open and we clambered up and peered inside. I was amazed at how small and tight the confines of the tank were.

Jumping down, we walked around the tank and I saw a mortar round lying on the ground beside it. On the left-hand side of the tank, a succession of armour-piercing rounds had hit the armour, peeling back its thick metal with apparent ease as the rounds had raked across it.

We walked around this historic battle site with our guide and came across an elderly American with another guide. We greeted him and he asked what we were doing with film cameras here. We explained about the video we were making and he told us that he had been a marine, one of the thousands who assaulted this small speck of coral and who had fought and spilled their blood here. He had wanted to come back after all these years to see this place again and to remember his fallen comrades.

We soon had a camera on him and, a natural before the cameras, he was regaling us with stories of how the whole area had had the jungle stripped away by the fighting until it was bare earth. He told us how the Japanese had retreated back to their final stand cave hideouts. At night they would rush out of their caves in fanatical attacks before retreating back again.

He pointed out a shot-up two-man Japanese tank of the type I had seen on the deck of the *Nippo Maru* in Chuuk Lagoon, and told us how the small barrel of the main gun was removable for transport. The small two-man Japanese tanks with their lightweight gun barrels had proved no match for the more heavily armoured American tanks.

'Once the Japanese were holed up in those damn caves up there we couldn't dig them out. When we tried to assault the caves we found that they had dug the caves sloping downwards and had set up firing positions inside. They were firing up an incline from protected positions, deep inside the caves, at our troops who were silhouetted and totally lacking in protection. We just couldn't break into those caves. Eventually, we brought up bulldozers and aviation fuel in barrels. The bulldozers got right up to the entrances of the caves and poured the aviation fuel into them. Because the caves were tunnelled downwards the fuel ran down the floor of the caves all the way to the bottom. Once it was in we lit the fuel and roasted those poor Japanese alive in their caves.

'Look over there,' he said, as he pointed out a Japanese cave. 'See how it's all blackened around the entrance – that's from when we had to burn them out.'

We paid our farewells – he had been a fascinating person to interview. Once a warrior, now grown old and frail, he was left with his memories of a traumatic time that was still as vivid and real to him that day as it was all those years ago.

We walked up towards the cave and, looking down from its blackened entrance, saw the field of fire it commanded over the lower flat lands where the American forces had been. In a circular man-made hole beside the cave entrance, protected by overhanging sheer cliffs, a large howitzer was still set on its mountings, sunk down into the hole in what would have been a very difficult target to hit.

Not far from the cave entrance was a Japanese shrine to the dead from this cave. All sorts of offerings were set on it, from cigarettes and bottles of juice to military relics plucked from the surrounding jungle, a battered US Army water bottle, a Japanese helmet and a frightening array of shells and ordnance.

As we made our way back to our plane for the hop back to Koror, I tried to imagine what a living hell this now beautiful tropical paradise must have been for both sides in this fight. The US marines, who had assaulted the beaches under heavy fire and who had fought their way to the base of Bloody Nose Ridge only to be held up by the Japanese last stand in the caves. And for the Japanese, who had been burned alive in those caves – this Paradise had become their own vision of the fires of Hell.

We passed by some American military memorials, still neatly maintained, over which a respectful silence hung. I realised here the scale of the losses on this one small island, set amid the vastness of the Pacific with its hundreds of islands. Each island had been cleared of its Japanese occupants in similar fashion with similar losses. I felt I gained a rudimentary understanding of the scale of human loss in the Pacific conflict as I imagined all the young soldiers who had given their lives more than 50 years ago.

The next day, back on Koror, we were up at 6 a.m. to breakfast and get back aboard our dive boat to be whisked out to an inlet where two nearly identical sister oil tankers, the *Iro* and the *Sata*, lie wrecked in relatively close vicinity to each other. One is upright and the other upside down. These two sister ships have no easily discernible or differentiating features on them. The one that sits on her keel was originally thought to be the *Iro* but now doubt surrounds this – it may be the *Sata* after all.

The *Iro* was built in 1922 and was sunk during the American raids in 1944. It took several bombing raids for the Americans to sink her, and the raids went on throughout the whole day. Even though the cargo of oil is long gone, a small slick still rises up to the surface, marking her grave.

We rolled backwards into the water off our boat and, as usual in these parts, I found myself looking down through crystal clear water to the upper works of a perfectly intact but rotted tanker, sitting directly below me. I drifted down through the clear water towards the wreck, its rusted brown metalwork an unmissable outline in the depths below me. As I reached the wreck, shoals of yellowtails moved gracefully over her works, parting to let me pass. Giant clams clung rooted to her in places, their huge zigzag mouths snapping shut in a single muscular response to our unusual intrusion into their realm.

The wreck was a vast coral foothold and everywhere I looked there were myriad explosions of colourful coral. I drifted spellbound through massive RAS masts with their cross bracing, and was able to explore the huge cavernous superstructures of this tanker.

That afternoon, to add a different touch to the proposed video, we were taken to Jellyfish Lake. Our dive boat moved into an inlet off a large island and we went ashore in a grey rubber Zodiac, jumping from it clad in our shortie wetsuits onto the sandy beach clasping fins, mask and snorkel.

Our guide led us up an overgrown path through the jungle to a large lake, which was covered for as far as the eye could see with white jellyfish. By now I was a confessed wreck-diver and, not liking jellyfish at the best of times, I was reeling with disgust at the thought of immersing myself in this jellyfish soup.

Our shortie tropical wetsuits left our arms and legs exposed. The guide told us that these jellyfish had lost the ability to sting as there were no natural predators here in the lake for them – they didn't need to sting to protect themselves. I couldn't accept that could possibly be true as I gingerly stepped into the shallow water to pull on my fins, mask and snorkel.

Dropping onto my front, I found myself in peaty water among the ancient roots of long-gone, large trees. There were no jellyfish here but as I looked out into deeper water I could see a vast swathe of them at all levels blocking my path. We all started to snorkel out towards the seething mass. I wished I were somewhere else.

As the mass of pulsating jellyfish neared I stared fixedly at the first ones as I approached, making sure that I gave them a wide berth. But, as we pressed on further out into the lake, the soup of jellyfish became so thick that I couldn't avoid them. I started pushing my way through them gently, bracing myself for stings as they were swept slowly down my body and bare legs by my forward motion.

Although the sensation of their jelly-like forms rubbing down my legs was uncomfortable, they were indeed, to my great relief, non-stinging. Soon I had overcome my fears and was able to hold them in my bare hands.

On the final day, we were taken to another island by our guides. After mooring and making it ashore we were led up through a dense jungle path for a number of miles. The path got progressively steeper and I soon regretted volunteering to carry the tripod for the topside camera that day. It became an awkward burden in the sweltering heat of the jungle.

Halfway to the top we became aware that we were actually moving through a man-made canyon and our guide explained that the Japanese had forced local islanders to work here to cut out a route to a fortress at the top of the hill through solid rock in places.

Slightly further on we came across two large 12-inch naval gun barrels lying beside the path. The guide explained that the Japanese were transporting these for installation in the fortress at the top of the hill when American fighters had swooped and attacked the procession. The guns had been so badly damaged in the attack that they were abandoned where they had fallen.

Eventually we got to the top of the hill where we entered the remains of the Japanese fortress now partly reclaimed by the jungle. All around, the buildings showed the traces of the fierce American attack that had wiped it out. Bullet marks still pockmarked the roofless buildings. Burnt-out buildings lay just as they had been left at the time of the attack, 60 years ago. Richard Cook, old enough to have done his National Service and know what he was talking about, spotted a mortar bomb lying just off the path. After checking it he knew it wasn't live and propped it up against a wall.

Everywhere we had been in Chuuk and Palau, we had seen so much evidence of the conflict that had engulfed these and countless other small beautiful islands strung out across the Pacific. It truly was a global war, and an understanding of the vastness of the conflict dawned on me as I realised that I had dived relics of this same war, from such distant places as the shores of Scotland to out here in a remote part of the Pacific. I had gained an understanding of how this war had touched all parts of the world.

When we at last got back to Scotland we were able to produce and start selling several videos from our expedition to Chuuk, Palau and Guam to add to *Dive Scapa Flow*. I left the company shortly thereafter but look back on my time in Chuuk and Palau with special affection. Had it not been for the videos I would probably never have got out to that remote piece of the Pacific, nor indeed spent so much time out there.

CHAPTER NINE

Blackout on the *Fram*

'It is easy to go down into hell . . . but to climb back again,
to retrace one's steps to the upper air – there's the rub . . .'

Virgil, *Aeneid*

The water beneath our orange dive boats was deep, dark and cold. It was April 1992 and almost a year had passed since our expedition to Micronesia. I was back diving in Scottish waters researching for my next book, *Dive Scotland's Greatest Wrecks*.

Two and a half miles out from shore, my diving partner Ewan Rowell and myself, with a team of trusted divers, were sitting above a well-known wreck in the Moray Firth, off north-eastern Scotland. We were about to dive 45 metres down into the darkness to explore the stern section of the wreck of the Swedish Second World War loss, the 2,491-ton steamship *Fram*.

The *Fram* had been en route from Stockholm, Sweden, to Cleveland, near Newcastle, in 1940, when it had been beset by a fierce south-easterly winter storm. In the face of biting winds, snow storms and heavy seas the *Fram* had limped close in to the Moray Firth to find some protection from the coastline to her south.

The *Fram* was under the command of Captain Sven Erik Rane who had been in charge of her since 1925, some 15 years. He had anchored his ship in Aberdour Bay, just under a mile offshore. The crew turned in for the night and a poor solitary crewman had been assigned to the anchor watch.

In the dead of night, a small coastal submarine, *U-13*, silently crept up on the *Fram* undetected. A single torpedo fired from *U-13* struck the *Fram* just aft of the bridge superstructure and exploded, killing several crew members. The explosion was so catastrophic that the ship broke into two sections immediately.

The bow section remained held at anchor, and started settling into the water quickly. The unfortunate crewmen launched life rafts as quickly as they could. Whereas just minutes previously they had been warmly tucked up in bed asleep, they now found themselves clambering into an exposed raft in a bitingly cold wind as their seemingly solid and secure home disappeared from beneath their very feet into the depths.

The stern section had remained afloat and, free of the restraining anchors on the bow section, now started to drift before the prevailing fierce south-easterly wind. Although the crew on this section also abandoned ship immediately, the stern section remained afloat for another 30 minutes, drifting downwind for a mile and a half. It finally sank beneath the waves two and a half miles offshore from the picturesque northeast fishing village of Pennan, immortalised in the film *Local Hero*.

As Ewan and I tumbled backwards over the side of our orange rigid inflatable dive boat, I looked downwards, my eyes peering into the depths, following the shot line that we had dropped to snag the wreck. This area of the Moray Firth was renowned for its good underwater visibility but it was immediately apparent that the water had not yet cleared, as it normally does, in the run-up to the summer months. I couldn't see very far down the line at all and my heart immediately sank a little. Ewan and I had had high hopes of doing some photography down on the wreck for the book and then spending the rest of the dive surveying it. This all looked in doubt now.

As the descent started it soon became clear that this was going to be a dark and gloomy dive where we would be reliant on our torches and our night vision, once it kicked in. As soon as we were just a few metres down the shot line the volume of particles in suspension in the water had completely stopped all ambient light from the surface filtering down to us. The further down we went, the darker it got, and then at a depth of about 25 metres it simply went pitch black.

We pressed on down the shot line, Ewan carrying his underwater camera and strobe on a lanyard round his neck. We had dived the *Fram* a few times before so we knew roughly what to expect. On this dive, the task we had allotted ourselves was to complete our survey of the stern section and get the photos I needed, on a short bottom time of 20 minutes.

When we were 20 metres down, Ewan, who was leading the descent, turned to give me the OK signal in his torch beam. Everything seemed fine – I gave the OK signal back and we pressed down further into the darkness. At 30 metres down I could feel the increasing water pressure squeezing my drysuit against my body and starting to cause a familiar discomfort. I bled more air into the suit to relieve the squeeze.

On this dive, before the introduction of helium and mixed gas diving to the sport diving world, Ewan and I were diving on compressed air. Air is fine on the surface but the nitrogen in it becomes increasingly more narcotic the deeper you dive. Your aqualung feeds you increasing amounts of compressed air to keep your internal air spaces at the same pressure as the water pressure surrounding your body. At a depth of 30 metres the water pressure is four times the atmospheric (or surface pressure) we all experience as we walk around on land at sea level. To counter this, your aqualung feeds you air at the same increased pressure. This means that four times as much air is going into your body with every breath, to keep the delicate pressure equilibrium between your lungs and the water around in balance.

The 79 per cent nitrogen in air on the surface does us all no harm, but at a depth of 30 metres, four times more nitrogen is going into your body, and this increasing amount of nitrogen starts to cause problems. At a depth of 50 metres, your body is getting six times as much nitrogen as on the surface.

The effects of this nitrogen loading, *nitrogen narcosis*, usually start to be noticeable at a depth of about 25 metres. Each diver has a different tolerance to the narcosis, the so-called 'Raptures of the Depths'. For me, at 25 metres the effects are mild. At 40 metres down I know I am significantly affected. Between 45 metres and 50 metres, the maximum recommended safe depth to dive on air, I know that I am hugely disabled by the narcs. Deeper than 50 metres and I become a space-trooper, hanging on to the last vestiges of reason and sanity. In my later 'deep air' days – before mixed-gas diving – I dived on air a couple of times deeper than that, once to 55 metres and once to 60 metres.

On the 60-metre dive, to a shipwreck off Stonehaven, the Second World War loss, SS *Cushendall*, I was hugely affected by the narcs. Initially, once I reached the seabed, I thought I was coping with the dive – just. It was pitch black and the underwater visibility was about 5–10 feet. But when, in the darkness, I lost sight of the bottom, and my buddy, I thought I had lost control of my buoyancy.

A huge overwhelming rush of panic swept over me and removed the last vestiges of self control. I wasn't able to deal with a simple situation. In my panic my vision closed in, so-called 'tunnel vision'. My heart rate shot up and my breathing accelerated until it was booming in my head. I panted for breath and quickly bailed out, seeking shallower water. I rose up far too quickly until at about 35 msw my head cleared and I halted my ascent. But my inability to deal with a simple problem at depth because of the effects of the narcs was terrifying and could have led to my death.

Diving to those depths on air is not something I would ever do again and I would discourage anyone reading this from venturing there. Your mental powers are hugely affected and when the slightest thing goes wrong it seems magnified in your mind. You can get euphoria, paranoia, tunnel vision and panic. People seriously affected by the narcs do the strangest and most out-of-character things.

I knew that this *Fram* dive was taking Ewan and me into a depth where we would both be significantly affected by the narcs. But we had done it before and with the familiarity to danger that breeds a dangerous contempt, we were plunging down into these risky depths, task-loaded with cameras and a self-imposed mental pressure to get a job done. We continued our descent to the *Fram* below.

At 35 metres down I was straining my eyes down into the darkness to catch my first glimpse of the wreck. Below me I couldn't see Ewan at all, although I knew he was only a few feet away from me. All I could see was his strong torch beam cutting through the darkness like a light sabre. When I swept my own torch over the area from where his beam was emanating, the black-clad back of his head and his twin scuba tanks materialised out of the gloom. Surely we would be on the wreck soon.

Some of our divers had already made it down to the wreck and one started taking photographs. Suddenly the enveloping darkness beneath was lit up by the brilliant flash of a camera flashgun. Even though the taker of the photo was some ten metres beneath us and hidden by the hulk of the wreck itself, the flash lit up the darkness for a blinding second and we saw the silhouette of the large stern section of the wreck. We had arrived.

On the surface, in our pre-dive talk through, we had agreed that when we reached the wreck we would turn to our right and head aft towards the stern to photograph the prop and rudder. In the enveloping and disorientating darkness however, we were both so affected by the narcs that when we reached the wreck we unknowingly turned to our left and started heading in completely the opposite direction to where we had wanted to go.

Instead of moving towards the photogenic stern with its rudder and unique square bladed propellor, we were finning along towards the middle of the ship – to where it had sheared off from the bow section in that fateful attack more than 50 years earlier.

When I realised our mistake, it was clear to me that there was not enough time left for us to get to the stern before we would have to ascend. I decided to get what photographs we could in this midships area – any photo would be better than no photos at all.

We had unfortunately, however, arrived down on the wreck in the area of the two aft deck holds. The *Fram* had been in ballast with rocks in her holds when she had been torpedoed and so there was nothing much worth photographing in them.

In between the holds however, mounted on the deck, was a large cargo winch. With time ebbing away I decided to get Ewan to take some shots of myself and another diver, John Tann, around the winch. It was just the right size to fit into a frame and would be quite photogenic.

John and I positioned ourselves around the winch and held our positions to allow Ewan to get himself into the best position to take a good shot. Once set on the winch, I turned to look at Ewan and saw him a few metres above me and off to my right, kicking his fins to get himself into position. I had worked with Ewan before, so seeing him getting ready, I turned back to look obliquely at the winch and started blowing air bubbles gently out of my breathing regulator. There is nothing worse in a diving photograph than a diver's face front on to the camera, and I wanted to avoid that. Also, photogenically, a diving photo looks better when there are bubbles rising up.

As I rested on the winch looking at an angle away from Ewan I saw the bright split-second flash of his flashgun going off once. The gloom was lit up for a brief moment. At least, I thought, we are going to get one photo from this dive.

I waited for perhaps a minute after this first flash, thinking Ewan would reposition himself for another shot. I wanted to avoid turning face full on to Ewan just as he was away to take another shot as this would spoil the photo. But I slowly became aware that no more flashes were coming. I turned round to look at Ewan to see what he was up to. Was he having difficulty with his camera? I saw him about five or ten metres away from me. He was perfectly weighted, hovering just above the deck with the tips of his fins just touching the deck itself.

As I looked at him, wondering what he was doing, his camera fell from his hands and his head went limp and fell loosely forward so that his chin rested on his chest. Either Ewan was larking about or something was seriously wrong.

I kicked off the winch as hard as I could, put my head down and finned like a bullet across to Ewan, who still floated upright, the tips of his fins on the deck. Even as I closed on him I was still thinking that he was pulling my leg, that he would look up and laugh at having put the wind up me.

As I reached him, I extended my hand and grabbed him by his buoyancy compensator (BCD) on his chest. I pulled him to me, raised his chin with my hand and looked into his mask. There was no expression in his face. His eyes were half open – but lifeless. I felt a rising fear swelling from the depths of my chest.

I had hardly stopped moving as I swept across and grabbed hold of him. As soon as I saw into his mask I knew he was out. I had to get him back to the surface quickly, where we could find out what was wrong and do something for him.

Dive training covers the *theory* of how to carry out assisted ascents from depth with a disabled diver and I had had some pool training on them in my initial dive training, years earlier. But assisted ascents are not practised for real in the sea – they are simply too dangerous. Too many things can go wrong for both victim and rescuer, even when it's just a drill.

I had never carried out an assisted ascent before on anyone – not many people have, in practice. Yet I was being pitched into this dire situation in the worst of conditions, in pitch darkness and from a deep depth of 45 msw, nearly three miles offshore. Thoughts of his wife and their recent child crowded my mind.

I knew that the air in our drysuits and BCDs would expand in volume by a colossal factor of almost five times as we headed up to the surface. Often air becomes trapped in undersuits and the folds of dry suits as well. If I couldn't get rid of that expanding air from both our suits and BCDs at the right time as we ascended, we would end up in an uncontrollable buoyant ascent. From this depth, such an uncontrolled ascent would see both of us exploding out of the water at speed when we hit the surface. Getting to the surface too quickly is definitely not a good idea for divers. You risk all sorts of medical dangers, from burst lungs and embolisms, to the dreaded bends – all of which from that depth would most likely result in a painful death. Perversely, if I dumped too much air, then we would become too heavy and would drop like stones down into the depths again. Neither was an option I wanted to experience.

It was going to have to be a slow, controlled assisted ascent – but the prospect of trying to manage the dumping of all the expanding air from our two sets of dive suits and BCDs, as well as holding onto Ewan the whole time with one hand, was daunting.

Keeping a firm grip of Ewan's BCD I signalled to John Tann that we were going up – and said a quiet prayer. I kicked up and, because Ewan's buoyancy control had been so good before he passed out, it was relatively easy to get going. I kept an eye on the breathing regulator in Ewan's mouth. Thankfully, as he passed out, it had not fallen out, which would have allowed water to flood his mouth, throat and lungs. I could tell he was still breathing rhythmically and steadily – at least he was alive.

By chance, in the enveloping darkness we came across the brilliant white anchor line for my dive boat, leading upwards at an angle of about 70 degrees to the boat above. This was immensely reassuring for, as I linked an arm round the rope I knew that this meant that we would surface right beside the dive boat where there would be assistance. At least we were not going to be carried by the current away from the anchored boat to surface some distance away, out of earshot. If that happened we might not be spotted on the surface and might end up drifting for some time with Ewan disabled and perhaps needing medical assistance. This was a good break.

From 40 metres to 35 metres I thought I detected movement in Ewan – nothing too much, but stirrings in his lifeless form sufficient to make me notice. At around 35 metres it became clear that he was starting to regain consciousness. I had never tried holding onto a 16 stone, 6 ft 2 in. diver as he regained consciousness, and the initial gentle stirrings gave way to some quite vigorous spasms and thrashings about. I held on for grim life – I didn't want to let go of him in case he shot up, or dropped down into the depths again.

The air in our BCDs and suits was expanding rapidly now and I tried to dump air from all four sources of danger. I could feel us starting to move upwards more quickly than I liked. Fear of a ballistic ascent made me halt, breaking our ascent with the fixed anchor line until I got our buoyancy back under control.

Two divers from another group that had obviously arrived topside came into view, descending our shot line. As they approached me from above they looked at me dragging an inert, unconscious diver up from the depths. I expected they would come to help, but, to my amazement, one gave me an OK signal. I couldn't really respond for fear of losing my grip on Ewan and the anchor line so I didn't give them the required OK signal back in response. I thought it apparent that all was not well and that my failure to return the signal should require them to investigate and look a bit more closely at the situation they were encountering. I shook my head vigorously, silently screaming that no, it wasn't bloody well OK – come and help me.

Seemingly completely oblivious to the seriousness of our situation, the divers simply continued their descent, swam round us and headed on down to do their dive. We were left in mid-water to continue our ascent on our own.

Between 35 and 30 metres from the surface, Ewan's thrashings as he came back to consciousness were so vigorous that I felt I risked losing grip of him. I wanted him out of this phase and seriously thought about punching him. I felt I had to do something dramatic to try and snap him out of this halfway-house between consciousness and unconsciousness. His eyes were wild and he still wasn't fully with us.

At a depth of 30 metres Ewan abruptly stopped thrashing about, settled down and suddenly he was my old mate again. His eyes changed and he now looked me quizzically in the eye – as if to query why we were halfway up the shot line with me half strangling him and trying to haul him up. I guessed he had no recollection at all of what had transpired.

Ewan then tried to break free from my grip and started giving me OK signals. I had heard stories of divers regaining consciousness only to black out again and drop into the darkness beneath never to be seen again. I refused to let go and eventually Ewan seemed to resign himself to the fact that I was going to rescue him, whether he liked it or not.

We rose up and carried out some safety decompression stops before breaking the surface. Inflating our BCDs and suits, we had a quick talk on the surface beside the boat to see if everyone was OK or starting to suffer symptoms of anything nasty.

We dekitted in the water and the cox took our scuba tanks and weight belts. We then pulled down with our hands on the grablines as we kicked with our fins to propel us upwards and into the boat. One by one we tumbled over the wide orange tubes into the safety of the dive boat.

As soon as our party were all aboard, we headed back to Rosehearty harbour at full speed. We wanted to retrieve the boat at the harbour and be heading home to Aberdeen as quickly as we could, lest anyone start to suffer any decompression problems from the ascent. The bends start to manifest themselves in a diver within half an hour to several hours after surfacing. The nearest recompression chamber was located conveniently in Aberdeen en route home.

Thankfully none of us developed any complications from the day's events. Ewan developed his underwater camera film and we got one shot – of John Tann and myself on the winch – this being the last thing Ewan saw before he passed out. It now features in the colour section in *Dive Scotland's Greatest Wrecks*, but few people know the drama behind that single photo.

The reaction for me set in that night, once I had completed all the physical tasks associated with the dive – rinsing my kit and running the outboard engine with fresh water to get rid of encrusting salt in the cooling system. As I lay in bed that night I found myself in a cold sweat, shaking with fear. My mind raced with all the 'what ifs', how I could have done better – and how it could all have turned out so differently.

Over the course of the next few weeks I suffered recurring nightmares of an ascent spiralling out of control and Ewan and me breaking surface at speed, my lungs bursting and unable to breath. Those nightmares passed and we now regularly bandy this story about on divers' nights out. I try never to let Ewan forget what happened – it's always worth a beer and you never know, he might have to do the same for me one day!

We later came to the view that the reason for Ewan's blackout was a carbon dioxide build-up which had essentially caused him to fall asleep. He had been under stress about the dive itself, the darkness and was task-loaded with having to take photographs to boot. His wife Alice had just given birth to their child Sam a few weeks before, and he had not been sleeping well. He was run down and was never comfortable diving on air beyond 40 metres anyway.

Nitrogen narcosis played its cruel part magnifying all the problems in the dive. Ewan believes he felt concerned at the rate he was using up his air supply on the bottom. He started trying to skip-breathe or pant, causing the carbon dioxide build-up. His body said 'enough' and out went the lights – literally.

For this book, Ewan has recollected the day's events in his own words:

> I was in a negative mood on the boat but decided I'd best get it over with as quickly as possible. The last thing I said to Rod before putting in my mouthpiece was, 'Look after me.'
>
> The next thing I remember clearly was running out of air. Up until then I'd not been thinking of very much at all except trying to get a photo. I was wearing small independent double cylinders and had drained one completely before I'd done anything productive. No problem; simply swap to the full cylinder, slow my breathing rate and concentrate on getting some pictures.
>
> The camera wouldn't work and I was getting confused. I'd left the lock on and was unable to operate the controls properly. I managed to frame a shot and fired at least one that included Rod and John looking at something. All the time I was skip-breathing to stretch my air as long as possible.
>
> As I lifted my eye from the viewfinder, I realised that something was very wrong. I felt a second or two of rising panic and then darkness came down on me like a great black velvet curtain. Time stopped. Then the curtain came away in layers and, as it lifted, I realised I was thinking clearly and was fully aware of what was happening, although it seemed to take a while longer before I could open my eyes or move.
>
> Suddenly I was in control again. I checked my depth gauge. It read 30 metres and was rising rather fast. Rod had me by the scruff of my life-jacket in some sort of wrestler's grip. A brief attempt to free myself just caused him to grip me tighter and rise faster, so I decided to lie as still as possible and try to enjoy the ride.
>
> Some divers came down past us, looked surprised, and asked if things were OK. 'OK,' I signed back and gave whatever signal I thought best said 'Rescue Drill'.
>
> If Rod hadn't pulled me up, I'd have simply slept on until my air was used up and things would have ended when the curtain came down.

Ewan and I learnt from this experience with deep air. In my view, any dive of more than a depth of 40 metres should be made, if possible, not on air but on a helium mix called Trimix. Trimix replaces a large section of the nitrogen in air that is so dangerous at depth with inert helium. This reduction in the amount of nitrogen going into your body in turn reduces the levels of narcosis.

We both qualified as Trimix divers in 1995 and, as we now dive routinely to depths of up to 70–80 metres, I now seldom dive on air. Evolution is a slow process.

Rod with the Ensign flown by Joint Services Expedition on the bridge superstructure of HMS *Repulse*, South China Sea.
(Guy Wallis)

1. Richard Cook and Claire Macdonald beside the remains of a downed Japanese Zero in the jungles of Peleliu, Micronesia. (Rod Macdonald)

2. Shot up American hardware at the foot of Bloody Nose Ridge, Peleliu, Micronesia. (Rod Macdonald)

3. A typical scene at Lochaline Pier in the Sound of Mull, as divers get ready to dive the *Rondo* and *Hispania*. Left to right – Rod, Peter Moir, Jim Burke and Richard Colliar. (Rod Macdonald)

4. A study in 'technical diving' as Tony Ray prepares to dive the RMS *Remuera*, eight miles off Fraserburgh. (Tony Ray)

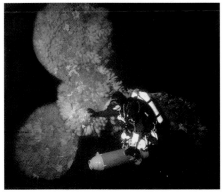

1. Rod examines the twin 15-inch gun barrels of B turret, HMS *Repulse*, South China Sea. (Guy Wallis)

2. Rod drifts beside the massive propeller of HMS *Hampshire*, which lies in 68 metres, 1.5 miles off Orkney. (Ewan Rowell)

3. Rod examines the remains of a circular life-raft, just aft of the bridge, HMS *Repulse*, South China Sea. (Guy Wallis)

1. Rod closes on the secondary armament, just aft of the bridge, HMS *Repulse*. (Guy Wallis)

2. Jim Burke flies under the aft 'H' main east of the SS *Hispania*, Sound of Mull. (Ewan Rowell)

3. Guy Wallis shot this photo with his back to B Turret on HMS *Repulse*, looking along the twin 15-inch gun barrels as Rod flies in on his Zepp. (Guy Wallis)

1	2
3	4

1. The Joint Services Trimix Expedition to HMS *Prince of Wales* and HMS *Repulse*. Left to right – Captain Greg Wilson, Squadron Leader Martin Payne, Sergeant Dave Taylor, 'Doc' David Adey, Major Guy Wallis, Paul Carvel, 1 Para, Dan Burton, Stuart McFarlane, 1 Para, Rod, Lance Corporal John Quinn, Royal Marines. (Rod Macdonald)

2. The spectacular limestone islands of Palau, Micronesia. (Rod Macdonald)

3. Rod and John Tann on the winch of the SS *Fram* – Ewan's last photo before the lights went out. (Ewan Rowell)

4. Dave Gordon (centre) and Ewan (right) sorting tanks and kit on the shores of Loch Ness before our first Trimix dive. (Rod Macdonald)

1	1. The RMS *Remuera*, the largest wreck around north-east Scotland now rests in 65 metres some 8 miles off Fraserburgh. (Rod Macdonald)
2	2. The SS *Gowrie*, lost 5 miles off Stonehaven during the Second World War. (World Ship Society)
3	3. The SS *Cushendall*, another of the Stonehaven '5-mile wrecks' lies in 58 metres. (World Ship Society)

1	2
3	4

1. *Stonehaven Diver*, heading north from Stonehaven to dive the mystery 'snag' off Newtonhill. Left to right – Dave Hadden, Rod (driving), Jim Burke. (Rod Macdonald)

2. The 10,850-ton armoured cruiser HMS *Hampsire*. (Imperial War Museum)

3. The haunting remains of HMS *Hampshire* lie in 68 metres of water, 1.5 miles off Orkney. (Rod Macdonald)

4. The *Hampshire* 2000 team in front of the salvaged propeller of the *Hampshire* at Lyness Naval Museum. Left to right – Rod, Ewan, Terry Waldron, Jim Burke, Chris Allen, Dave Taylor, Stuart Ward, Andy Garrick. (Rod Macdonald)

1. Rod examines the massive twin 15-inch gun barrels of B turret, HMS *Repulse*, South China Sea. (Guy Wallis)

2. The massive wreck of HMS *Prince of Wales* lies in 70 metres in the South China Sea. The three starboard torpedo impact sites can clearly be seen. The Ensign flown by Joint Services team is attached to the starboard side, outboard propeller shaft. (Rod Macdonald/Guy Wallis)

3. The haunting remains of HMS *Repulse*, South China Sea. The Ensign flown by the team can be seen on the bridge superstructure. (Rod Macdonald/Guy Wallis)

CHAPTER TEN

Coll, Tiree, and the SS *Labrador*

'It had ceased to be a blank space of delightful mystery . . .'
Joseph Conrad, *Heart of Darkness*

Two years later, in 1994, Ewan and I were setting out from Stonehaven towing my RIB, now named *Stonehaven Diver*, towards the west coast of Scotland. A five-hour drive took us to Kilchoan, on the Ardnamurchan peninsula, on the northern shores of the sea loch, Loch Sunart. We had agreed to join Peter Moir and Ian Crawford, the co-authors of *Clyde Shipwrecks*, who were actively researching wrecks around Coll and Tiree for a chapter on that area in their new book, *Argyll Shipwrecks*.

We reversed *Stonehaven Diver* down the small slip there and launched her. Once she was in the water, we were able to pull her round to the side of the slip and tie off the bow and stern ropes. This would keep her held firmly flush against the slip whilst we loaded dive kit and dry kit for a week's stay in the small cottage on Tiree we had booked.

Peter and Ian had gone across by ferry, with their boat *Tornado*, a few days before and had started doing some inshore work.

Their book, *Argyll Shipwrecks*, was going to cover the whole Argyll coast with its countless small islands and reefs, the graveyard for many ships. They had been writing the book for about three years already and had many trips to Kintyre, Gigha, Islay, Mull, Oban, Loch Sween and Loch Melfort already under their belts. But the main target for the week was going to be locating the graveyard of the SS *Labrador*. She had come to grief in 1899 on Mackenzie Rock, a small rock miles out to sea that is dry at low water and completely submerged, but menacingly close to the surface, at high water. Mackenzie Rock is a treacherous rock for mariners and lies some 12 miles or more south of the tip of Tiree in the middle of nowhere. Once you have seen this rock, it is easy to understand how, in the nineteenth century, in the days before precision navigation, this rock could have ensnared the *Labrador*.

Peter and Ian had taken a Land-Rover across with them and Ewan and I weren't going to need any land transport. We had decided to cross to Tiree by sea, heading across the Passage of Tiree from Kilchoan to Coll, some 12 miles. There we would turn south, running down Coll's eastern coastline. We would then leave Coll and cross Gunna Sound to reach Tiree. Our cottage was at the southernmost tip of Tiree. In all, the journey by sea would be nearly 30 miles.

We had to carry everything we needed for the week in *Stonehaven Diver*. We had two 12-litre dive tanks each, net dive gear bags, dive suit bags and dry bags holding daytime clothes along with sleeping bags, food and provisions. By the time the boat was loaded up there wasn't an inch of floor space left. It was filled to the gunwales with kit. Even although the sea conditions that day were a moderate Force 4 westerly, as a safety precaution we ran blue, nylon anchor rope across either side of the boat, through the tube grablines and back, to create a latticework of webbing through gear bag handles.

I gingerly clambered over the kit and got astride the console seat. I fired up the engine, letting it warm up for a few minutes. This crossing from the mainland to Coll and then down to Tiree was the most significant piece of exposed water I had crossed with this boat. Once we left the safety of Loch Sunart we were on our own.

Once satisfied that the engine was running well and that there was a strong jet of cooling water from the water pump outlet, Ewan untied us and we cast off and moved out into Loch Sunart. To the south of us the northernmost opening of the end of the Sound of Mull passed us by. I could see the familiar haven of the small sheltered harbour of Tobermory and the Rubha nan Gall Lighthouse to seaward of it. Peter and Ian knew we were to be leaving Kilchoan to make the crossing that day and we agreed that they would call us on the VHF radio on the hour every hour, on channel 16, the call channel.

As Kilchoan passed well astern of us, I motored *Stonehaven Diver* out of Loch Sunart. The wind was from the west, which meant that the seas were being driven towards us over the 12 miles of open sea from Coll, which was a sliver of dark headlands on the horizon. The westerly winds had created a sizeable swell and the bow of *Stonehaven Diver* rose up rhythmically with each wave before dropping heavily down into the trough following on. The sky was a leaden, overcast grey and the ambient light was poor. I thought how exposed and vulnerable we were out here in our sailing gear astride this small speck of orange rubber and fibreglass.

I throttled *Stonehaven Diver* up and she moved onto the plane. The westerly wind brought a moisture-laden clinging wetness to my face and I started to feel a chill. I pulled up the hood of my sailing gear, wriggling into it as far as possible. My torso was snug and warm in my Thinsulate dive undersuit.

At 3 p.m., some 20 minutes into the journey and bang on time, the VHF crackled into life.

'*Stonehaven Diver, Stonehaven Diver, Stonehaven Diver,*' came the call. '*Tornado, Tornado.*'

I pulled my VHF handmike from its mount and gave the usual reply.

'*Tornado, Tornado, Tornado. Stonehaven Diver, Stonehaven Diver* – channel 10 please.'

I rolled the channel select switch until channel 10 came up, backlit against the red LCD display.

'*Stonehaven Diver, Stonehaven Diver. Tornado.*' Peter's voice was loud and clear as he continued. 'How are you guys getting on? Where are you? Over.'

'Hi, Peter. Ewan and I are just leaving Loch Sunart and heading over to Coll. We should be nearing Coll in about an hour's time. What are you guys up to? Over.'

'Rod – Ian and I are on the east side of Tiree, diving on a small wreck close inshore. We'll keep an eye out for you – we should see you running down the Tiree coast. We've been past your cottage and you can forget about having to tie up in the harbour at Scarinish. The cottage is right down at the rocks and there's a fantastic wee creek where you can moor your boat in. Over.'

'Excellent Peter – we'll call you once we're running down Tiree. *Stonehaven Diver* – out.'

As our small boat heavily ploughed and bashed its way against wind and waves out into the Passage of Tiree, it was comforting to hear Peter's voice and know that we had good radio contact even though we were some 20 miles apart. The Passage of Tiree was a wide expanse of very dangerous water. I now had the security of knowing that if my engine failed in any way, at least there was another well-equipped dive boat which could come to our aid.

The wind roared as we sped out into open water and Mull receded on our port beam. Coll was a distant target but it was soon getting perceptibly bigger. The engine roar competed with the sounds of our sea crossing to make conversation impossible other than shouted snippets. Ewan and I lapsed into a comfortable silence and just enjoyed the sheer beauty and moment of this sea crossing.

Once we were about half way across the Passage of Tiree, Coll itself was now clearly defined and we could start to pick out land points. Encouragingly, the landmass of Coll and Tiree was blocking the westerly winds and the nearer we got to the islands the calmer the waters got. I was able to throttle *Stonehaven Diver* up to 25 knots and we flashed over, starting to head southwards to move down from Coll to the more southerly island of Tiree.

Very soon we were a mile or two offshore from Coll speeding down its easternmost coast towards Gunna Sound, the strip of water that separates the two islands. Once across Gunna Sound we headed down the east coast of Tiree, our cottage being near the southernmost tip.

I got back on the radio and called up Peter and Ian on channel 10.

'*Tornado, Tornado, Tornado, Stonehaven Diver, Stonehaven Diver.*'

'Hi Rod,' replied Peter's voice over the air. 'I'm looking at your boat just now. I can see the bow splash and the orange of your boat. You're just to the north of us. Over.'

'Excellent, Peter, we'll head inshore – it's a bit dusky over your way and I can't see you yet against the headlands. Can you put on your navigation lights or shine a torch and we'll come over. Over.'

'OK, Rod – lights on. Do you see us? Over.'

'Yep, got you – will be with you shortly. Out.'

With that, we turned the boat and headed directly inshore towards some black and foreboding cliffs, at the base of which I could see Peter's navigation lights on *Tornado*.

Very shortly I was taking *Stonehaven Diver* in beside the anchored *Tornado*. We tied off to it and switched off our engine. The Yamaha 60hp outboard hadn't missed a beat on the way across.

I attempted to get up but found myself stiff and unsupple as I tried to move off the console seat. I had been sitting astride it, fixed in position, for too long. I clambered over the mass of kit webbed down on the deck and reached over to shake Peter's hand. Ian was still in the water, but soon was clambering into *Tornado*. We cracked open a thermos of coffee and warmed up, four divers in two boats, sitting under broody, leaden skies, cliffs towering above us.

After sorting out how we were going to meet ashore, I kicked our engine back into life and got Ewan to take the RIB the rest of the way down the coast of Tiree to the south.

Our cottage sat by itself some miles south of the main town of Scarinish. Rashly, we thought we should be able to spot it from the sea fairly easily but I was unable to be sure exactly where we were along the coastline, as I couldn't pick out any very recognisable features. Dark grey clouds continued to darken both the sea around us and the rocky shoreline. Black rocks lined the coast, freckled with white water breaking on them. Here and there rocky spurs and outcrops ran out to sea.

Ewan had our chart out and, with his sailing background and a sighting compass, soon had worked out exactly where we were. Lights were coming on here and there ashore, and this helped us pick out from the chart where we were.

We spotted what looked like an isolated cottage down by the shore, which seemed to be in the right location and to fit the bill as being our booked home for the next week. We headed towards it keeping a watchful eye on the echo sounder. As we ran in towards the cottage, the most wonderful small creek formed before our eyes, about 100 feet across and totally protected on either side by dry rocky outcrops. This would be a perfect mooring. The cottage was barely 100 feet from the shore.

Once we got as far into the creek as we could, we saw evidence that human hands had once worked the rocks of this inlet as there was a rough landing area on the southern side. We tied up here and offloaded all our kit onto the rocks. Ewan, being Ewan, then put his dry suit on and tied off a long length of spare anchor rope to a fixed outcrop on our side of the creek. He pulled his fins on, dived into the sea and swam across, towing the rope to the other side of the creek. Once there, he clambered out of the water and tied the rope off securely to another fixed rocky outcrop, the rope now being slung right across the creek to make a secure mooring line.

Putting on my dry suit I motored the empty RIB out to the middle of our new fixed rope and tied it off securely with the painter. For good measure I also put my anchor down. This boat wasn't going to go anywhere without us.

The following day, Ewan and I were up early, to be met with a blustery fresh wind, which brought the waves to a slight white-crested chop not far offshore. After breakfast we were out getting *Stonehaven Diver* free from its overnight storm mooring and loaded up with our dive kit ready for a 9 a.m. departure when, right on cue, Peter and Ian's boat, *Tornado* appeared round the headland from the north. We motored out of our creek and rendezvoused with them out at sea. A mile or so offshore, the seas were very lumpy and we made the snap decision that it would be too dangerous in our small boats to try crossing the 16 miles of exposed and notoriously treacherous Atlantic waters to get to the *Labrador* wreck site. If the conditions were doubtful here, out there in such an exposed location diving could be ruled out.

We abandoned any thoughts of the *Labrador* that day and decided on our Plan B, which was to locate, dive and survey the wreck of the SS *Cairnsmuir* on the western side of Tiree. Soon both our boats were screaming round the very southernmost tip of Tiree at 25 knots, en route for the site where we believed the *Cairnsmuir* to lie.

History records that the *Cairnsmuir*, a 1,123-ton steamship built in Glasgow in 1876, had set out for a long journey from Hamburg to China in 1885. She had crossed to the Orkney Islands and passed through the Pentland Firth before heading down the west coast of Scotland. She ran onto Bo Mor reef on the west side of Tiree and became a total loss.

We arrived at the reef and leaving one diver in each boat, two divers entered the water and started searching around the reef for signs of the wreck. We soon started finding evidence of a wreck, but it was clear that it had been heavily salvaged, and what was left had been pulverised by the fierce unbridled Atlantic storms. The only traces we could find were scattered metal plates wedged in the narrow gullies of the reef.

After having psyched myself up for the *Labrador*, this shallow dive on a barren debris field was a bit of a let down. But as we headed back from the morning dive the skies cleared and the sun broke out. We were treated to a perfect west coast day and we rued the fact that we hadn't gone for the *Labrador*. Perhaps we would go tomorrow.

Tomorrow came – and we were greeted with the same grey skies and blustery sea conditions, which made us rule out the *Labrador* once again. We decided to survey the wreck of the *Nevada II*, a large 3,499-ton steamship, some 420 feet in length, which had been wrecked on north-west Coll in 1942, bound for West Africa with a varied general cargo of NAAFI stores.

Our two dive boats took us up the east side of Tiree, across Gunna Sound and up the west coast of Coll to its very northernmost tip. We soon had the large silhouette of a wreck beneath us, quite close into the rocks in about 16 metres. We dived this wreck in pairs – the most visually stunning structure being the massive steering gear quadrant, which rose up ten metres from the seabed.

That afternoon, at the same time as the day before, the skies cleared, the winds died, the seas settled and another fine west coast day thrust itself upon us. In glorious conditions we dived another of Peter and Ian's hit list of 16 wrecks off Coll, the famous wreck of the 4,411-ton *Tapti* lost off south Coll in 1951. As we headed back towards Scarinish our thoughts turned once again to the *Labrador* for the following day. We had completely circumnavigated Coll and Tiree in one day, a distance by sea in our small boats of some 50 miles.

The following day came – and we got the same blustery start. We again took a decision to leave the *Labrador* to the next day in the hope of better conditions – and to get on with locating and diving some more of the 16 target wrecks.

We had soon located and dived the *Nessmor*, a 2,216-ton steamship wrecked in 1895 at the southernmost tip of Coll, and the *Bickley*, a small 401-ton steamship wrecked in 1884 off Crossipoll, Coll. That afternoon brought the same pattern of settling seas and weather. It finally dawned on us that there was a definite weather pattern here. Tomorrow: the *Labrador*, we thought – whatever.

The next morning, the now familiar sight of Peter and Ian's orange dive boat coming round the headland from the north greeted us. We were already loaded up in *Stonehaven Diver* with enough tanks for a day out at sea and two dives each out on the *Labrador*. Scuba tanks, net kit bags and dry bags competed for deck space with food, water and spare fuel.

As with the preceding days the morning greeted us blustery and grey. We came up abeam of *Tornado* and both boats throttled up to about 20 knots, as much as was comfortable in the lumpy, choppy seas. The bow of my boat rose up high as it bounded up and off the crests of waves before slapping down into the next wave or trough. At each impact a spray of water whipped up either side of the bow to be blown across the boat and onto our faces by the wind. The water looked black and foreboding in the poor light.

As we headed south past the southernmost village on Tiree, Hynish, on the southern horizon, I saw a tall pencil-like black line rising up. At first I thought it was a trick of the light or the clouds. But when it didn't move, I began to think it was the mast of a tall sailing vessel, hull down on the horizon.

'Rod, do you see Skerryvore Lighthouse? Over,' crackled the VHF on our working channel, channel 10.

'I'm looking at that tall object on the horizon that looks like a mast just now Ian – is that it? Over,' I replied.

'It is indeed, my boy. It's about 14 miles away just now; 150 feet high and built in about 1844. Amazing really.'

Our boats pressed on bashing into the seas, the bow spray billowing up at each impact. Hynish, with its deserted buildings and small harbour used by the men who built Skerryvore lighthouse, dropped away astern of us as we pressed on southwards. As Tiree and Hynish receded behind us we left the shelter of the Tiree landmass and the seas got even lumpier. *Stonehaven Diver* was flying off the crests of waves before slamming down with a backbreaking impact onto the next wave. I looked across at *Tornado* and was surprised to see just how high their bow was lifting as it leapt over the waves. We weren't going to be able to keep up this speed in these conditions, so I throttled back to about 15 knots and this immediately reduced the ferocity of the impacts.

The silhouette of Skerryvore Lighthouse on the horizon grew as we fought on, bashing against the seas. With each mile we covered it seemed to grow in height and width. Soon we could see the outline of the treacherous black rocks at its base, which were exposed at low water and on which it had been built 150 years before. These rocks had claimed at least 30 recorded ship losses. Stuck out here, seemingly in the middle of the Atlantic, they were really in harm's way and almost undetectable at high water. It was little wonder that they were such a graveyard for ships.

As we motored on, heading inexorably towards the lighthouse, we saw a first chink of blue sky in the grey clouds above us. Soon the wind had perceptibly eased and the seas had dropped to a short chop. I was able to throttle up again to between 20 and 25 knots and speed on with our approach to Skerryvore.

The seas settled further as we pressed on – it was amazing just how quickly the sea conditions were changing. If they could ease this quickly, I chided myself, then no doubt they could worsen just as quickly. Out here, with nothing but America to our west, there was nothing to lessen the full might of the Atlantic. I tried to visualise what a westerly Atlantic storm must have been like for the keepers of the light. The expert design of the lattice work structure of massive, solid granite blocks, had given the lighthouse amazing strength. It had endured 150 years of Atlantic storms seemingly untouched. The difficulties faced by the workers, who had to live on Tiree and be ferried out by boat to build the lighthouse, were incredible. Initially, when the base was being laid, they could only work at low water.

Finally, after about an hour's motoring, we arrived at the rocks and entered a small rocky inlet to the sheltered side. Hundreds of black, inquisitive seal eyes stared at us impassively as we approached and moored up at a little jetty.

Leaving the boats to stretch our legs, we walked over the rocks towards the base of the lighthouse. I found scattered pieces of rusted iron struts and spars lying in small gullies, and wondered if these had come from any of the many shipwrecks on these rocks.

As we approached the base of the lighthouse we saw a metal ladder which ran up for some distance to a steel platform grating, and that the door of the lighthouse there was open with a toolbox lying on the platform outside. The lighthouse had long since been automated but someone must have been in it, perhaps doing maintenance or repair work. One of our number shinned up the ladder and called out into the open door to see if anyone was about. There was no reply – whoever was working here surely could not hear us through the solid granite walls. He picked up the toolbox and moved it to the opposite end of the platform. If the workman hadn't heard or seen our approach, we hoped that he would come out eventually and find that his toolbox had, apparently, moved itself – the Ghost of Skerryvore?

As we strolled back to our boats I asked Ian, who had planned the day for us to the last detail, where the dive site was.

Pointing south he replied, 'You see that little black spot on the horizon over there, Rod?'

'Ye-es,' I said cautiously.

'Well, that's Mackenzie Rock – that's it.'

'Bloody hell,' I replied. 'That's another few miles down to there – we're a long way from home if the shit hits the fan, Ian.'

In fact, Mackenzie Rock lies three miles further south from Skerryvore

Lighthouse and is one of the most remote places I have dived. We were already 14 miles south of Tiree out into the Atlantic and the bows of our boats were turning towards another speck on the horizon – black ominous rocks, which only showed at low water. It is not a place for the inexperienced, poorly-trained or ill-equipped. If you get it wrong, if you get separated or have an engine failure, the next stop is New York.

Our two boats skipped over the three miles in almost flat, oily, calm conditions. Soon we were in the middle of nowhere. Our only company was a part-submerged rock being washed by an oceanic surge, despite the calm surface.

Passing around the rock and checking the echo-sounder we found that a reef ran out from the rock for some way to the south, with a depth of only a few metres. The rock was like an iceberg, with only its tip showing. On the southern and western sides of the reef, it dropped away dramatically in what appeared to be a wall, down to a depth of 35 metres.

We dropped anchor on the reef and tied the boats up together. The historical reports narrated that the *Labrador* had run onto the reef and stuck there at first. We hoped to see some evidence of this on our first dive.

'This is not going to be as easy as I thought,' was Peter's first reaction.

By now it was about 11 a.m., and time to get on with the diving. The first two divers, Peter and myself, got kitted up.

I rolled off the dive boat and immediately found myself in five metres of water in perfect crystal-clear visibility. I could see for at least 30 metres all around me. Scanning the reef below me there was no sign of any wreckage, nor of grinding impact damage from the massive keel of the *Labrador*.

I kicked my fins and headed off southwards to check out the wall. The reef shelved off slowly until I found myself at a depth of about 20 msw. Then the reef came to an abrupt end and dropped vertically downwards. I stopped myself on the edge of the reef and looked down. I could clearly see the bottom of the wall down at about 40 metres, and there was no sign of the 2,998-ton, 401-foot-long *Labrador* down there.

I swam along the reef top for some way checking the bottom of the wall, but of the *Labrador* there was still no sign. There was no need to go down the wall, much though I was tempted. After checking this area I surfaced and got back into the boat. Peter had drawn a blank as well.

We moved the boats to another section of the reef and Ewan and Ian went in. Twenty-five minutes later they were up – also having drawn a blank.

We sat on our moored boats eating a light lunch. The sun blazed down on us as we enjoyed a surface interval in this most remote of locations. It was so hot we had to peel our drysuits down and unzip our undersuits to cool down. As we let the nitrogen from the first dive escape from our bodies I got Peter to tell me the full story of the wrecking, hoping this might give us some more clues to its whereabouts. We were all determined to find it.

Peter relayed the information he had gleaned from his research on this vessel. She had run onto Mackenzie Rock on 2 March 1899, near the end of a voyage from America to Liverpool. Most of her final, fateful trip across had been uneventful, but as she reached the eastern side of the Atlantic after her crossing, the weather closed in. Captain Erskine was unable to take the sun for the next three days and had to navigate as best he could by dead reckoning.

During the night of 1 March and the early hours of the next morning, he had worked out that he was somewhere off North Ireland. In fact he was some 60 miles off course – and heading at full speed towards Mackenzie Rock.

At 7 a.m., the 62 passengers were rudely awoken by a slight shudder in the vessel. Many dismissed it as inconsequential and continued as normal, but the truth soon flashed round the ship. They had run aground and preparations were being made to disembark the passengers into the ship's lifeboats.

The boats were launched without any panic, and all could tell that the ship was badly holed as her cargo of grain was bursting through her decks, swelling as it consumed the tons of sea water flooding into her hull below.

Luckily, the sea in this hugely exposed place was fairly calm that morning. Even more luckily, shortly after abandoning ship, the Norwegian steamship *Viking*, herself well behind schedule, by chance arrived on the scene and was able to pick up all the passengers and crew – with the exception of one boatload who had already started off for Skerryvore. It is remarkable that in this exposed and fragile location, the complete loss of the ship did not involve a single loss of life. If sea conditions had been poorer that night, all those aboard her could easily have perished.

The *Labrador* sat on the reef for several days but by 6 March she had broken her back amidships, disappeared below the seas and become a total wreck.

On our morning dives, we had been searching the southern and western sides of the rock. Going over the story again it was clear that we would have to search the eastern and northern sides of the rock in the afternoon.

We chatted through a couple of hours of a surface interval before it was time for the second dive. We felt totally isolated out there, seemingly in the middle of the Atlantic. The languid surge of the swell washed over the rock. In the distance, three miles away, Skerryvore Lighthouse stood tall, marking our way back to distant Tiree, some 17 miles away and well down on the horizon.

Taking a compass bearing I rolled backwards out of *Stonehaven Diver* and dropped down to the bottom of the reef at about five metres. I checked my compass and headed off on the northerly bearing that would, I hoped, lead me to the *Labrador*'s resting-place. The reef shelved off gradually and soon the flatish table top effect gave way to a series of gullies running down hill. It was in here that I started to see the scattered remains of small parts of a ship. A few broken and rusted spars lay jammed and bent into a groove by some incredible force.

As I swam downwards, the gully widened and I started to see more and more of the debris of a ship's passing. Broken and buckled plates, pieces of the ship's side, pipes, flanges and valves lay scattered around in no discernible order. I came across a clump of brass condenser pipes for a donkey boiler and, to mark this area for the rest of our divers, I unclipped my reel and wrapped it round the pipes. I took my regulator out of my mouth and wriggled it into the open bottom end of the attached delayed deco buoy, a bright orange, six-foot high nylon sausage.

The deco buoy filled rapidly with air and I held on to it as long as I could, until it almost started to lift me upwards. There was a noticeable current running around the site, so if I didn't fill it properly, the bag could easily be swept horizontally and not make the surface. Once full, I let go of the bag and it rocketed up to the surface some 25 metres above me. At least, I thought, that's the site marked.

Free to continue my exploration I continued along the canyon which had now bottomed out at about 25 metres and which then petered out to a wide open expanse of flat seabed. Here the trail went cold.

Taking a 90 degree bearing on my compass I moved eastwards to the next parallel canyon along, and suddenly it was pay day. As I turned into this canyon I was met with the sight of a seabed that seemingly shimmered with polished brass ship's fitments.

Everywhere I looked the seabed was covered with flattened ship's side plating on top of which were jumbled all sorts of pieces of ship. Complete sides of deck-houses lay flattened with pipes, anchor capstans, mooring bollards, massive anchors and large 100-year-old portholes strewn all about.

I came across her huge boilers and main condenser with its hundreds of brass cooling pipes, which lay about 50 metres from the rock. The stern steering gear, the massive quadrant that moved the rudder, we located in the centre of the wreck site.

It was clear from the flattened remains of this once-proud ship that she had been pounded remorselessly by the heavy Atlantic winter storms for a hundred years, and this had reduced her to a flattened mass. Those same storms had managed to move the massive steering gear from the very stern of the wreck site to midships and managed to kick around enough sand to polish the exposed brass of portholes, flanges, valves and the like. Many of the fitments didn't have the usual green coating of verdigris, the green look you normally get with brass when it has been exposed, or underwater, for a long time.

As I moved around the debris site I came across a huge section of the side of the ship, underneath the prop shaft, which had been flattened and seemingly welded onto the rocky seabed. Rows of intact portholes, most with their glass still in place, lined the ship's side.

I finned slowly to another area nearby, and soon worked out that I was in the vicinity of the bathrooms as the remnants of marble sinks were scattered all around. Amidst the shattered marble, intricate brass latticework combing, which presumably ringed around the rim of the sinks, lay torn and bent. In another area I found piles of broken crockery, some still bearing the fluttering flag symbol of the Dominion Line.

My allotted bottom time had soon expired and it was time for me to make a slow ascent to the surface. Ewan, attentive to my whereabouts and bubble stream as ever, came jetting across in *Stonehaven Diver* and helped me and my kit aboard. Peter was soon aboard *Tornado*, and we briefed both Ewan and Ian on what to expect and where to find it. My deco bag still bobbed, rather precariously, in the strong current at an angle of 45 degrees marking the westward start of the debris field. Once Ewan was ready, I motored up to my deco buoy and Ewan dropped in and followed the line down to the site. Thirty minutes later, both Ian and Ewan were back on the surface after an amazing dive.

Ewan and I had planned to make the return trip to mainland Scotland the next day, but having found such an amazing and seldom, if ever, visited dive site, in the middle of nowhere, we decided to shelve our return for another day. We would return to the *Labrador* again tomorrow.

As *Stonehaven Diver* and *Tornado* were powered up and surged up onto the plane we fixed the towering Skerryvore Lighthouse as our marker to lead us home. About an hour later we were approaching the south coast of Tiree and running up the east coast to our cottage and creek.

The following day, the same weather conditions prevailed. We toughed it out against blustery winds and a heavy swell as we bashed our way towards the *Labrador*. The sun came out later in the morning, the wind died and the seas settled. We were blessed with another fantastic day's diving on the remains of the *Labrador*, which still ranks high on my list of most exhilarating dives, because of its location, the abundant oceanic sea life and the fantastic wreck.

With sad hearts we said adieu to Tiree, Coll and the *Labrador* the next day and, after refuelling at Scarinish harbour, we started out for the crossing of the Passage of Tiree back to Mull and the mainland.

A stiff easterly was blowing from the mainland across the Passage towards Tiree. The wind drove on the seas from the mainland to the east, the waves building in intensity and size the nearer they got to Tiree. They were monstrous by the time they actually reached Tiree.

There was little hope of getting *Stonehaven Diver* on the plane in these conditions and we had to plough on, heavily-laden, beating our way against the seas. After half an hour of bashing our way through these seas, when I looked behind me back to Tiree, it was as though we had hardly left. Slowly, we made our way across the Passage and the more distance we put between Tiree and ourselves, the more the seas noticeably started to diminish. The closer we got to Mull, the more its high terrain gave us a lee.

Once we were halfway across the Passage, the wind had dropped away to a Force 3–4 and the seas were reduced to a short chop, precisely the conditions *Stonehaven Diver* rode best in.

I asked Ewan to take over the driving and as he guided us round the west side of Mull towards the northern entrance to the Sound of Mull I sat back on the double console seat and watched the fantastic Scottish scenery flash past.

We rode well in towards Mull and by now the seas were a glassy calm. Seagulls whirled above us and seals played around the rocks inshore. We sped past the port side of a charter dive boat packed with waving divers. I waved back and wondered what they had been diving – and what they would think of what we had just done.

Later as the evening's dusk started to descend, we rounded the northernmost tip of Mull and headed back to the slip at Kilchoan, our starting point so long ago.

After offloading our gear into our car we nipped across Loch Sunart in *Stonehaven Diver* to the sheltered harbour of Tobermory on Mull. After offloading a few dry clothes we tied up at a mooring buoy about 50 feet off the quayside. Clad in my drysuit, I pulled on my fins and plopped over the side into the water and finned ashore. After a welcome shower, a change of clothes and some food, Ewan and I drank a gallon or more of beer each and talked long into the night with the many groups of divers that seem to congregate at the famous maritime pub, the Mishnish. Where better to end a monumental week's diving?

CHAPTER ELEVEN

The *San Tiburcio* and the Yellow Helicopter

'I must go down to the seas again,
For the call of the running tide
Is a wild call and a clear call
That may not be denied'

John Masefield, *Sea Fever*

In November the same year, 1994, we arranged a dive trip out of Findhorn, a small old fishing village just past Elgin in the Moray Firth. We planned to dive the wreck of the Second World War Eagle Fleet tanker *San Tiburcio*.

Setting off early from Stonehaven, Ewan and I towed *Stonehaven Diver* for two hours up to Findhorn Bay, before meeting up with the two other divers who were joining us that day, Dave Hadden and Kevin Dodds. This would be one of the last big dives of the season – the days were rapidly getting shorter and darker, the water cooling off towards winter's icy grip.

We arrived at Findhorn, a large natural bay that fills at high water and almost completely empties at low water, save for a channel around the main collection of houses and a few hotels that dot its shore, at the northern and seaward side of the bay. It is a small village much favoured by old hippies, who in the 1960s established the Findhorn Community, the legacy of which still exists in the village.

Launching *Stonehaven Diver* at the small slip, we loaded her up with our air tanks, gear bags and all the increasing amount of paraphernalia that goes into the sort of dive we were now doing. Although it was only 10 a.m., the sun was well up and its weak warmth washed across a tranquil silent bay. We were in luck with the conditions today; the sea was a flat, oily calm.

Our target wreck for today was the 8,266-dwt British steam-driven tanker *San Tiburcio*. She lies about 30 minutes by RIB from Findhorn Bay

142

on the other side of the Moray Firth, some four miles south of Tarbat Ness lighthouse.

The *San Tiburcio* was launched in 1921 by the Standard Ship Building Corporation at Shooters Island, New York. She was delivered to the Eagle Fleet and registered in London. She is a large vessel of 5,995 tons gross, 413 feet in length with a beam of 53.4 feet.

The tankers of the early part of the last century, like her, were of a simple construction. Essentially they were a basic, long, steel box divided into a series of compartments. The engine room was located at the very stern, to avoid having to run the propeller shaft from a midships engine through the oil tanks with the risks that would entail.

The *San Tiburcio* was divided into a total of 33 separate compartments, which gave her exceptional strength and stability. This strong construction allowed her to be loaded far more heavily than a conventional vessel, to the extent that she would sit so far down in the water that her decks would be washed by the waves in any sort of heavy sea.

To allow her crew to move in bad weather, to and from her 'three islands', the fo'c'stle, the midships bridge superstructure and the engine room superstructure at the stern, a 'flying bridge' was created. This was an elevated walkway that ran fore and aft along the full length of the vessel, some eight feet above the main deck.

The *San Tiburcio* was constructed with an eye on serving the growing oil market of South America. She was built with a shallow draught of 31.1 feet, which would allow her to navigate up the shallow channels through the River Plate Estuary and reach the shallower ports further up river – where the large 15,000-ton tankers, common at the time, could not pass.

During the Second World War, most of the Eagle Fleet were requisitioned or chartered by the Ministry of War Transport for the war effort. The war would be devastating for the Eagle Fleet, as some two thirds of it would be destroyed by enemy action.

On 4 May 1940, the *San Tiburcio* set off on what was to be her last voyage from Scapa Flow. Under the command of Captain W.F. Fynn, she was bound for the port of Invergordon in the Cromarty Firth, the sheltered inlet that runs off the larger Moray Firth. She was loaded with a cargo of 2,193 tons of fuel oil and 12 aeroplane floats.

After crossing the Pentland Firth and running down the east coast of Scotland she entered the Moray Firth. When she had reached a position about four miles south of Tarbat Ness, and level with the small village of Rockfield, a tremendous explosion rocked her, and she ground to a wallowing halt. She had hit a mine laid three months earlier, on 9 February, by the Type IIB German minelaying submarine *U–9*.

The explosion was devastating. The stricken tanker broke her back just aft of the central bridge superstructure – a clean break as though cut with a knife. However, the two halves of the ship did not sink immediately. Her system of watertight compartments managed to keep both sections afloat for 45 minutes, allowing all her crew to abandon ship safely.

The two sections finally sank to the seabed and now rest upright in about 40 msw. The *San Tiburcio* is widely regarded as one of Scotland's greatest wreck dives. This large, relatively intact wreck sits in an area of good visibility. She is covered in life and has become a home for countless sea creatures. This wreck would be well worth the long drive across Scotland to Findhorn.

Once *Stonehaven Diver* was fully loaded, I clicked the engine into gear and we motored slowly forward, past the village, heading towards the narrow bottleneck exit from Findhorn Bay into the Firth. Once in the channel we followed the channel markers keeping us away from the sandbanks that shoal out some way from land on either side.

Findhorn Bay has a natural bar across the entrance, a firm sand bank, peppered with rocks and shale, which has become home to a carpet of mussels. Once we had passed over the bar, we were out into the Moray Firth and I throttled *Stonehaven Diver* up. We powered up onto the plane, our speed leaping up from nine knots to twenty knots almost instantly.

The water was still an oily calm and the weak sun beat down on the four of us as we sped forward, straight out of the bay, towards the middle of the Firth, before heeling to the east towards the *San Tiburcio*. The cold November air drew tears from our eyes.

Once we were about a mile out of Findhorn Bay and out of the shadow of the land, I slowed *Stonehaven Diver* down and let the trailing wake catch up with us gently. Pulling out the VHF handmike I made a safety call to the coastguard on channel 16.

'Aberdeen Coastguard, Aberdeen Coastguard, Aberdeen Coastguard, *Stonehaven Diver, Stonehaven Diver.*'

'*Stonehaven Diver*, this is Aberdeen Coastguard – channel 67 for routine traffic and standby,' came the alert reply almost instantly.

'Six seven and standing by,' I replied and rolled the channel select switch until channel 67 came up on the VHF's LCD. Whilst I waited for the coastguard to call back, I clicked the boat into gear again and started moving forward slowly. Shortly, the radio buzzed into life again.

'*Stonehaven Diver*, this is Aberdeen Coastguard. Go ahead. Over.'

'Aberdeen Coastguard – *Stonehaven Diver* Mike, Romeo, Mike, Whiskey, November Six (MRM WN6)' I replied. 'I have some safety traffic for you. This vessel is registered under your small boat scheme so you have my details. We have just left Findhorn Bay and will be diving four miles due south of Tarbat Ness Lighthouse. There are four persons aboard and we will be returning to Findhorn Bay at 1700 hours. Over.'

'*Stonehaven Diver* – message received. Please call us when you return. Out.'

With the safety traffic ended, I throttled *Stonehaven Diver* back up onto the plane and soon we were skipping over the sea, the bow starting to turn eastwards towards the unmistakable white stonework of Tarbat Ness Lighthouse, glinting in the bright sunlight.

We had raced on for another few minutes when all of a sudden there was a jarring thump and the engine stopped abruptly. We surged forward, powerless, for a few seconds before the heavily laden boat settled down into the water and wallowed to a halt.

I tried turning over the engine again with the ignition key. There was plenty of power in the battery but the engine wouldn't fire. I tried again and again but the engine was still dead. Something was seriously amiss and this would take time to resolve.

I looked out the anchor and threw it over the side to hold us in position whilst we checked out what was up. I didn't want to be drifting freely in the middle of the Moray Firth.

There was a cluster of activity at the stern of the boat as we hauled the Yamaha 60 outboard up out of the water. I tried turning the engine over again but the propeller didn't move. Making sure the throttle was in neutral, I tried spinning the prop but found that it was locked solid. This was not good. It was our only engine and we were more than a mile out into the Firth.

I dropped the shaft of the engine back into the sea and, taking off the engine cover, I tried to pull start it using the white starting lanyard directly on the top of the engine. I was trying to manually turn it over. But it was to no avail. The engine was still jammed solid.

At first I suppose I was denying to myself that we had a serious problem. I was sure, given our equipment and the knowledge of the people aboard, that we could sort out whatever was wrong. But as time passed and all our efforts to fire up the engine failed, it was slowly dawning on me that we might not be able to get out of this under our own steam.

Something catastrophic had happened inside the engine. The drive shaft seemed to be seized, locked in position. The fault could lie in anything from the crankshaft in the main head of the engine to the gearbox. In any event, after about half an hour's futile attempts, we finally accepted that the engine was dead and started to consider what our options were.

We could call the coastguard, but we were in no danger and that would result in tying them up in our little predicament. If there was any way of getting out of this under our own steam I wanted to go for it. Involving the authorities was a last option.

The tide was flooding into the Firth. *Stonehaven Diver* was fitted with two large wooden oars located on the inner sides of the side tubes. They were really just for basic manoeuvring and paddling about in harbour and not intended for any serious work. It would be difficult to paddle our heavily laden RIB in anything other than flat calm conditions, but we had an oily calm today so it might just be possible.

We decided to see if we could paddle the RIB back to the nearest land, the large sandy beach to the immediate west of Findhorn Bay. If we could get ashore there, then I could go and get my 4x4 and trailer. If there was a track through the forest, I might be able to get down onto the beach with my trailer and retrieve the RIB.

If that wasn't possible then we would anchor the boat up safely and walk round to the Findhorn Bay itself and see if we could persuade one of the many boat owners there to come out and give us a tow round the point into Findhorn. The decision being made, I pulled up the anchor and stowed it away.

Ewan and I sat down, one of us astride either side tube, and started to paddle away with long, slow strokes. I watched the sea at the side of me and found that, almost imperceptibly at first, the boat started to move forward – very, very slowly. We began to inch our way towards the distant land.

The tide carried us to the west of Findhorn as we kept on paddling inshore, but it was hard work, pushing the heavy mass of boat, divers and dive kit through the water. Our arms soon became tired as the paddling position astride the tubes was difficult and uncomfortable.

After about 20 minutes, Ewan and I took a break and Dave Hadden and Kevin Dodds took over. After another 20 minutes or so, they were feeling the strain and we rotated paddlers, again, and again and again. It was back-breaking, uncomfortable and hard work. We paddled on in this fashion for about two long hours. Gradually the long expanse of golden beach, flanked by dense green forests that run for miles and miles to the west of Findhorn, grew steadily bigger.

By about 1 p.m. we were just a few hundred yards offshore. I reckoned we were now some three miles west of Findhorn Bay. On either side of us, for as far as the eye could see, was desolate, uninhabited beach. There was no sign of any habitation, nor of any break in the back-lying forests that would indicate a track along which we might get our 4x4. At least we were going to make dry land under our own steam and save the embarrassment of having to involve the emergency services. The sandy beach was completely devoid of rocks and seemed an ideal place to land.

We kept paddling towards the shore. As we approached, even though it was still a flat, oily calm, we started to see a disturbing line of breaking waves at the beach, not visible from offshore. The surf would make landing difficult.

Twenty minutes later and we were close inshore and in shallow water. As we had reached the shallows, the shelving seabed was causing waves to break all around us. Slowly surging white water lifted our boat and sent us surfing towards the beach. Ewan jumped out of the boat, painter in hand, up to his chest in water and set foot on the seabed.

The dunes and a dense forest proved to be an impenetrable barrier for miles either way, so we hastily abandoned our idea of retrieving the boat on the beach. We talked about our position and decided that we would try walking in the surf, towing the boat for the few miles back to Findhorn Bay. If we could get round the point then the flooding tide might carry us into the bay and we could paddle to shore. Two of us grabbed the painter and the other two took hold of the moulded carrying handles, one either side of the hull. We started to walk eastwards towards Findhorn doing a good impersonation of Humphrey Bogart in *The African Queen.*

Immediately we found the going was very tough. As we pulled the boat parallel to the beach, the breaking waves hit her beam on. As each wave hit it threatened to overturn the boat, which still held all our dive gear. The waves were breaking over the side of the RIB with some force, making life towing it uncomfortable and filling the boat with water and increasing the drag.

We tried moving out into deeper water to get past the worst of the surf. It was easier out beyond the point where the waves were breaking but the water was up to our chests. It was almost impossible to get any forward movement or purchase because of the buoyancy of our drysuits. Nevertheless, sensing an end to all this we struggled on for a mile or so.

It was now nearly 4 p.m. and the early winter sun had started to drop low on the horizon. The darkness of a late November afternoon was starting to find its way towards us.

We were all starting to get seriously fatigued. We had now been paddling and fighting the surf to paddle and tow the boat for almost four hours. Findhorn itself was still not in sight, but we knew it was round the next wooded headland. We were only about a mile away from journey's end.

We continued our efforts to tow the boat in the surf, but it was getting repeatedly swamped and threatening to overturn with every breaking wave.

By about 4.30 p.m. darkness was starting to become a real threat. We were exhausted and still making little progress against the sea. I had to accept that we were not going to be able to finish our task in daylight – and we could not go on if it was dark. I decided to just halt where we were.

Seeing that everyone was getting very tired, Ewan decided to go ahead on foot to Findhorn Village to see if he could find a boat owner who could come out and give us a tow round the headland and into the bay. He strode off along the beach clad in his black drysuit. Soon he became a distant figure, his black suit standing out against the golden beach.

We paddled our boat for about 50 yards out to sea to get back into calmer water beyond the breakers and put the anchor down. Ewan would not yet be at Findhorn and there was no guarantee that he would be able to secure help. Fearing that darkness was going to overcome us and make any rescue more difficult I decided to call the coastguard and report our predicament. They might be aware of a way we could get a tow round the headland into Findhorn Bay.

Picking up my VHF handset on channel 16, I called in.

'Aberdeen Coastguard, Aberdeen Coastguard, Aberdeen Coastguard, *Stonehaven Diver, Stonehaven Diver.*'

'Diver vessel calling Aberdeen Coastguard – you are very weak and broken up. Channel 67 for routine traffic.'

I gave the usual response and flipped to channel 67. It was worrying that we must be in a poor radio coverage area. They had not been able to even make out the name of our vessel.

'Diver vessel calling Aberdeen Coastguard. Go ahead. Over.'

'Aberdeen Coastguard – this is *Stonehaven Diver* MRM WN6. I called in earlier today to report our diving from Findhorn Bay. Our engine has broken down. We are safely ashore a mile west of Findhorn – but need assistance to get a tow back from where we are to Findhorn Bay. Can you assist? Over.'

'*Stonehaven Diver*, you are still very broken up. We hear your engine is broken down. Are you in any danger? Can you repeat your message? Over.'

I tried repeating our message but it was clear that the coastguard were not picking up all we were saying and were concerned that we might be in danger.

As I sat hunched over the VHF having this disjointed and broken conversation with the coastguard, I became aware of a yellow RAF Sea King helicopter hovering, at the periphery of my vision, less than a mile away inland, over what looked like a small inland loch. It looked like they were either carrying out a rescue over there or doing a drill. Either way, if we could talk on the radio to the helicopter crew they could perhaps relay our plight.

'Aberdeen Coastguard – there is a RAF Sea King helicopter hovering less than a mile away inland. Would it be possible to route the radio traffic via him?'

'Yes, got that *Stonehaven Diver*. Standby.'

A few minutes later the radio crackled loud and clear.

'*Stonehaven Diver, Stonehaven Diver*. This is Sea King,' came a clipped and assured English accent. 'I am coming to your assistance. I will be approaching you from the west. Standby.'

'Sea King. I will put on my navigation lights to assist you. Standing by.'

I watched as if in a dream, as the yellow Sea King pulled up from its position over the loch and banked seawards to the west of us. Soon it was level with us, about a mile away down the beach. It flew straight along the water's edge towards us, very low. Its nose was tipped down and the 'whoppita, whoppita, whoppita' of its rotor blades flew through the dusky evening air towards us. It was surreal sitting there in the dusk with a helicopter scene unfolding around us like a clip from a Vietnam War movie.

I flipped on my red, green and white navigation lights and the helicopter screamed low, towards us. It slowed as it arrived in our vicinity, its nose lifting up as it approached and came to a stationary hover beside us. It then moved directly over us, its large front tyre seemingly in reach, just a few feet above us.

My radio crackled again as the pilot of the Sea King tried to contact me. I couldn't make out what was said because of the deafening din the chopper was making directly above me. I tried to speak into the radio and indicate that the noise of the chopper was so deafening that we couldn't hear anything. My radio crackled again with the sound of the pilot's throat mike. I could only barely make out what was said but it was the last thing I expected – or wanted.

'*Stonehaven Diver* – I am now going to use the downdraft of my rotors to blow you to the beach and safety. Over.'

I grabbed at my VHF handmike – being at anchor we could be flipped over by that. There was a lot of heavy dive kit stacked up in the boat, which could cause a lot of damage to us if it got thrown around.

'Sea King. Do not attempt that manoeuvre. We are at anchor and are safe. We can get to the beach any time. I cannot make out your radio traffic properly for the noise of your engines and rotors. Can you back off a bit?'

The Sea King moved away for a few hundred yards. The pilot came back on the radio, his voice now clearly made out in the relative quiet – clipped and seemingly bony in the throat mike. I thought I detected a sense of disappointment in his voice that he hadn't been able to practise driving us onto the beach.

'*Stonehaven Diver*. I need to establish proper communications with you. Could you please stand up – that's fine. Now, if the answer to my question is affirmative will you please raise your arms above your head and cross them? If the answer to my question is negative please keep your arms down by your side. Now, do you understand that? Please indicate with the signal.'

I now had a growing suspicion that we were being treated as a training exercise by this chopper which had apparently been doing a drill when we had fallen across its path. We had been in good radio contact with the chopper until it had come so close that we couldn't hear anything. Now that it had moved away from a few feet above our heads we had re-established good communications. I could clearly hear the pilot's voice booming out from my VHF speaker. Why on earth were we being asked to disregard the radio and give hand signals? Nevertheless, we were in no position to question what was going on so I obeyed the pilot's command. I raised my arms straight above my head and crossed them.

'Good, *Stonehaven Diver*. Now, is anyone injured?'

We all stood with our arms straight down at our sides.

'No one is injured. Are you in any danger?'

We stood arms down by our sides.

'I count three persons in your boat. Is that the total number of persons in your party?'

We remained with our arms down by our side.

'Can you confirm – there are more than three persons in your party?'

All three of us in the boat raised our arms and crossed them.

At this, I decided that this system, although exceedingly clear, had no way of explaining what Ewan was doing. I didn't want to alarm the pilot, as he might think that someone was in the water. I pulled up my VHF handset and spoke into it.

'Sea King, this is *Stonehaven Diver*. There are three persons aboard this vessel. One other has already gone ashore and is walking along the beach to Findhorn to see if he can get a boat to come out and tow us round into the Bay. Neither he nor us are in any danger. Over.'

The pilot of the Sea King came back on the radio.

'*Stonehaven Diver*. We will now designate the three of you in the boat as the 'Survivors' and the person ashore as the 'Casualty'. If you are in no danger we will go and rescue the casualty. Standby.'

With that, the Sea King dipped its nose forward and, picking up speed, went shooting down the beach towards Findhorn about 50–100 feet above the ground. As it disappeared along the beach after Ewan, I wondered what was going to happen next. It all seemed out of my hands. The three of us just sat in the boat looking at each other glumly. I wondered what Ewan was going to make of this.

Ewan later recounted that he had just about got to the corner of the headland before Findhorn when he heard the sound of a helicopter approaching him. He turned round to see where it was going, not suspecting for one minute that it was coming for him.

However, as he watched, the helicopter made a beeline for him. He neither needed nor wanted a ride in a chopper but amidst a whirling sandstorm from its down draft it descended and settled on the ground beside him. The crew gestured that he should come over and jump in.

Once in the chopper, he was given a RAF headset to wear and sat down as the chopper lifted off and went screaming back up the beach towards our boat, from where he had just spent the last 30 minutes walking. As the chopper approached our moored boat, he heard one of the crew on the radio ask the pilot what they should do with him.

'Throw the bugger out!' came the laughing reply.

'Ah, skipper, he's got a headset on – and can hear you.'

'Ah, ****,' came the skipper's reply.

The chopper slowed to a hover and dropped down to the beach opposite our moored boat. Not knowing what was going on, we watched bemused as Ewan jumped out and walked into the water and then swam out and got into our boat again.

'Well that was a bloody waste of time, lads – I was almost at Findhorn when this chopper came after me. I didn't really want to be rescued and almost felt like running off into the woods.'

'*Stonehaven Diver* – Sea King. We have now recovered the casualty. A lifeboat is now on its way to you and will give you a tow. There is no further need for assistance from us so we will depart.'

'Sea King – thank you for your assistance. *Stonehaven Diver* – Out.'

After the Sea King departed, all four of us sat in our anchored boat as darkness fell. What seemed like an eternity later, we heard the noise of a small outboard engine heading our way. We soon saw the phosphorescent white bow wave of a small inflatable inshore lifeboat. Soon the RNLI inshore lifeboat arrived beside us and we were greeted by its crew of two. In the darkness I couldn't make out their features – only shadows and silhouettes.

'Hi guys – are you all OK?' asked the cox.

'Yeah, thanks,' I replied. 'We're tired and hungry but there's nothing coming over us.'

'We're here to give you a tow,' said the cox after they had tied up beside us. 'But we didn't realise your boat was so big – or that you had so much heavy kit in it.'

I looked at the outboard motor of the small inflatable, which was smaller than *Stonehaven Diver*, and which only had a 40hp outboard on it.

'It'll be a slow tow,' I said. 'But at least we don't have far to go to get into Findhorn.'

'Sorry, we can't take you in there in darkness. We're from Nairn and don't know the entrance to Findhorn well enough. It's a tight entrance with sandbanks either side, and a bar across it. It can be tricky at the best of times, but now, in the darkness, it's too dangerous – we'll have to tow you to Nairn.'

My heart sank at this. We were less than a mile from Findhorn – but I knew they were right. The narrow entrance to Findhorn Bay is a difficult channel to navigate even in daylight. We had had to get out of our boats on past trips and walk, towing our boats across the bar at low water. In the dark we could get well and truly stuck.

I wasn't sure how far exactly Nairn was away from us but guessed that it must be about 12–13 miles. With that small inflatable and its 40hp outboard, the tow was going to take a long, long time. Even if we were alone speeding along on the plane at 20 knots in good conditions it would take a good 45 minutes. Being towed at a few knots meant a long cold open tow in the chill air of a late November evening. But I could understand why they wanted to do it – and still had no real choice in the matter.

As we clipped my painter to the towing hook on the RNLI transom the cox leaned over. 'You guys are lucky – there's an RNLI exercise ongoing at the moment in the Moray Firth and there were four lifeboats in the vicinity. They *all* wanted to get to you – but we were the closest.'

Once they started the tow they throttled their inflatable up. The small engine laboured as it took the strain of my rigid hulled inflatable, all our twin sets, dive weights and my own redundant engine. Even when they were at full throttle we moved slowly through the water at four to five knots. But at last we were finally moving.

It was by now about 6 p.m. and pitch dark. There were no lights on the deserted beaches ashore, but I could see the orange twinkle of the small villages on the other side of the Firth. Ahead of us there was an orange halo, the glow of the lights of Nairn and Inverness beyond.

In the darkness, the red, green and white glow of my navigation lights dimly lit the faces of Ewan, Dave and Kevin, throwing coloured shadows across them. It had been a long, arduous day already and we were all exhausted and hungry.

Soon Kevin, the thinnest of the four of us, started becoming very chilled despite his dry suit. Dry suits, as well as keeping water out, tend to keep moisture from your body inside. This can condense, cool you down and chill you.

I gave Kevin the spare cagoule I kept on the boat for emergencies and a spare hat and gloves to try and keep the chill November air off him. When he still complained of being cold, I looked out my orange exposure bag and he wrapped it round him to keep the now biting damp air off him. He seemed to warm up at this but even so, tired, hungry, cold and low in blood sugar, we all lapsed into a resigned silence as the RNLI engine laboured away trying to pull its heavy charge.

Two long hours later, at about 8 p.m., we were finally approaching Nairn harbour. The lifeboat crew of two had done a stoic job towing us through the darkness towards their homeport and I was sorry for having dragged them out on a Sunday night, wrecking whatever social plans they may have had.

Although we were still well offshore, we had now started to head in towards the port. Already I was beginning to conjure up in my mind the feast I was going to have shortly at the nearest fast food outlet around. Just as I conjured up the food being put down in front of me, with lashings of hot tea, the RNLI lifeboat engine note changed.

The cox throttled down the lifeboat and we wallowed to a stop. I called over through the darkness, to the silhouette of the boat ahead of us, lit up against the orange lights of Nairn, and asked if there was a problem.

'The engine has been labouring and guzzling our fuel heavily,' came the reply. 'I don't know if we have got enough to get us into harbour. We're calling one of the other lifeboats, which is on standby nearby to come and stand off us in case we run out. Bad rocks around here. What fuel have you got aboard?'

'Two full tanks of pre-mix 100:1,' I replied 'Is that any good to you?'

'No,' came the swift, shouted response from the darkness ahead. 'Our engine is oil injection – we need clean petrol. We'll just wait off here until the other lifeboat arrives.'

A few minutes later we heard the steady hum of diesel engines and soon a large orange lifeboat appeared out of the darkness. A searchlight was switched on and swept over towards our two boats. At that, the towing inflatable throttled up their engine again and we headed further in towards Nairn harbour escorted by the larger lifeboat.

Half an hour later we were inside the small harbour, being towed through its winding passages to a slip where a cluster of people were standing.

As soon as we had tied off and stiffly stepped ashore, two ladies came up to us and introduced themselves as the wives of the two crew who had towed us. They had come down to meet us complete with flasks of hot tea and some biscuits. After what we had just been through, the warm tea was gratefully received and flooded down through my body warming from within.

I apologised to the crew for having spoiled their Sunday. Magnanimously, the cox told me not to worry. They had been on exercise that day anyway and when a real incident had happened, it had just made their day. He explained that they didn't get called out that often and had volunteered to do the work as they liked it. These two men were first rate, unassuming chaps, who had just got the job done professionally and without fuss. We are lucky to have people like this, all volunteers, on standby around our shores.

After tying up *Stonehaven Diver*, the cox then gave me a lift to Findhorn Bay where I at last got back into my car and drove the empty trailer back to Nairn. In the low glare of the harbour lights we finally winched *Stonehaven Diver* out of the water onto its trailer.

After that, we headed off towards Aberdeen and pulled in at a Little Chef at Forres where we ordered seemingly everything on the menu, twice.

Once we had eaten our fill we got back on the road for home. Two hours later, I had dropped Ewan off at his home and made my way down to Stonehaven to stow away the boat and tumble into bed at 1 a.m. Work was going to be a bit dull the following day in comparison.

CHAPTER TWELVE

Trimix – the Door Opens

'Push on – keep moving'
Thomas Morton, *A Cure for the Heartache*

After Ewan's blackout on the *Fram*, despite intense peer pressure, and to his great credit, he very sensibly never again ventured deeper than 40 metres on compressed air.

Thinking back now, we had had a warning before the *Fram* episode about the dangers of diving deep on air. At the time we didn't think too much about it. But now, with hindsight, it is clear that it was something we should have taken heed of. Like Ewan, my own deep air diving career would give me a subtle warning followed by a very serious incident – one which would stop me diving deep on air once and for all. Deep air kills, as we now know.

Ewan's first, more subtle, warning, took place with me near the bows of the legendary wreck of the *Rondo* in the Sound of Mull on the west coast of Scotland. The *Rondo*, a First World War vintage 'standard ship', was driven from her moorings near Tobermory in a furious storm in 1935. The sheltered harbour of Tobermory lies at the north end of the Sound of Mull, the narrow channel, some 13 miles long and a mile wide, that divides the Isle of Mull from mainland Scotland. Powerless, the *Rondo* was driven before the wind for ten miles down the Sound. It is a miracle that she was able to drift so far, as the Sound is peppered with dangerous reefs and rocks.

Eventually, her luck ran out and she ran aground on a six-metre-deep reef, projecting from the small rocky islet of Dearg Sgeir. She drove onto the reef and came to a grinding halt perched atop it. Stranded, high and almost dry, she was eventually declared a total loss by her insurers.

Salvers started stripping her *in situ*. They had removed all of her upper works, and a considerable portion of her hull, when six weeks later she was driven over the side of the reef by the seas. She slithered down near-vertical underwater cliff faces until her bow impacted on the bottom at about 50 metres, where she came to an abrupt halt.

The *Rondo* is now one of the most remarkable dives in Scotland. She stands almost vertically on her bows. Whilst they are in 50 metres, the uppermost parts of her – her rudder and prop shaft – rise up until they are only a few metres beneath the surface.

On one dive on the *Rondo*, as Ewan and I headed for the bows, Ewan started feeling distinctly uncomfortable at just short of the 40-metre mark. He gave me the recognised hand signal that he was feeling unwell. At that, we called the dive there and then. We turned and headed up to the shallower parts of the wreck where the narcosis affecting him eased and then disappeared.

This incident was a first warning. The subsequent *Fram* blackout was a more serious warning – one that we could not ignore. Ewan knew he had a sensitivity to nitrogen narcosis and just stopped diving deep on air. It was the right decision.

Unfortunately that decision coincided with my own progression into increasingly deeper air diving. It was the early 1990s and the 'technical diving' mixed gas revolution had not yet arrived.

I had looked for many years at the wreck symbols far offshore from my own Stonehaven and Aberdeen coastline and wondered what stories these wrecks, hidden from view since the First and Second World Wars, held.

As my diving career progressed, I was getting into deeper and deeper air diving. Wrecks had become my main underwater interest and the lure of being the first to discover and dive virgin wrecks enticed me intoxicatingly further offshore and into deeper water.

Ewan, although not diving any of the deeper wrecks, was still part of the team. His sound sailing, offshore oil industry and commercial diving background was a huge help to us in locating and allowing us to dive on the deeper wrecks, in the days before Global Positioning Systems (GPS) became popular and inexpensive.

Ewan shares my passion for the sea, and together we spent many a long day at sea in *Stonehaven Diver* endlessly checking approximate wreck positions 3–5 miles offshore, working with a sighting compass on fixed land positions. We worked out of Gourdon, a small coastal fishing village about ten miles south of Stonehaven. The locals were always interested in what we were up to, as divers were not a common sight for them. They talked with awe of a Second World War wreck, the *Roseberry*, which had been sunk in 1940. She had been part of a large convoy that had wheeled round the north of Scotland and was heading to the south-east English ports when she was attacked by German aircraft from Norway.

I checked the Hydrographic records for the area, but no wreck of a vessel called *Roseberry* was listed. However, there was a ship lost in the area from that convoy, listed as the *Queensbury*. I wondered whether the name of the vessel had simply been mixed up and corrupted over time.

In 1993 we started looking at trying to trace and dive the several deep wrecks charted off Gourdon. After one long day out at sea, Ewan and I managed to run over a large wreck in 50 metres, some 2–3 miles offshore from Gourdon.

This wreck was charted as the First World War loss, the tanker *Baku Standard*. Interestingly, although the depth to the seabed was 50 metres, the shallowest parts of the wreck rose up to 39 metres. That meant the wreck rose up for more than 30 feet. This was a big wreck, and I tried to persuade Ewan to dive it with me. We had found it together, and it was fitting, in the diver's code of honour, that we be the first of our group to dive it. I tried to reason with him that at the shallowest parts he wouldn't be too badly affected by narcosis, even though we knew it was right at his level of tolerance. Ewan stuck to his guns and refused to dive – but he would boathandle for us.

A few weeks later and we had *Stonehaven Diver* hooked into the unknown wreck that possibly was the *Baku Standard*. The echo-sounding trace was large enough for it to be a small early tanker, very different from modern-day tankers. Dave Hadden, another regular dive mate of mine, and a seasoned deep diver, had volunteered to dive it with me.

We rolled backwards off our RIB simultaneously and headed over to the down line. After a round of OK signals we started the descent. As we finned downwards, the eternal darkness of our east-coast waters, a result of run off from the many rivers that empty into the sea here, enveloped and then consumed us.

We hit seabed at 50 metres and in the darkness our powerful torch beams lit up the chain and eventually the anchor on a flat sandy seabed – there was no sign of the wreck. As I reached the anchor, the first wave of narcosis caught up with me and washed over me. After a quick descent to this depth, it hits like a gallon of Guinness being injected straight into you. Initially I felt a crushing disappointment that the anchor had been pulled off the wreck by us, or by the current – I thought we were going to miss the wreck altogether and end up diving HMS *Inthevicinityof*.

As I stared into the gloom, I became aware that a few metres ahead of me there seemed to be a large black mass towering over us. I gestured to Dave and we finned forward, to be confronted with a wall of rusted steel rising up a few metres.

I swam up and over what turned out to be the gunwales of a large wreck, well settled into the silty seabed. I found myself on the main deck of a large merchant vessel. Sweeping my UK 800 torch around, the intense beam lit up a silt-filled hold some 25 feet square, with attendant cargo winches set on the deck and derricks, fallen to the deck. Forward of the hold, I could see a large tubular mast collapsed down onto the deck. We were on the main deck of a large merchant vessel – not a tanker.

We moved off in the opposite direction from the hold and collapsed mast, not knowing if we were heading aft or forward. As soon as we passed over the rim of the hatch, a large rectangular deck-house, rising up more than five metres, appeared in front of me. As I stood on the deck staring up at this wall of rusted steel, covered in sponges and dead man's fingers, I could make out the silhouette of the entire deck-house, contrasted against the faint green of the distant surface above me.

I had arrived at the base of what appeared to be a bridge superstructure. I found two forward facing doorways, the doors long ago rotted and fallen from their mounts. Portholes, some in place, some missing their brass fitments, which had fallen from their rotted mounts, lined the front of the deck-house.

We moved cautiously inside through one of the doorways, sweeping our torches around. Any internal partitions had long since rotted away and the area was one common space, covered with a deep layer of silt. The brass and glass opening lights of portholes hung open; white porcelain toilet bowls and sinks gleamed in the darkness.

We moved outside again and rose up to the next deck level, and then another deck above that, until we came to the top level of this deck-house. Moving round to the back of what had been the navigating bridge, at the starboard wing I found an open aft-facing doorway covered with the remnants of a fisherman's net, lost aeons ago.

There had obviously been some sort of deck-house on top of this deck level, which had collapsed. The top of the bridge was a debris field and large sections of rusted steel wall lay flat on top with portholes still fixed in position. Large rectangular smooth cornered bricks, some 12 inches by 6 inches, lay scattered everywhere. When I took out my knife and scraped one I found that it was made of a thick black bituminous material. This was a cheap way of giving a modicum of protection to the roof of a bridge in wartime.

As I looked at these bricks I saw a glint of green – the telltale sign of brass underwater. I moved a few of the bricks and found myself looking at a large starboard-side docking telegraph. Leaving the telegraph for posterity I moved over towards the aft-facing doorway. I took my knife and cut into the degraded netting obscuring the doorway, finding it quite easy to remove. Once I had cleared a path for me to squeeze through, I wriggled in through the doorway and entered the bridge proper.

As soon as I was inside I was staggered to see that nearly all of the large thick glass rectangular bridge windows were still in place, set in greened brass frames. As I peered out through one of these and looked down, with my night vision having kicked in, I could now make out the first foredeck hold beneath me, where we had arrived. I could see the cargo winches and then the massive foremast, fallen forward over another foredeck hold. I turned, and looked to my left-hand side. Here lay a large brass compass binnacle, half buried in the silt.

As I left the bridge and started the long slow ascent to the surface, I was completely blown away by what we had just done. We had located our first deep wreck and had now dived it. It seemed obvious that it had not been dived much, if at all, in the past. Had it been, it would have been looted. But everything was still *in situ*: telegraphs, compasses and portholes. It was the quintessential virgin wreck. I realised how the wrecks I had dived in shallower waters had been almost completely picked clean of all artefacts and anything brass. When we got back ashore, we sketched up what we had seen, to try and get an idea of what sort of ship it was we were diving on.

Slack water the following weekend found us anchored into the wreck again and diving on the section aft of the bridge. Here we found a second long low deck-house, with what had been cabins along either side. Again, portholes hung open and we managed to glimpse into the engine room and see the tops of the seven cylinders of a massive oil-fired engine. The engine dropped down into the innards of the engine room for about 40 feet and was ringed with catwalks.

Just aft of the engine room we came to the end of this deck-house, and here we found two aft-facing doorways. Entering the starboard side doorway, Dave Hadden and I cautiously moved forward trying to avoid stirring up the thick layer of silt. When we were about 25 feet inside what appeared to be the galley, I saw the outline of the tops of three tea chests sticking out of the silt. I wondered what would be in them and stuck my hand into the first one and wriggled it down into the silt. I felt crockery and pulled out a small plate. It had an unusual shipping logo on it, one that I hadn't seen before. I took that piece to the surface with me.

Later, once it was cleaned up, I was able to make out the crest of the Wilhelmsen Line, a Norwegian shipping line still in existence today. I was clear that we were now diving a Second World War era, Norwegian merchant vessel, and by the time we had finished sketching it once back ashore, we had a good idea of the layout of the whole wreck.

The Hydrographic printout showed that there was a Norwegian vessel listed as having been sunk a few miles away from the position we were diving, the Wilhelmsen Line vessel MS *Taurus*. I wrote to the Norwegian Maritime Museum in Oslo who helpfully came back to say that they had more than 200 photos of this vessel under construction. It was a famous ship, and had been Ship of the Year in 1935 when she was built. They sent me prints of the best photos – and lo and behold, it was identical to the wreck we had dived and surveyed. We had identified our virgin wreck.

I now had wreck research coursing through my veins and soon teamed up with George Mair, another deep air diver who lived in Aberdeen and who had a Rigid Inflatable Boat as well. Being so far offshore it was best to have two boats working together. George came out and dived the *Taurus* with us. He seemed very switched on at depth on air and seemed hardly affected by the narcs at 50 metres.

George took to wreck finding and spent a lot of time out at sea checking marks and positions. Working as a pair we dived regularly on our local wrecks over the next couple of years.

One week he called to tell me that he had located a large wreck in about 60 metres, some 5 miles offshore. The top of this wreck rose to 50 msw so it was right at the limit recommended for air diving by the British Sub Aqua Club (BSAC).

Soon we had a party of two boats going out to dive this new wreck. The Hydrographic department printout indicated that this mark might be a German U-boat but the echo-sounder trace seemed too big for that. Once down on the wreck we found it was the First World War tanker *Baku Standard*, which was charted as being lost in the position we had now established was the *Taurus*. I was beginning to see how muddled up all the wreck identities were.

I must admit that I found the dive to 50 metres and just over on air in the pitch dark to be a very difficult experience. I was at the limit of my own personal tolerance to nitrogen narcosis and was just hanging on in there. It was difficult to rationalise what I was seeing down on the wreck and indeed, once back on the surface it was hard to even remember much of it.

A diver's tolerance to nitrogen narcosis can vary from one day to the next and depends on a whole host of environmental factors such as fatigue levels, underwater visibility, the darkness and work levels. If a diver is working hard, finning against a current at depth, he will be more affected by the narcs.

In retrospect, this uncomfortable dive on the *Baku Standard* was a parallel to the first warning Ewan got on the *Rondo*. Like Ewan's it went unheeded.

Later that month, Dave Hadden and I went on a dive trip out of Girvan with some old friends of his from England. They had chartered a hard boat for the weekend to exclusively dive wrecks.

The first dive was on a virgin wreck located recently by the skipper. When we got over the wreck, I was dismayed to see that the depth to the seabed on the echo-sounder was 55 metres and that the wreck rose up to only 50 metres. Having just had an unpleasant time down on the *Baku Standard* at 50 metres, here I was away to dive down into these serious depths again.

On this occasion the shot had landed, or bounced, just off the wreck. As Dave and I dropped down through 50 metres there was no sign of the wreck. Eventually we landed heavily on a muddy seabed at 55 metres, way beyond the BSAC recommended safe limit. I didn't feel too narcosed this time and looking upwards and around me I made out the silhouette of a smallish wreck nearby. We finned slowly over to the wreck and rose up mercifully to the 'shallower' depth of 50 metres. Here we had a fantastic but short dive on another virgin wreck – complete with navigation lanterns *in situ.*

Having carried out that dive successfully, when I got back to Stonehaven, George Mair told me he had located another wreck five miles off Stonehaven and asked if I wanted to dive it. I agreed immediately. This was one of the locally fabled 'five-mile wrecks' that local fishermen talked of. It was a wreck off my part of the coast, and I wanted to see it for myself.

George told me that the depth to the seabed was 58 metres and that the shallowest part of the wreck rose up to about 52 metres. I initially balked at these depths, but then my enthusiasm to dive another virgin wreck took over. I reasoned with myself that these depths were only a few metres deeper than the dive I had just done out of Girvan. I had coped well enough on that dive – what could another few metres do? I agreed to dive it.

Our two boats arrived above the new wreck on a fine summer evening just before slack water. George and Eric Ronsberg would dive it first – George had found it and it was fitting that he should go down on it first. Dave Hadden and I would then go in as the second wave.

George and Eric were inwater for more than an hour. When they eventually surfaced, I learned that they had indeed successfully got onto the wreck. He described its layout and the depths we could expect of 54–8 metres. George and Eric had done something like 55 minutes of air decompression stops – that is, after they had spent their allotted dive time down on the wreck, they had had to take 55 minutes for the ascent to let the nitrogen bubbles saturating their tissues escape harmlessly. To surface earlier risked an attack of the dreaded bends.

These were serious depths and dive times – the longest I had spent in decompression during an ascent at that stage was about 25 minutes. I immediately felt a stab of apprehension at what I was about to take on. I felt a definite wobble of my resolve to dive. This was way beyond my experience. Nevertheless I was committed, and in the perverse, face-saving, macho world of diving, I wasn't going to bottle it now and call off.

So Dave Hadden and I rolled off our boat and started heading down into the darkness, lights switched on, piercing the inky blackness beneath. From time to time I flashed my torch beam onto my dive computer and watched my depth increase. It all seemed to take an eternity and I started to feel the first insidious pangs of narcosis affecting me. I was at 25 metres when I first swept my torch over my computer – I usually didn't feel much at that depth.

When I next checked, I was still descending – it was 35 metres. Next check and I was at 45 metres. By now, I knew I was well narcosed and in the danger area. There was no sign of the wreck below me – just impenetrable darkness, but I knew it was close to me now.

My next check was at 50 metres – I was feeling in control but apprehensive as we plunged into the darkness. Then I was down at 55 metres. I had hoped that the anchor would be on or near the wreck. If so, I might be able to see the wreck and leave the anchor line before I hit the bottom and make my way up the wreck to its shallowest point. The wreck would give me something I could cling to – something man-made and recognisable that would make me feel secure. But of the wreck there was no sign, and it dawned on me that I would now have to go all the way to the seabed at 58 metres. I swept my torch down and suddenly there was the anchor, lying on the sandy seabed. I landed in a cloud of silt beside it and Dave arrived beside me. It was now pitch black and the underwater visibility was 5–10 feet.

By now slack water had passed, and there was a slight current running. George had told me that the wreck lay not far ahead of the anchor, so I determined that I would tough it out and fin forward from the anchor to see if I ran into the wreck. I signalled to Dave and kicked my fins.

We swam together forward against the current and as I did so I tried to rise up a few metres to minimise my depth. I had wanted to stay in sight of the seabed but after finning forward for perhaps a minute or so, I swept my torch downwards – and there was no sign of the seabed.

For some inexplicable reason this produced a huge surge of panic from deep within me. I instantly became convinced that I had started having a buoyant ascent to the surface. From this depth such an ascent would lead to my certain and painful death. My breathing started coming in panted gasps. I felt my vision close in, until I could only see a tunnel of vision ahead of me. I was overwhelmed by a huge wave of narcosis and lost all control of myself. I managed to turn towards Dave, who was still beside me. It never crossed my mind that if I was having a buoyant ascent, he wouldn't be there. I signalled with the 'thumbs up' signal that I was going up and started to rise up from the bottom.

I can't remember how long the ascent took – I know I shot up to about 35 metres very quickly and then everything swam back into focus. I cannot remember the ascent from 58 metres to 35 metres at all. One minute I was on the bottom, the next minute my mind was clearing and I was putting on the brakes to halt my ascent at 35 metres. What happened in between I don't know. My breathing calmed and I regained control. The wave of narcosis disappeared just as fast as it had overcome me.

Dave, like a seasoned buddy diver he was, had stayed right beside me as we rose up – probably wondering when I was going to stop or whether he was going to have to stop me going up. As it was, when I reached 35 metres and the narcs disappeared, I dumped air from my buoyancy wings and suit and reached neutral buoyancy, a perfect equilibrium where we hung motionless in the water.

Dave took out his delayed deco reel and fired his buoy up to the surface for the boat cover to see and follow. We carried out a normal ascent after that without any complications.

Ewan had been given a gentle warning on the *Rondo*, followed by a severe warning on the *Fram*. Now I too had had my gentle warning on the *Baku Standard*, followed by what could have been a fatal incident on this wreck – which we later identified as the SS *Cushendall*.

As technical divers we now have an expression, 'Deep air kills'. It is very true and I, like Ewan, had just found out the hard way. Like Ewan, I resolved that I too would never dive to these extreme depths on air again.

After Ewan's *Fram* blackout, as our team ventured further out to sea, diving deeper wrecks, Ewan had stayed in touch, boat handling when he could and sharing his knowledge of the sea with us. I had always felt a tinge of sadness that we had essentially left him behind as a result of his decision to stop diving deep on air.

In the summer of 1995 however, Ewan came on the phone to me, hugely excited and firing words at me rapidly. The diving authorities had now accepted the introduction of mixed gas diving in the UK, after blocking it for years. Various technical diving associations were now going to start offering courses. He wanted us to sign up for the first of these courses to be run in our area by an American training agency which was setting up in the UK – Technical Diving Incorporated, TDI.

As an ex-commercial diver, Ewan was intimately familiar with the ins and outs of mixed gas diving. Dave Gordon, a diving instructor with our local dive shop, Aberdeen Watersports, and one of our group of deep air wreck divers, had just been trained up as a mixed gas instructor by Rob Palmer, one of the original exponents of technical diving. Rob, a huge name in technical diving, then and now, had got involved with TDI and was going to set up the UK side of their training agency.

Just as soon as Dave Gordon had qualified as a Trimix instructor Ewan and I signed up for the three courses that we would need to qualify us as Trimix divers.

We first had to do a Nitrox course. Nitrox is basically oxygen-enriched air. By increasing the level of benevolent oxygen in the gas mix and reducing the level of harmful nitrogen in the mix, Nitrox extended bottom times for 'no-stop' diving hugely, and increased safety factors against problems like the bends and narcosis. A common Nitrox mix we use for decompression after a deep dive is called Nitrox 50. This is comprised of 50 per cent oxygen and 50 per cent nitrogen, as opposed to the usual 21 per cent oxygen and 79 per cent nitrogen in air. The only reason for learning Nitrox theory and application was to use it as a decompression gas for Trimix diving.

After sitting and passing our Nitrox exam, we started on an Extended Range Course. This was designed to introduce us to extended or deeper diving and teach us about the benefits of carrying separate Nitrox tanks slung under our arms to accelerate the decompression stops we had to carry out. Using Nitrox, as opposed to air, for decompression meant that we could get out of the water more quickly and far more safely. Decompressing using air as I had done throughout my deep air diving career, with its high nitrogen level, was all that had been available to me, but it wasn't the best gas for decompression. Nitrogen is your enemy.

I found the whole concept of 'accelerated decompression' using separate Nitrox tanks, containing Nitrox 50, 60 or even 80 (i.e. 80 per cent oxygen and only 20 per cent nitrogen), absolutely fascinating. At first I was suspicious and cautious of the significantly shortened decompression stops the theory claimed I could do, but soon I had embraced the new wisdom.

On a dive to 45 metres on air with a bottom time of 21 minutes, the decompression stops recommended by the standard Buhlmann air tables would mean that a diver would take 29 minutes to complete them during the ascent. Therefore, a diver, after spending 21 minutes on the bottom would be able to safely leave the water after 50 minutes.

Doing the same 21 minutes on air at 45 metres, but using Nitrox 60 for decompression, shortened the total dive time to 30 minutes, i.e. the ascent would only take 9 minutes as opposed to the 29 minute ascent using air to decompress. In addition, by using Nitrox 60 to decompress, divers also hugely minimised the risk of the bends. The leap forward in decompression diving was staggering.

After passing the Extended Range exam, Ewan and I were now onto the serious stuff of the Trimix course proper. The first two courses, Nitrox and Extended Range, had just been the foreplay.

The idea behind Trimix is that nitrogen is your enemy at depth – it is the cause of nitrogen narcosis. Helium, on the other hand, is your friend. To reduce the narcotic effects of nitrogen, a large percentage of the nitrogen is removed and replaced by helium, which is inert. Helium is a very small molecule in comparison to nitrogen and passes in and out of body tissues very quickly. With helium escaping quickly and easily from tissues, the risk of rogue bubbles hanging around and causing the bends is reduced. Most importantly, at depths of more than 40 metres, where nitrogen is seriously affecting and impairing a diver's mental abilities, helium has no easily discernible narcotic effect.

We were taught about air equivalent depths. As you dive deep on Trimix the smaller amounts of nitrogen build up and still produce a narcotic effect. To understand how great that narcotic effect is going to be, we relate it to the narcotic effect air produces at any given depth.

A typical Trimix I use for dives in the 50–80-metre range is 16 per cent oxygen, 45 per cent helium and the balance of 39 per cent nitrogen. (We also reduce the level of oxygen in the mix from 21 per cent in air to 16 per cent, as oxygen too becomes toxic at depth.)

At 70 metres, on this mix, my body feels a narcotic effect the same as if I were diving on air at only 29 metres. At 29 metres, the narcotic effect of nitrogen is felt, but only mildly. Trimix thus allows us to dive deeper than ever possible on air, and far more safely.

Dave Gordon patiently took us on a series of training exercises in cold, dark quarries where we learned about the tools of our trade. The main rig consisted of a stainless steel backplate and webbing harness which supported two 12-litre steel tanks on our back and two 7- or 9-litre Nitrox tanks, slung one under either arm and fixed to our harness, called 'stage' tanks. They are breathed at different stages of the dive.

We learned techniques to prevent us breathing from the wrong tank at the wrong time. If you get too much oxygen in your body, the oxygen becomes toxic. Each gas was safe in its own working depth but potentially lethal if breathed at the wrong depth. The oxygen in air, 20.9 per cent, becomes toxic when you dive to depths greater than 80 metres.

Each of the various Nitrox mixes we use has its own safe working range. Nitrox 50, one of our common decompression gases, can only safely be breathed at depths of less than 20 metres. If, by mistake, you put the regulator for it in your mouth and breathe it any deeper than that, you run a very real risk of an oxygen toxicity hit, which produces unmanageable convulsions and almost inevitably underwater, death. Many, many technical divers have died in this way.

I chose to have one type of breathing regulator, the hugely reliable Apeks valves, for each of my decompression stage tanks and completely different regulators, for my 'bottom mix' in my twin set. I hoped that there would be no chance of mixing the two types up – even in zero visibility when I would be working by touch alone. For my bottom mix I chose Poseiden Jetstreams, which easily deliver large amounts of breathing gas even in deep, hard-working conditions.

Very soon, Dave had us doing calculations to work out the best gas to breathe at various depths of a dive, the air equivalent narcotic depths for those gases – and 'run times' for the dive. It was no longer a simple case of strapping on fins and leaping into the water with forgiving air in my tanks. Dives now had to be run like a military operation with gas mixes and decompression stops being worked out on computers by specialist decompression software.

The total run time for the dive was worked out in advance. We knew exactly how long we were going to spend on the bottom; we knew at what speed we would ascend and at what depth we would halt for our first decompression stop. Each minute of our dive was precisely scheduled. We knew when we should arrive at each predetermined decompression stop and exactly when we would leave that stop depth to move up to the next stop depth.

A common dive profile for a dive to 60 metres goes something like this:

Minute 1:	leave surface breathing Bottom Mix
Minute 3:	arrive at bottom
Minute 18:	leave bottom
Minute 20:	arrive at first decompression stop at 36 metres – spend 1 minute there, leaving at minute 21
Minute 21:	arrive at next decompression stop at 33 metres – spend 1 minute there
Minute 22:	arrive at next deco stop at 30 metres – spend 1 minute there.
Minute 23:	arrive at 27 metres – spend 2 minutes there
Minute 25:	arrive at 24 metres – spend 2 minutes there
Minute 27:	arrive at 21 metres – change over to decompression mix and spend 1 minute there
Minute 28:	arrive at 18 metres – spend 2 minutes there
Minute 30:	arrive at 15 metres – spend 2 minutes there
Minute 32:	arrive at 12 metres – spend 2 minutes there
Minute 34:	arrive at 9 metres – spend 4 minutes there
Minute 38:	arrive at 6 metres – spend 13 minutes there

Surface at Minute 51

Having learnt all the theory from Dave, it was time for our first Trimix dive proper. The three courses we had been doing had extended over quite a number of weeks and we were now moving into November. The seas were too rough around our shore to easily get the depth needed for our first scheduled training dive, which was to be a 50-metre dive on Trimix. But Dave had already sussed out a good site up at Loch Ness where he and Rob Palmer had dived during his training. The bottom shelved out gradually for a short distance before dropping away in a sheer wall to a depth of 100 metres or more into the depths of Loch Ness.

Ewan and I left Stonehaven early one Saturday morning for the two and a half hour drive across Scotland to Inverness. From there we wound our way down the narrow road that leads along the shores of Loch Ness. Passing the fork at Drumnadrochit for the road to Skye and the west coast of Scotland, we continued southwards towards Fort William.

Driving past Drumnadrochit, we passed the ruined and picturesque

Urquhart Castle on our left-hand side, already teeming with several large tour buses and scores of tourists eager to catch a glimpse of the Loch Ness monster. Little did they know that we were going to dive deep down into the loch's peaty black water, just a few miles further down the road.

Very shortly we arrived at a small youth hostel and pulled off the road into a small gravelled car park. Aberdeen Watersports' white transit van was already there and a few helpers were ferrying a number of tanks, and training paraphernalia down a small path that wound down to the loch. Sticking an arm through my harness and hoisting my heavy twin set onto my back, I picked up my weights harness and in a rather ungainly fashion, struggled down the path through the trees. A short distance later the path opened out onto a flat, shelving, stony beach with the wide expanse of Loch Ness nearby. Returning to the car we brought down our gear bags and then started getting changed into our dive undersuits and dry suits.

Once ready, I picked up my twin set and set it in the very edge of the loch and positioned one stage 9-litre tank either side of it – ready for me to clip on. I then sat down on my backside and wriggled backwards into my twin set harness. Clipping on my stage tanks I was now fully rigged.

Dave and Ewan then stood up and got ready to enter the water. I tried to stand up and immediately found that the combined weight of my heavy steel twin set and stage tanks allied to my weights and other dive kit made it almost impossible for me to get off the ground. I struggled away and eventually with assistance from some helpers, managed to get onto my feet. I walked into the welcome, supporting embrace of the water to join Dave and Ewan.

Sticking my bottom mix regulator in my mouth I took a few deep breaths of the magic Trimix, not knowing what to expect. There was no discernible difference to breathing air, but when Dave took his regulator out of his mouth to speak to us, it was like he was talking after breathing helium balloon mixture as a party trick. He did a passable rendition of Donald Duck as he explained that we would swim down a 45-degree shelving slope. This would then take us to a sheer wall, which dropped down to some unimaginable depth in the Loch. We would descend down the wall to a depth of 50 metres and halt our descent there. We would then swim laterally along the wall at 50 metres, before ascending again. A couple of support divers were going to follow us down halfway on air.

Seeing we were OK about his briefing, Dave turned and splashed forward into the water. Ewan followed and I brought up the rear. The water was a dark, peaty brown, and visibility was only at best about six feet. I spent the next five minutes or so following Ewan's fins, the only thing visible ahead of me as he swam down the slope.

At a depth of about 25 metres we came to the edge of the wall. The slope just stopped abruptly at a sharp edge. There was nothing but a pitch-black void beneath me and it was daunting to fin out over it.

I shone my torch down the wall but the powerful beam of my UK 800 torch made little headway against the darkness of the peaty water. I could see that Ewan and Dave had their torches on and Dave signalled for us to go down.

In a close group we descended vertically in open water keeping a check on our buoyancy. Dropping straight down a sheer wall is always exciting. Factor in for this dive the darkness, all the new equipment and new breathing gas, and the Loch Ness monster, and it is little wonder that I felt hugely alive as the stone cliff face drifted upwards past me.

When I reached 45 metres I suddenly realised that I felt as fresh and clear-headed as on the surface. Normally I would be well narcosed at this depth. We arrived at the 50-metre mark and Dave halted our descent. The three of us hung suspended in the darkness above the abyssal depths of Loch Ness.

I felt immensely clear-headed and swept my torch around the wall, taking in its contours and simple little things like twigs and leaves trapped in crevices – things I'd never have noticed if I'd been hanging on for grim life on air at this depth. It slowly dawned on me how big an effect mixed gas was going to have on my diving career from the point of view of taking in and understanding what I was seeing on shipwrecks. The difference felt like trying to work out a complicated mind puzzle sober, as opposed to doing it having just consumed a gallon of Guinness.

We swam uneventfully along the wall for about ten minutes, keeping our depth perfectly at 50 metres before Dave turned and signalled that it was time to ascend. At this time, TDI training advocated a rapid ascent to the depth scheduled for the change over to decompression gas, to create a pressure gradient to force the helium out of our tissues. (We no longer observe this and are now fans of 'deep stops' along the way to the first scheduled decompression stop.)

Ewan and I followed orders and finned up the wall hard, before cresting it and heading on up the slope at speed to the 20-metre change over point. As my depth got quickly shallower I thought I could hear squeaks and groans from my body as the helium rushed out of my tissues.

Once we got to 20 metres, we swapped over to our deco mix stage bottles and started carrying out decompression stops at depths of 18 metres, 15 metres, 12 metres, 9 metres and lastly a long hang at 6 metres.

Here at 6 metres when I was halfway through the allotted stop time my hired deco regulator suddenly exploded from my mouth with some force and a blast of deco gas was fired down my throat.

I was temporarily stunned at what had just happened. This had never happened to me before. One minute I had a regulator clenched in my teeth, the next it had been blown right out by some catastrophic failure. The regulator itself was disgorging a huge torrent of breathing gas and was thrashing about with the forces working on it.

After a second or two of staring at my regulator, as if in a dream, it dawned on me that I had in fact no regulator in my mouth and that I was holding my breath. I should be doing something positive about this. Unfamiliar with the hired kit and new rig set-up, I was slow to react. All I needed to do was to swap over to my other redundant deco mix tank and regulator.

Dave was over in a flash and, grabbing hold of the free-flowing regulator, followed the hose back to find which tank it led from. He then switched off the pillar valve and the gushing bubbles stopped.

There was no danger at any time here. We were just hanging around in six metres not far from the shore in easy conditions – but it was a reminder of how the unexpected can happen at any time underwater.

We completed the rest of our decompression stops without incident. When we got back ashore we stripped the 1st Stage of the regulator, the part that connects directly onto the pillar valve in the neck of the scuba tank. The nylon seat in the 1st Stage had ruptured, allowing high-pressure Nitrox to blast its way down to my breathing regulator with such force that it blew the regulator right out of my mouth.

Back on the stony shores of Loch Ness, as I dekitted after my first Trimix dive, the main feeling I had was a sense of wonder at what I had just done. After diving on air at this depth for a number of years I had become used to the huge rush of narcosis that sweeps over a diver as he descends beyond 40 metres to the then recommended air limit of 50 metres. I had become accustomed to diving to 50 metres or beyond, with my brain only partly functioning – like a drunk man. Like the drunk driving a car, you felt you could control things well enough. It is only when something goes wrong that, sometimes tragically, we learn how little control we have.

I had learned to survive in an alien liquid world on air at these depths – not to function well, not to control them – but simply to get by. Now, standing on the shores of Loch Ness, reprising the dive I was struck by just how clear-headed the whole dive had been. Instead of being well narcosed at 50 metres, it was as though I was walking in a park on a summer's day. Everything was sharply in focus.

I had been in more control of this dive than I had ever been on a dive to this depth. I had been able to spend time to look around and take in and assess my surroundings. If narcosis levels were hugely decreased, so too was the risk of the dreaded bends. Less nitrogen – less risk.

I felt that a door had just been opened for me and as Ewan and I chatted on the long drive back to Stonehaven after the dive, the miles flew past as I wondered where this new departure for my diving career would take me.

We carried out a series of further Trimix dives over the following weekends and then it was time for the exam, which we sat at Aberdeen Watersports' shop and classroom at Aberdeen harbour. Ewan and I were the first to go through the new TDI set-up in the UK. Rob Palmer asked Dave to send him our exam papers so that he could check and see how we responded to the questions set. In the event, both Ewan and I scored over 90 per cent and we soon received our TDI Trimix certification cards. We were Trimix divers at last and new frontiers awaited us. Tucked away in the TDI training manuals was a phrase that stuck with me however: 'If you walk the Frontier – you will meet Indians.'

Sadly Rob Palmer, who had been such a leading exponent of the new wave of technical diving and the dangers of deep air, died a few years later in the Red Sea whilst trying to set a new world deep air record. He was last seen by support divers, heading downwards at the incredible depth of more than 120 metres. He was never seen again and his body has never been recovered.

CHAPTER THIRTEEN

Evolution is a Slow Process

Having qualified as Trimix divers in 1995, Ewan and I had soon acquired the full technical divers' rig and were ready to launch ourselves far offshore to explore a vast treasure trove of wrecks previously too deep for ordinary scuba divers to reach.

As a reality check, our first dive following our training would be on the stern section of the *Fram* where Ewan had blacked out in 1992 and to which we had not returned since. Nothing like confronting your demons.

The dive went uneventfully enough but in that one simple dive on this half ship section, I learned more about her than I had done in the ten or so dives I had carried out on air, whilst researching for *Dive Scotland's Greatest Wrecks*. Simple, large-scale things like the orientation of the rudder, the square-bladed prop, the internal layout of the intact stern itself were things I had picked up on when diving on air. But it was the small detail, like the tiny pitched roof of the engine room, with its small, brass-rimmed glass fanlights still *in situ* that stood out. When you are struggling to survive you just don't notice things like that.

On the way back to the line to ascend we spotted that someone had stacked a couple of spare porthole glasses, probably robbed from a porthole locker, under the hull intended to be picked up at a later date. I just never noticed small things like that on air at that depth.

Once aboard the boat we talked through the dive. It became clear that what, on air, had been a deep, dark, scary dive, on Trimix, turned out to be a simple to manage, not so deep dive on what now just looked like a pile of rusted metal plates. The narcosis being stripped away stripped away the hype of my own mind.

At the end of that year we returned for a weekend in the Sound of Mull. We enjoyed fine diving on the SS *Hispania* and SS *Shuna*, perhaps the finest, air diveable wrecks in Scotland outside Scapa Flow. We then dived down past the 40-msw mark on the *Rondo* where Ewan had had his warning, and made our way right to the tip of the bow in 50 msw. Again, as we stood on the seabed with the hull of the *Rondo* reaching vertically 50 metres up to the surface above, we wondered what all the fuss was about this wreck. Sure, it was a dark, scary dive, but on mix, it was just the stripped-down shell of a ship standing on its bow.

The following year for us was one of numerous explorations of virgin undived wrecks. This is what divers dream of – to be the first to dive a wreck, to establish its identity and to identify why she sank.

For some years Ewan and I had looked at the Hydrographic Department's printout of wrecks around Rattray Head and the corresponding Admiralty chart. Rattray Head is near the triangular corner of north-east Scotland, between Fraserburgh and Peterhead, and was a favourite Second World War hunting ground for German U-boats, as well as planes from Norwegian air bases. Convoys heading for London and the English east coast ports, from all over the world, would wheel round the northern Orkney Islands, rather than risk the dangerous English Channel, before heading down the east coast of Scotland and England.

A channel for this maritime traffic, half-a-mile wide, was laid out and marked with buoys every half a mile and swept regularly for mines. This 'swept channel' was situated about five miles offshore. Further offshore, the swept channel was protected by the great Northern Mine Barrage, a wall of mines intended to prevent incursions by enemy U-boats against Allied shipping in the swept channel. At first the Northern Mine Barrage ran only from London to Fraserburgh, just a few miles further north-west from Rattray Head. Later in the war, seeing the losses around Rattray Head, it was extended right the way up to the Orkney Isles.

In all, during the Second World War, some 52 Allied vessels were sunk around north-east Scotland alone, concentrated on Rattray Head. There were so many wrecks around, some in shallow water, that the Admiralty had declared the whole Rattray Head area unsafe for navigation for two miles offshore. I grew up in Fraserburgh and I can remember walking with my family on a bright summer's day out across the flat sands drained and exposed at low water in strong spring tides and seeing brown rusted parts of ships sticking out of the sand.

Ewan had purchased a magnetometer to help us in our wreck finding quest. It detects variations in the earth's magnetic field caused by large lumps of metal on the seabed. It can detect these large lumps – wrecks – on either side of the sweep of its track for up to 1,000 metres. We thought that if we got into the charted approximate position for a wreck we would be able to home in on it using our new toy.

We arrived at Inverallochy, which has the nearest harbour to Rattray Head to launch our RIB, early one Sunday morning ready for a search offshore. By this time Global Positioning Systems (GPS) had come on the market that were suitable for small open boats like ours, so we had punched in a number of possible wreck coordinates from the Hydrographic printout. We had optimistically taken all our dive kit with us and had given ourselves two or three hours before slack water arrived, in which to locate a suitable wreck to dive.

We were very conscious that when these ships were lost during the Second World War, they did not have the sophisticated navigational tools available nowadays. Seamen navigated by dead reckoning and by taking bearings on fixed land points. If visibility at sea was poor they could be well off with their navigation. However, we had found that there was usually something around in the vicinity of a Hydrographic position. Sometimes the charts revealed that the position had been surveyed or wire-swept, and these marks proved far more accurate. But, more often than not, the wreck was sometimes up to a mile or more away from its reported position. A mile is a lot of water at sea and we would use Ewan's magnetometer to home in on the target wreck.

In addition to *Stonehaven Diver*, Dave Gordon of Aberdeen Watersports, who had trained us in mix diving, had come along in the shop's own RIB as well. Two divers would go down from each boat leaving one cox in each.

Ewan and I got our boat organised first and motored out of Inverallochy harbour into the wide expanse of Fraserburgh Bay. I throttled *Stonehaven Diver* up onto the plane and turned to the south-east, heading the five or so miles along towards Rattray Head. We punched in the coordinates for the first target wreck site into the GPS and hit the GOTO button before orientating the RIB onto the LCD Highway on the GPS. The Highway feature would let us drive right up to the site.

As we skipped along an oily surface at about 20 knots, to the south of us I could see the tall masts and flare of the St Fergus Gas Terminal. Dimly, in the distance beyond that, I could make out the fishing port of Peterhead.

As we motored south, Ewan sat behind me on the double console seat, giving me directions from the handheld GPS. It was so new that we hadn't had time to fix a bracket on the console for it yet. Steve Collard, an air diver, had just returned from working abroad in the Gulf and having heard all the fuss about Trimix diving had come along to cox our boat and see how it was done. I wanted to get out of the harbour and down to the site as quickly as possible to give us a chance of locating the wreck. A magnetometer search of a box zone would be time consuming – and slack water waits for no man. There was every chance we might not find any wreck at all.

Once we got down to the precise location of the Hydrographic position, there was nothing showing on the seabed but a flat undulating sandy bottom. Dave Gordon's boat hadn't come into sight yet to the north of us. Ewan unreeled the torpedo-like magnetometer transponder fish and plopped it over the side as I motored forward. It ran out for some way behind us on its cable. Soon he had the magnetometer calibrated and we were off searching.

Ewan sat on the starboard-side tube of the RIB watching the LCD of his magnetometer closely, as it read out the information from the transponder fish. I started doing a grid search pattern from the GPS and Ewan was able to guide me as the strength of the readout got stronger or weakened.

Very quickly, the magnetometer's beeping started to get more and more intense and the LCD graph on the instrument box started to give a large sine wave. We were very close to something very large and metallic. I stared at the readout on my console-mounted echo-sounder until finally the trace jumped up, marking the presence of something large directly underneath. Fixing the position with the MOB (Man Over Board) function on the GPS, we got Steve to drop the anchor once we were right over the largest part of it. The anchor plunged down and then snagged on something solid. Checking the ground speed on the GPS showed a ground speed of zero knots. Although the tide was still pushing water past us, and creating ripples around the anchor-line and a wash down the side of the boat, we knew we were fixed solid in position. The outline of the wreck stayed fixed on my echo-sounder.

I switched off the engine and checked my watch. The whole search had only taken 15 minutes, far less than I had expected. We were way too early for slack water, so we had time to relax, to fiddle with our gear, eat some food and hydrate for the coming dive. As I looked to the north I saw the bow splash of Dave Gordon's RIB heading our way.

When Dave arrived he was mightily impressed, as indeed we were too – all our new toys had worked. I casually remarked the wreck trace looked big enough for it to be a 4,000-ton ship. The echo-sounding trace had jumped up from a seabed of 60 msw to a least depth of 50 msw – these were the same dimensions as the MS *Taurus* – and she was about 4,000 tons. So we christened her the 'Four Thousand Tonner' for the time being, until we established her identity.

An hour or so later, the current sweeping past us had noticeably dropped away. Slack water was approaching and it was time to get ready to dive.

Ewan and I sat opposite each other on the tubes of the RIB, as Steve helped us rig up in our technical gear. It was still all new to me, and I still felt ungainly, complicated and heavy. Once I was rigged, I had my twin set on my back, a stage Nitrox tank under either arm, four regulators hung at different parts of me, two torches stowed on me and my chest looking like spaghetti junction with the hoses for my various mixes, suit and wings inflation, running all over the place. I felt as though I couldn't move. And here I was away to drop over the side of a boat about five miles offshore. I had to be mad.

But then, Ewan was shouting over 'You ready, Rod?'

'Yes,' I replied. 'Let's get it done.' This was still a 60 msw dive and I was still breaking all my ingrained taboos about the depth I could dive to. This was my deepest dive to date and I felt the familiar surge of apprehension mingled with anticipation. The thrill of the chase, the search for and successful finding of the wreck were still there but a feeling of unreality overcame me. I had one of those moments when you feel that you are outside your body. I was observing myself getting ready for the dive in a dispassionate third-party way. I was on the dive treadmill, intent on getting my kit on and sorted. When I was rigged up, I swung one leg over the side of the tube and sat there resting my twin set on the tube.

Ewan rolled into the water and without thinking I followed his lead. As soon as I was in the water my apprehension disappeared. The weight of my ungainly kit was instantly supported by the buoyancy in my wings and suit. The water looked crystal clear and I could see a good 20 metres or more down the anchor line. The good visibility and bright blue underwater seascape instantly calmed my beating heart.

I was floating, suspended about two metres beneath the surface. I looked up at the RIB and could see every detail of its hull. I could also see Steve's face staring over the side of the boat down at me. I gave him a wave, not knowing if he could see me, turned over and finned across to the down line – our guide into the depths.

I travelled down breathing from the seven-litre stage tank under my left arm, which was filled with Nitrox 32. Once I got down to about 35 metres I took that regulator out of my mouth, stowed it under its bungee, stuck in my bottom mix regulator of Trimix B (16 per cent oxygen, 45 per cent helium) and took a few long deep breaths.

Above me, the bright sunshine illuminated the anchor line all the way up to the surface, where I could still see the outline of *Stonehaven Diver*. Something special was going on here. I had never had such good visibility on the east coast of Scotland before. I gave Ewan an OK signal and got the OK reply back. I turned and headed downwards again.

As I approached 40 metres, I thought I could see a brown-coloured seabed about 10 metres beneath me. I started to fear that the current might, after all, have pulled our anchor off the wreck. As I pressed on downwards, the brown seabed slowly parted like a pair of curtains and I found myself passing through a huge shoal of fish. As we passed through it, the shoal closed again above us.

I looked down, and was staggered to see a huge shipwreck resting on a clean white sandy seabed. I could easily see down to the seabed at 60 msw, and could see perhaps 25 metres laterally either way, fore and aft along the ship. Three huge boilers sat amid a scene of devastation and loose portholes lay scattered everywhere.

We swam up to one of the boilers and Ewan drew my attention to some copper piping coming out of one of them. We could see where some commercial diver had neatly hacksawed it off, aeons ago, as the engine room had been plundered for its precious non-ferrous metals. The ship had clearly been blasted to pieces here, to allow access for salvage divers, hence the loose portholes, which had been sprung from their mounts.

Of the roof and sides of the engine room and indeed any of the usual superstructure above, there was no trace. This was a method favoured by the famous, and now defunct, salvage company Risdon Beazly Ltd, who salvaged nearly all of the accessible war wrecks around the British shores in the post-war years. Divers would set charges around the hull and then return to the surface. Once the charges were blown, a large grab would be deployed which would lift off the entire upper section of the engine room and superstructure above and dump it at the side of the ship.

I finned up to the side of the hull and stared out across the sandy seabed at either side, but I couldn't see the superstructure. I knew it must be lying there somewhere, tantalisingly out of sight. It would hold endless clues as to the identity of the wreck. The salvers would have removed everything brass down here in the engine room, which may have borne a clue to the ship's identity.

We finned forward and very soon were rising up at the end of the blast area as the ship's hull, which sat on an even keel, reformed before our eyes. We finned aft past an open hold and then were at the very stern.

Intent on having a good exploration of the ship, we then headed forward along the other side of the hull at about 50 metres, the seabed easily visible 10 metres beneath us. If we stayed this high we reduced our decompression times which had been worked out for the worst case scenario of a full dive at 60 metres.

Passing beyond the blast area again, but in the other direction, first one, then a second, open cargo hold appeared before us. There was no sign of any bridge superstructure, and I realised that the whole superstructure must have been removed and dumped, not just the engine room deck-house.

I finned over the open holds and looking down saw that they contained neatly stacked steel railway tracks and piles of coiled warps of steel cable. The fo'c'stle was intact, but the hull had cracked just aft of it, causing the fo'c'stle to roll slightly backwards. Two open, black, aft-facing doorways offered easy entry into the fo'c'stle, but because of the cracking and collapsing, they were well beneath my present depth of 50 metres. I didn't want to go deeper again, and load up on decompression requirements at this late stage of the dive, even though there was the tantalising prospect that the bell, if not taken by the salvers, might lie somewhere down there in the debris. That unmistakable clue to the wreck's identity would wait for another day.

Ewan and I called the dive here and made our way back to the anchor line for the slow ascent. I always preferred the security of the anchor line on these new technical dives – I was still getting used to my unfamiliar equipment and it was something fixed to hold onto if I suddenly found myself too light and taking the elevator to the surface.

As I made the slow ascent to the surface, I went over what I had learned about the vessel on this one dive. She was a single-screw steamship, some 4–500 feet long with a beam of about 45 feet. She was carrying a cargo of railway tracks and warps and from her layout was clearly a Second World War loss. I couldn't wait to get back to the Hydrographic printout to see if I could identify her from this information.

That night Ewan and I pored over the printout. This vessel was just too large to be the ship charted as being lost in that position. The wreck of the SS *Port Dennison* fitted the bill size-wise, as did a few other ships lost in this area. It was a bit of a muddle and no one ship leapt out as a positive identification.

In Aberdeen Watersports that week, getting my tanks filled for the next week's dive, a diver who worked for a government marine institution approached me. Dave Gordon had reported what we had found and done in the shop and everyone wanted to know about this new wreck.

As I talked to this chap and mentioned that the *Port Dennison* was a possibility he told me that that may well be correct as he had heard that she was carrying a cargo of steel. That was enough to temporarily identify her for the time being and we started calling her the *Port Dennison*.

I have been back to dive this wreck on a few occasions since but have never found anything on her which would categorically establish her identity. It has been suggested to me that a better candidate for her identity might be the Second World War loss, *Anvers*, as the *Port Dennison* is in fact charted as having been sunk far further out to sea. It is possible that she drifted in towards shore after being abandoned, before sinking, but our identification of the wreck was very tenuous.

However, it is now clear that our wreck is not in fact the *Port Dennison*. In Moya Crawford's compelling book *Deep Water* she mentions that her husband, the famous commercial salver Alex Crawford, actually came across the wreck of the *Port Dennison*. She reports that it was intact with its bridge *in situ*, and that they conclusively identified it by a Remotely Operated Vehicle (ROV) when, on the hull at the bow, they found the ship's name, *Port Dennison*, in large letters. So, we know that the fabulous wreck we found and dived is not the *Port Dennison*, but we don't know yet which one it is.

A number of other divers were now qualifying as Trimix divers and we tended to come together as a small group to share knowledge, experiences, boats and beer. When Dave Gordon said he wanted to try and find the RMS *Remuera* about eight miles off Fraserburgh later that summer, we all said we were up for it. Dave chartered a fishing boat out of Fraserburgh for an evening dive. The target, the Royal Mail Ship *Remuera*, is the largest ship lost off the north-east coast of Scotland. Photos of it show an elegant vessel with massive superstructures rising up amidships and at the stern for several deck levels.

After work, on the assigned evening, we all drove the hour or so up to Fraserburgh and rendezvoused at the harbour and started loading our kit aboard. By this time, Steve Collard who had been blown away by the *Port Dennison/Anvers* dive had got himself qualified as a Trimix diver. We were also joined by a Royal Marine commando, John Quinn.

Once loaded up the boat ambled gently out of the harbour and set off on an hour-long journey out to the site as we all set about rigging our kit. The skipper assured us he could drop us on the *Remuera*. I knew that the *Remuera* was possibly the most exciting wreck on the north-east coast of Scotland and was very interested in finding it. She was a large twin-screw vessel, some 502 feet in length with a beam of 62 feet, built on the Clyde in 1911 for the New Zealand run. She saw service in the First World War as a troopship and in the inter-war years served as a migrant ship. On 26 August 1940 on a return voyage from Wellington, New Zealand, she was attacked by four Heinkel 115s and eight Ju-88 German aircraft based in Norway. She took a fatal, direct hit from an aerial torpedo.

The photograph we had of her showed her superstructure rising up for five deck levels. If she was sitting upright, exploring her would keep me happy as a diver for the rest of my career! I imagined drifting through a latticework of encrusted rooms and entering an intact liner's bridge with everything still *in situ*.

By the time the engine slowed as the skipper reached the site, we were all sitting rigged up in our twin sets waiting to pop our masks on and leap over the side. It was almost slack water and if we didn't get in the water soon we would find ourselves working in a terrible current.

The skipper started searching for the wreck . . . and he searched . . . and he searched. Forty minutes later, there was a total air of despondency aboard as we realised we were missing slack water and not going to get to dive the fabled *Remuera*.

By now it was getting on in the evening and the first hint of nightfall was hovering over the eastern horizon. Eventually the skipper admitted he couldn't find the wreck and turned his boat to head for home. About 15 minutes later on the run ashore however, the engine note suddenly changed and the boat slowed. Dave Gordon came running out of the wheelhouse and threw a large shot weight, line and pink Dan Buoy over the side.

'We've just run over another wreck – it's a bit away from the *Remuera* site but who wants to dive it?' I had already learned that fishermen are good at avoiding wrecks by large margins with their trawl nets, but sometimes, accurately pinpointing them was not their forte. It was just possible that we had run over the *Remuera* by chance.

We all leapt at the prospect of getting a dive in after having mentally resigned ourselves to no dive at all. Ewan was aboard that day, I can't remember why, but was not going to dive. I was relieved, as I didn't know anything about this skipper or his seacraft. It was good to have an experienced hand like Ewan staying aboard to let the skipper know what we were doing.

I was diving with John Quinn that evening and we jumped from the gunwales of the fishing boat, splashing heavily into the water. With the sun low on the horizon there wasn't the light penetrating down from above that we had had on the *Port Dennison* dives. As I reached 25 metres down it became like a night dive, pitch black with us reliant on our torches. My eyes strained into the darkness looking for snagged trawl nets suspended on buoys that would be a danger to us.

At 50 metres down my torch picked out the keel strip of an upturned vessel 5 metres beneath. Thankful to have got on a wreck, I saw immediately that this was the keel of a sleek, narrow and far smaller vessel than the *Remuera*.

John and I sat astride the keel strip as I adjusted all my kit and got comfortable. After that, picking the starboard side at random, we headed over to the side of the ship and dropped down the vertical, rusted steel wall of its hull until we landed on the seabed at 60 metres.

The hull disappeared into the seabed on this side and John and I finned forward just above the seabed. We found little of interest until, abruptly, the hull ended, about 40 feet aft of the bow. The whole bow was gone as though someone had simply sliced it off with a giant knife. The innards of the ship were opened up for us and we spent some time exploring in and around this area.

I came across piles of spare porthole glasses stacked up and gleaming in my torch – the porthole locker. The beam of the ship worked out at about 35 feet, a far cry from the 62-foot beam of the *Remuera*.

In the darkness, with our allotted bottom time gone, John and I rose up to the 45-metre mark and fired off our delayed deco bags to show our position to the boat above. As we drifted in an accelerating current down the wreck, we actually passed the anchor line visible in the distance but unattainable in this current.

Just short of an hour later, John and I had completed our scheduled decompression stops and broke the surface of the water. I could see the fishing boat, which seemed about a quarter of a mile away in the distance, picking up other divers who perhaps had ascended the shot line.

As John and I bobbed in the water, waiting to be picked up, I was struck by the immensity of my surroundings. The land, some eight miles away, was but a sliver of darkness far in the distance. It disappeared from sight as each swell passed over us. It was very dusky to the east of us, and over the land to the west, the orange glow of the setting sun lit up the horizon. A pair of seagulls flew in and landed in the water close to us and simply sat there beside us, staring at us and trying to make out what we were.

The surface cover in the boat should have seen our delayed deco buoys and be aware where we were down current, but I realised they would be looking east into darkness and perhaps could not see our fashionably black wetsuit hoods and kit in the swell.

I inflated my suit and buoyancy wings as far as I could, to lift me as high as possible out of the water. Then, as a large rolling swell came towards us, we crested its languid top and I switched on my large dive torch. Pointing it directly at the boat, I traced a large 'O' – the OK signal. I got a signal back from the boat and was hugely reassured that someone was looking in our direction and knew where we had ended up.

About ten minutes of bobbing in the water later, the fishing boat turned and started coming towards us. Soon it was alongside and welcome hands were helping us up over an absolutely useless ladder and tyres at the stern. All the other divers were there aboard safe and well.

My post-dive euphoria was dampened when Ewan took me aside and told me that the skipper hadn't had a clue about how our diving worked. He had no idea that we would drift downstream hanging free on our buoys for about 45 minutes. When it was time to pick us up he had headed off in the wrong direction, upstream. I wondered what would have happened if Ewan had been in the water with us and not onboard to guide the skipper. We might have reached Norway by now. This was another lesson for us. Never use skippers you don't know and trust on extreme dives like this, far offshore.

That same season, 1998, we returned to dive the five-mile wreck off Stonehaven that I had bottled out on at 58 metres on air in 1994, and which had led me into mixed gas diving. By this time I had managed to obtain photos of the three Stonehaven wrecks that make up a triangle one or two miles long on each side. The one we had dived was the most northerly of the three. The local fishermen called this one the *Gowrie*. But we wanted to find all three and dive them. I still had the GPS coordinates from my air dive and arranged a return visit.

We anchored above the wreck with a couple of RIBs and an increasing band of divers. Soon, we were descending into the darkness below, in good midday visibility of 10–15 metres. When I got to a depth of about 35 metres I was met by the top of aeons-old trawl nets still floating, suspended on their buoys. The currents had spun the nets into a column that stretched up from the wreck in 58 metres to 35 metres. Once spun into a tight column the nets had been largely covered over by encrusting marine growth and could never now be unfurled. They were hard and safe and represented no danger at all.

Two of the three Stonehaven five-mile wrecks are steamships sunk by aircraft attack in the Second World War, the SS *Gowrie* and SS *Cushendall*. Both are small ships of some six or seven hundred tons and just over 175 feet in length. The third of the triumvirate is the *Matador*. Some authors have claimed that the *Matador* is a 4,761-ton steamship sunk in 1924 whilst under tow for scrapping at the end of her life. Now, a steamship of that size and vintage off our own doorstep would be worth locating and diving. We had photos of the *Cushendall* and *Gowrie,* and knew that the wreck we were diving was not a large 4,761-ton steamship.

Once down on the wreck, we found that we had arrived near the bows. The bows were a magnificent sight as the vessel had settled on an even keel. As we moved aft over the foredeck holds, we came across swathes of monofilament netting trapped on the wreck. Whilst the large gauge trawl net suspended above us didn't pose any danger, these monofilament nets are a diver's nightmare, as once trapped in them they catch and cling to you in a hundred places – the more you struggle to get free, the more you become ensnared.

A single fishing line once snagged me, and that had stopped me dead in my tracks. The prevailing wisdom is that you don't struggle if you get snared. You make yourself buoyant and then see which strand of the net is holding you – it's the taut one and is easy to cut. You then repeat the exercise until you see the next line holding you, and so on. I knew the theory but had no wish to try it out in reality. I gave the netting a wide berth.

Beyond the hold and netting we came to where a single storey bridge and engine superstructure had once stood. These deck-houses, on small steamships, were often predominantly made of wood and so disappear soon after the vessel sinks. Here there was no sign at all of the bridge superstructure, only a solitary boiler sitting totally exposed.

Beyond the boiler, the sides of the hull swept round to meet at the stern. From this one dive, we now knew the length of the vessel and her beam. We knew she had her engine room and bridge superstructure at the very stern of the ship with holds forward. But it was her very distinctive bows that gave it away. They were so characteristic of the Edwardian era of shipbuilding.

The SS *Cushendall* had been built in 1904 and was an old vessel by the time she sank. The SS *Gowrie* was far more modern, so it was clear that this wreck was the SS *Cushendall* and not the SS *Gowrie* as the local fishermen believed.

Hot on resolving the mystery of the remaining two wrecks and possibly finding ourselves a large 1924 steamship loss right off our doorstep, we dived a few weeks later on the inshore wreck of the triangle.

The visibility on this dive was poor. By the time we got down on the wreck it was pitch black and I secured a strobe light to the anchor line with Velcro so we would all see to return to it on our ascent.

Six divers dived that day, Steve Collard and Ewan among them. We found that we had landed the anchor just a few feet off the very tip of the bow and that this ship lay on her port side. I swept my torch around the seabed looking for the lucky sight of a bell, fallen from the fo'c'stle, lying on the seabed. But of that there was no sign, only scattered large chunks of coal littering the seabed.

Ewan and I were in the first of our group to get down on the wreck and we started to move aft past an 'on its side' hold. Like the *Cushendall*, here too was a curled up, vertical column of trawl nets. As I swept my torch up it, the column rose up beyond the limit of my beam.

I moved up to the upper starboard side of the hull and started to see the very characteristic gunwales and scuppers of the *Gowrie* straight out of our black and white 60-year-old photograph. There was no mistaking this one either.

We moved beyond the foredeck holds and arrived at the aft superstructure and engine room. The superstructure was largely rotted away but I managed to glimpse the auxiliary steering helm, still *in situ* at the stern. I also came across the pitched roof of the engine room itself.

Being a small 689-ton steamship, the engine room wasn't that big and my torch easily picked out the complete triple expansion engine still projecting out horizontally above the ground, on the centre line of the vessel. Catwalks ringed the engine. There was plenty of room for me to move around inside, but the fanlights, which make entry to engine rooms on bigger vessels easy, were too small to allow entry for me in my bulky technical rig. I vowed to return another day and find my way into the engine room.

After making it round the whole wreck, Ewan and I got back to the anchor line, led there by the bright flash of the strobe, which lit up the inky darkness momentarily. As I grabbed hold of the line and started to make my way up it, with my night vision now well kicked in, I could make out the silhouette of perhaps half of the wreck lying there in the darkness.

In the distance, I could see the other four divers making their way back to the anchor line like ants, their torch beams flashing around in the dark. Stonehaven wreck number two – identified.

I learned later that the captain of the *Gowrie*, at the time of her loss, hailed from Gourdon, the small fishing village just a few miles down the coast, which we had been using to launch and retrieve our boat for some years.

The last of the five-mile wrecks to be identified was the outside wreck of the triangle. We had identified the *Gowrie* and *Cushendall,* so this must be the *Matador*, the 4,761-ton steamship. This would be an exciting dive.

But events intervened, and it was a few years later before I got organised to dive the *Matador*. When we did eventually get to dive it we were in for a surprise.

Our dive group of two RIBs arrived over the *Matador* and we anchored into it. By this time Chris Allen, a former chairman of the BSAC, who had been living abroad for some time, had returned to live in Stonehaven and a new younger diver, Tony Ray, had joined our group.

Although this was another virgin wreck dive, Ewan and I, who had located it, asked if they wanted to go down in the first wave and be the first divers to see and touch it. They jumped at the chance.

When they came back an hour later, it was clear that it wasn't a 4,761-ton steamship, but a far smaller vessel. Ewan and I then dived and found that it was a 120-foot long steam-driven trawler, very similar to HMS *Strathgarry*, the Boom Defence Vessel in Hoxa Sound, at Scapa Flow.

The small wheelhouse had completely disintegrated and we were left with the simple hull and decking stringers and ribs. It was a pity we hadn't found our own large steamship, but at least the final part of the jigsaw had been added.

In 1998 another diver from slightly further north, who Ewan had known in his earlier days, bumped into us by accident on Hogmanay at Boddam Quarry just as we were coming out from our final dive of the year, something of a ritual for us up there.

Boddam Quarry is set high up a horribly exposed hill, face on to the sea, which is less than half a mile away. On 31 December it is windswept and freezing cold and the water is usually around 2 degrees above freezing – enough to send pinpricks of cold stabbing at your scalp through cold-water dive hoods. In these conditions, my Poseiden Jetstream regulator constantly fires small pellets of ice into my mouth as I inhale.

Anyway, Jim was there with an old mate of his, Andrew Garrick, from England, doing exactly the same as us. When Ewan and Jim recognised each other after the dive, we quickly retired to the warmest pub in Boddam in our thermal undersuits for a couple of pints.

Jim listened avidly to our stories of virgin wrecks and caught the bug. Soon he too was a qualified Trimix diver and was turning up for our almost weekly virgin wreck dives. Jim, a solid, strong guy, with an easygoing personality, soon proved himself to be an immensely capable and very brave technical diver, with a workshop to die for and a passion for wreck diving that equalled that of Ewan and myself.

We formed ourselves into a loose group, which we casually called the Stonehaven Snorkellors – because none of us carries a snorkel. We then added the moniker Deep Cave Rescue Team to become the SSDCRT, not that any of us then particularly liked going deep, or into caves, or indeed had rescued anyone in the last ten years or so.

Our team, consisting of myself, Ewan, Jim Burke, Tony Ray, Chris Allen, Mike Rosie, Richard Colliar, Dave Hadden, Steve Collard, Dave Gordon, John Quinn and Roger Mathison were diving in a privileged time for the sport. The boundaries had just been moved – the 50-metre limit of air diving had just been stripped away and we could venture in depths up to 100 metres in Scottish waters. Some hardy souls in other groups were diving beyond the 100-metre mark, but the decompression times they were incurring were phenomenal and not really suited to cold Scottish waters.

In 2000, one of the fishermen I knew in Stonehaven, Ian Balgowan, had given me the position for a 'snag' believed to be a wreck some seven miles off Newtonhill, a coastal village five miles north of Stonehaven. Andrew Garrick was up for the weekend staying with Jim and we had set up a dive out of Stonehaven on one of the three five-mile wrecks. I had picked up an ear infection and wasn't diving that day – I would boat handle.

When Ewan, Jim and Andrew arrived at the harbour just as I was launching *Stonehaven Diver* I told them about the new position I had been given. I didn't know the precise depth but we could go and check out the position – it might be a new wreck after all. I left the choice to them. They leapt at the new wreck.

Soon, we were speeding over short seas up north towards Newtonhill, heading out to seaward all the time. As I looked at my echo-sounder I could sense anxious faces looking over my shoulder. All three were rigged with gas mixes and tables for a 60-metre dive. The echo-sounder passed the 60-metre mark and the depth kept scrolling down all the way to 68 metres.

I slowed the RIB as I approached Ian's GPS position and just as we arrived at it, the echo-sounder trace jumped up by five metres. We had arrived over a wreck right enough, but not a big one.

Jim, Ewan and Andy splashed into the water and set out upon what was, at this time, Jim's deepest dive. I sat in *Stonehaven Diver*, anchored above the wreck, enjoying the sunshine and seas, which had settled since we left.

After 20 minutes their delayed deco bags appeared clustered around the line. All three were safe and as the bags stayed at the line I knew they were all ascending the anchor line.

An hour or more later, three smiling faces appeared beside the RIB. As I got their gear off them and got them aboard, the chatter was heated as they tried to recount what they had seen.

Once back in Stonehaven we retired to our unofficial HQ, the Marine Inn on the harbour front, where Ewan sketched the wreck for us. The most salient feature was that there was a substantial fixed naval gun, larger than a 12-pounder, set at the very stern. This meant that she was defensively armed, a wartime merchant ship rather than a military ship, the gun being designed to ward off U-boats stalking her on the surface whilst she used her speed to outrun them. What's more, there were shells lying around the base of the gun, some loose, some in boxes. It looked as though she had been in action at the time of her sinking.

The following weekend saw our two boats anchored back above the same mystery wreck. I was dive fit again and was to be diving in the first wave with Jim Burke. I travelled down on my strong helium bottom mix, TDI's Trimix B, made up of a reduced oxygen level of 16 per cent, with 45 per cent helium and the balance nitrogen.

I had a comfortable descent into the pitch-blackness of our coast, adjusting my buoyancy all the time to stop me dropping too fast. As I approached the 60-metre mark, there was no sign of the wreck around. It is easy to plonk the anchor right on top of a 400-foot long, 50-foot wide 4,000-ton steamship. It is a lot more difficult this far out and in these depths, to shot exactly a small narrow steamship. As the shot or anchor descends it is carried along slightly by any current, despite its weight, and can often end up just off the wreck – as it transpired was the case here.

I dropped down past 65 metres and then hit bottom at 68 metres. Visibility in our torch beams was about 4–5 metres. I was surrounded by darkness standing beside Jim Burke on a sandy seabed, 250 feet underwater with no sign of the wreck.

The gentlest of currents was running southwards and assuming that that had carried the anchor with it we left the line and headed northwards against the current.

Within a minute or two, a large, overhanging stern, rudder and propeller of a steamship appeared out of the darkness. We had only been at best 50 feet away from it when we hit bottom, not far in topside terms, but in the eternal darkness of these depths it was plenty far enough to get us confused and possibly lost.

With a whoop of delight through my regulator to Jim, we rose up the sheer side of the wreck and found ourselves on the aftmost piece of decking staring at an old-fashioned defensive gun which was pointing forward and upwards, deployed in an elevated position. That wasn't in itself conclusive of anything, as fishermen's nets sometimes get snagged on defensive guns and are known to have pulled gun barrels into all manner of elevations and directions.

The look of the gun made me begin to feel that this was a First World War vessel. I searched on the gun itself and in the debris surrounding the base of the gun for the brass firing panel, which might have some identifying features on it, but of that I could find no trace.

The shells that Ewan, Jim and Andy had reported on their dive the week before were strewn about and there were boxes of stacked shells sitting near the base of the gun.

Gesturing to Jim, we left the firing position and moved forward. I moved from the starboard side of the wreck to the port side and estimated that its beam was 30–5 feet. So far, we knew she was a narrow in the beam, defensively armed, single-screw steamship – possibly from the First World War. But I wanted to find something tangible to confirm her identity.

As we finned past the gun, we came to a large boiler exposed from above. A forest of struts and stringers of a long vanished stern superstructure stuck up here and there.

We passed in between the struts and moved forward through what had been at one time the forward facing bulkhead of the bridge superstructure. In front of us were a couple of holds about 20–5 feet square with a cargo winch set on a dividing piece of deck, where a foremast would once have stood. Conscious that our permitted bottom time was rapidly disappearing we kicked forward, anxious to see the whole ship from stern to bow in this one dive.

Passing beyond the foremost hold we came to a small raised fo'c'stle with another cargo winch set atop it. I kicked over the side of the bow to see if the ship's name might still be discernible, possibly embossed on the side of the wreck, or perhaps, rather hopefully, still gleaming, albeit green, in large brass letters. But there was no sign of her identity here either.

With our bottom time now gone we had to start our long ascent to the surface. As we rose upwards from the fo'c'stle, its rusted lines seemed to blur beneath us, and then it was consumed by its eternal cloak of darkness and hidden once again from human sight.

Jim and I were still cocooned in the enveloping blackness. We moved slowly upwards, seemingly blind in the darkness, with no visual references to tell us where we were. Everywhere we looked: up, down or to the side, the same unyielding inkiness gave us no clues to whether we were heading up or sinking down to the seabed once again, even in our torch beams. We were entirely reliant on the phosphorescent glow of our depth gauges to regulate our ascent.

As we headed up and halted at 45 metres for our first 'deep stop', I ran over the dive in my mind, pleased that we now had seen the entire ship and had a good idea of her dimensions. Perhaps some long-lost vessel would leap out of the history books as a suitable candidate once we got ashore.

Initially, when we looked at the Hydrographic printout for the area, we suspected that the vessel, from her dimensions, might be either the SS *Arno*, the SS *Kaprika* or the SS *Susanna*. The problem was that these vessels, although fitting the bill size-wise, were all charted as having sunk some considerable distance away. There was just no vessel charted as wrecked at our position – or indeed within about five nautical miles. But ships sometimes stayed afloat for long periods after being abandoned. It was possible that if there had been an attack and the ship had been abandoned that she could have drifted inland on a prevailing easterly wind for several miles before being consumed by the sea. There was only a small 'snag' symbol in the vicinity on the Admiralty chart, to reveal the presence of some danger for fishermen's nets on the seabed.

The more I looked at these wrecks the more I realised that our mystery wreck was not any of them. She looked like a First World War loss to me and these were all Second World War losses. As I trawled through some old reference books on war losses a name suddenly jumped out: the SS *Norwood*.

The SS *Norwood* had set off from Aberdeen during the First World War and quite simply had never been seen again. No one knew where she had been lost and she was recorded simply as being lost 'off East Scotland'. She had been built by a local firm of ship builders in Aberdeen at the turn of the last century, and I was able to get hold of the records of her construction. Her dimensions fitted the bill exactly for the uncharted vessel we had dived on.

We now started tentatively calling her the *Norwood*, but as with so many other wrecks, we simply had not had enough time down on this wreck because of her great depth, to find something that would conclusively establish her identity. A true identification of this wreck awaits the next generation of deep divers, when the next quantum leap in diving technology is made.

In one of life's little coincidences, the following week I was reading my local newspaper, the *Press & Journal*. When I turned to the letters section, I almost spilt my coffee – for here was a letter from a lady in Aberdeen, thanking the *Press & Journal* for running a story sometime previously, which I had missed, 'Tragic loss of the *Norwood* recalled'.

The letter recounted that the lady's elder brother had been a crewman on the *Norwood*, when it had set out from Aberdeen on its last voyage, during the First World War. The *Norwood* was sighted just to the north of Aberdeen but then was never seen or heard of again. The lady wrote that she was pleased that, after all this time, her brother's loss had been remembered. An address was given.

As I walked down to work that day, after much heart-searching, I decided to contact the lady and see if she was interested in hearing our story and talking to us. I wrote her a polite letter making her aware that we had located an uncharted wreck off Newtonhill which we were presuming was the *Norwood* because of its dimensions, layout and age. Very conscious that this was a very sensitive issue despite the passing of such a long period of time, I concluded the letter by advising her that if she wanted to talk to me about this she could contact me by phone and I gave her my number.

The letter went in the post that night and in all reality I expected that I would not hear from her. Divers sometimes get such a bad press that she might be mightily offended by the thought of us exploring what might be her brother's last resting-place.

A week later, our receptionist at my law practice rang through and told me there was a lady on the line who wanted to talk to me. Being in work mode, the name didn't leap out as an existing client, so I asked our receptionist to go back and try to elicit what the call was in connection with. She came back to report that it was a personal call related to diving – and the *Norwood*. She got put straight through.

As I answered the call I found the most delightful, elderly lady on the other end of the phone. I went over how we had located this fisherman's snag and dived and found it to be a wreck. From our basic survey of it, the vessel that most fitted the bill was in fact the *Norwood*. I tried to convey to her the difficulties of working in pitch darkness at those depths.

She was very switched on. Far from being difficult that we were possibly diving on her brother's last ship she was absolutely delighted about what we had found. She had wondered all these years where her brother lay and now we had given her a mark on a chart that she could point to.

This lovely lady, who was now over 90, told me that she last recalled seeing the *Norwood* leaving Aberdeen harbour alongside the ferry *St Ola*. It was sometime later that the vessel was reported as being overdue. Her mother took the loss of her son very hard, and never accepted that he was not coming back. For years after the loss, she left the door of their house open, in case he should arrive during the night, so he could walk in.

We chatted for perhaps half an hour and I told her that if we did positively identify the wreck I would be in touch with her again. So far, we have not returned to dive this mystery wreck again to conclusively establish its identity – but the *Norwood* remains our best guess.

CHAPTER FOURTEEN

Submerged

'Fierce raged the tempest o'er the deep'
Rev. Godfrey Thring, *Hymn*

Amid the succession of fantastic dives to increasingly deeper virgin wrecks we seemed to be embarking on nearly every weekend when weather permitted, there was one occasion when, on what was a relatively simple shallow dive, the sea came back at us and taught us a lesson. Never get complacent with the sea – it will lull you into a false sense of security, and then, just when you feel you are mastering its ways, it will bite back at you and show you who really is in charge.

Ewan and I had planned to dive one of our east-coast wrecks but, as the weather unfolded as the weekend approached, the east coast got blown out by a south-easterly wind. We changed our plans and arranged to dive on the bow section of the SS *Fram* which lies in shallower water than the stern section where Ewan had his blackout.

The weather was set to turn for the worse later that day, but as we drove up to Rosehearty to launch *Stonehaven Diver* it seemed that it was turning rather earlier than forecast. The wind had already moved to the west by the time we arrived at the harbour.

Dave Gordon, our old Trimix instructor, was still doing the training for Aberdeen Watersports and was instructing a couple of divers at Boddam Quarry that morning. He had rung us to see what we were doing that day. When he heard that we were going to dive the *Fram* bow section he asked if he could come along with his two trainees to give them their first sea dive. He would not be clear of the Quarry for some time, but could meet us at 1 p.m. at Rosehearty harbour. We agreed to delay going out until he arrived.

Ewan and I went for a walk, talking about the strengthening wind, which was now starting to make the seas build up. We decided to simply wait until Dave arrived and then assess the conditions and see whether the dive was possible or not.

We offloaded our kit and slowly rigged up everything. Then we launched *Stonehaven Diver* and parked up the jeep and trailer. Come 1 p.m. there was no sign of Dave and I was anxious about the increasing wind and sea state. We got hold of him on a mobile phone and found that he was on his way and would be with us shortly.

By the time he had arrived, we were all rigged up and sitting in the safety of Rosehearty harbour. The crests of the waves were now breaking white water and a swell from the west, driven by the strong westerly wind, was building up. The waves were hitting the breakwater with such force that spray was being driven right over the top of it. Admittedly it's not the largest breakwater in the world, but it was still a sign we should not have ignored.

We talked about the situation. I was hesitant about doing this dive just for the sake of it. It was a well-dived wreck and would be exactly the same next week, next year in fact. But everybody was up for the dive and wanted to give it a go – so rather than let everyone down, I agreed to try heading up to the wreck site, a few miles to the west.

The *Fram* bows lie in a bay, which can be sheltered from some winds. If the *Fram* wasn't diveable, then we might be able to find a lee close inshore and at least let Dave take his two trainees in for their first sea dive. I warned them that if it was *really* bad when we got to the site, I would turn and come back.

There were six of us in my boat and we motored out of the harbour entrance, as spray whipped over the breakwater high above our heads. As soon as we were out of the protection of the breakwater, I turned the bow of *Stonehaven Diver* into the large swell and we started bashing our way up to the west, against the prevailing seas. It was a rough, laborious passage, the boat rising up large swells to slam down once over the crest. There was no chance of getting on the plane and we wallowed along at about seven knots as the seas got more and more unkind.

More than 30 minutes later, my GPS was beeping to advise me that we were approaching the *Fram*. All around, the wind whistled past me, and waves were breaking as we made our way through them. The bow of my boat pitched down into troughs, with green water sometimes coming right over it. Then we laboured up the next wave and through its white capped crest of breaking water.

When we got to the site we dropped our anchor and paid out as much line as we could. We huddled together and discussed the situation. There was white water breaking all around the boat and even with a lot of line paid out it was still very uncomfortable in the anchored boat as we were pitched around. Finally I decided that it was too risky – and told them there was no prospect of diving the wreck today.

We looked across to the sheltered east-facing side of the headland to the west of us. We had thought that we could find some sheltered water in the lee of the wind, but the motion in the seas was now so much that white water was dashing and frothing against the rocky headland all along it. We would find no shelter there today for the trainees.

I motored upwind to slacken off the anchor and Ewan pulled it in and stowed it. This time, no one seemed particularly disappointed at my lack of enthusiasm.

Once the anchor was in, Ewan jumped onto the double console seat behind me as I chose my time carefully to carry out a 180-degree turn to head for Rosehearty. I didn't want to have my RIB flipped over by a wave if I went beam on at the wrong time.

Once we had turned round and were running back home with the seas everything seemed to change. Of course the wind seemed less, we weren't bashing against it. OK, there was still white water breaking around us but it's never so bad when you are moving with it instead of against it. Sure, we were two or three miles offshore in a storm in a small piece of orange rubber and fibreglass. But we had been in worse and were well equipped. We would be back in the safety of Rosehearty harbour in about 20 minutes, half the time it took to get out to the site.

The homeward sea conditions that day proved quite hard to steer in. The swell was so big that we had to motor up the wave we were pursuing. Once we reached the crest, we had to slow and let ourselves almost surf down the leeward side of it, before hitting the bottom of the trough and throttling up to rise up the windward side of the next wave.

We were moving with the seas, and for the first ten minutes or so we toddled along in this fashion. As I went over the crest of a wave I was probably doing about three knots and we were almost stationary by the time we started to surf down the other side.

Halfway home, we rose up the windward side of a large wave reaching for the crest, its white water being whipped away ahead of us as spray towards our destination, Rosehearty.

As *Stonehaven Diver* crested the wave, we hung there balanced on its peak. This wave top seemed bigger than the rest. Then I realised that the bow of my RIB was sinking into it. It flashed through my mind that the top of the wave had been driven out over the trough by the wind.

As we went through the wind-blown crest there just seemed to be a big hole in the sea directly beneath us. My old physics teacher's lectures on the laws of wave motion and interference came to mind. Where waves meet and interact you can get double-sized waves and double-size troughs – wind against tide can produce severe sea states. Bugger me, I thought, what's going to happen here.

It seemed like we were on a ride from a theme park roller-coaster, as

Stonehaven Diver plunged downwards – except on a roller-coaster, people scream with delight. Here there was not a sound from anyone. I braced myself at the wheel. This was something different.

After dropping heavily downwards for what in truth must have only been a second or two at the most, the bow hit the bottom of the double trough. I expected a hell of a shock – and then that the boat would level out and we would continue on our way. I was more concerned that if we came to a sudden halt, standing up on our bow, then all our heavy kit, steel tanks and weight belts, at the stern of the boat, would fall forward and cause someone some damage. Not so on this occasion.

After the bow hit, I was immediately slammed in the chest and face by a wall of green water that drove the wind out of my body. My mind, confused, didn't register the reality of what had happened.

I must have closed my eyes instinctively as we hit the bottom of the trough, for the next conscious thought I recollect, is opening my eyes to find myself with the blurred vision of being underwater with no mask on.

I looked around and found that the whole boat, and all six of us, were completely submerged. We had augured right through the bottom of the trough and were now several feet under water. This was not good – underwater, three miles offshore, in a storm.

Unbeknown to us, the inbuilt buoyancy of *Stonehaven Diver*'s large orange side tubes was doing its job and lifting us towards the surface gently – as my mind raced, confused with a thousand thoughts and unable to do anything constructive.

As I sat there gripping the wheel and wondering what to do, my head broke through the surface of the water. I looked around as five other heads broke the surface. Ewan was still sitting behind me – with a quizzical look on his face – and the four others were still aboard. The two trainees looked a bit shocked – was this what all first sea dives were like?

It was a surreal sight; six heads poking out of a storm-tossed sea, sitting in an orange, totally submerged, dive boat. I half wished that an underwater photographer had been there to capture it on film. Now that would have made the dive photo of the year for sure!

As we continued to sit in stunned silence I realised that our boat's buoyancy tubes were lifting us higher and higher up in the water. My neck became exposed – then my chest.

But then, just as the tops of the tubes were about five inches beneath the surface of the water, the RIB reached an equilibrium. The weight of all our heavy gear, added to the water in the open hull, was too much for the buoyancy tubes to lift any further. We might have to ditch some of our heavy gear.

Just then, the first voice in all of this, Dave Gordon's, shouted out, 'Rod, the engine's still running!'

I turned round to see Dave peering over the stern of the boat at the submerged outboard, and I could see exhaust bubbles bubbling up underwater beside the engine.

Without thinking about it, something made me throttle the engine up. We were still in forward gear. I pushed the throttle forward and the boat moved forward, albeit still underwater. Now this was interesting.

Seconds later, I saw that the bow of the boat had broken the surface. I could see the beautiful orange of its fabric clear of the water for the first time. Realising that the shape of the hull was lifting the bow upwards, I throttled forward harder and more of the bow became exposed.

Water cascaded aft past me. Soon the complete bow and then the console steering position were clear of the water – but the stern and engine were still submerged.

I throttled harder still and the whole console seat became exposed. Then all the side tubes were clear of the water, and then, finally, the top of the engine appeared. The whole engine head was exposed, beautiful Yamaha blue, the engine still purring away. It hadn't missed a beat during the whole episode. I am really impressed with Yamaha engines, as you may be able to tell.

I understand that what saved us was that we kept our forward momentum and the engine was kept running. If a car exhaust is submerged, as long as the engine is kept running, the positive pressure of the exhaust fumes is sufficient to stop water back-filling into the engine itself. Outboard exhausts are exactly the same and our Yamaha, no doubt like all other outboards, is designed for periods of immersion such as this. No water at all got into the hood and at the spark plugs and electrics.

Once *Stonehaven Diver* was fully up, I motored forward allowing the remaining water inside the boat to pass out through the transom-mounted elephant trunk self-drainer at the stern. And then it was all over and we were back heading homewards.

We checked our kit and found that miraculously, even though we had just about been standing on our very bow as we augured in, we hadn't lost anything. All that was missing was my black woollen hat, which had been swept off my head by the initial plunge into the water.

I motored even more gingerly back to Rosehearty harbour. As I turned to head southwards into the harbour entrance, we were once again hit by the full force of the storm. I had learned another valuable lesson – when you are in charge of a boat, if you don't feel right about doing something, then just don't do it. If in doubt, do nowt, as the saying goes.

Another lesson we learned about boats and the sea on a different occasion was that you should never leave just one man alone in a single boat on boat cover, no matter if it's an RIB or a 75-foot-long hard boat. A simple accident aboard the boat could spell disaster for the dive party in the water.

In 1999, we were diving off Clark Ross's superb hard boat, the *Seacraig* out of Arbroath. We had been introduced to Clark a few years previously. He is an ex-commercial diver with a colourful career who had heard via one of our group, the then Arbroath-based marine, John Quinn, of the sort of 'out there' diving we were up to. He had come up to Stonehaven with his boat, which he uses to take divers out around Arbroath. We had had a good couple of days diving with him on a couple of our local deep wrecks, the MS *Taurus* and *Baku Standard*.

Diving out of RIBs is one thing, but to surface after a dive in brilliant sunshine to be met with the aroma of bacon sizzling in the galley before having a bacon roll thrust in your hand as soon as you get your suit off was simply too much. Clark looked after us. Cheese and biscuits and a glass of red wine would follow.

Clark got in touch with us that year, to say that he had been out looking for wrecks in the *Seacraig* and had fixed a huge wreck ten miles offshore from Arbroath in more than 60 metres of water. He suspected that he had located the Second World War loss, SS *Nailsea River*. Clark no longer dives deep, but his passion for wreck finding remains undiminished. He wanted to know what he had found and set up a dive for our group on it.

We arrived at Arbroath harbour at 7 a.m. one Saturday morning to find the *Seacraig* with its engine running and Clark keen to get us and our kit loaded aboard. He had got us to meet that early so there would be enough water left in the harbour for his 75-foot boat to successfully get out – and also to allow time for us to get the ten miles out to the site all in good time for slack water.

Loading all the kit, heavy twin sets and the like into a boat well down a harbour wall is always difficult, so we were running a bit late when Clark was finally able to cast off his mooring ropes to make his way out. It was touch and go whether we would get out, as his keel grounded on the soft, silty bottom of the harbour a few times while he skilfully manoeuvred this large boat out of the rapidly emptying harbour to sea.

Once out of the harbour we all settled down to the familiar routine of getting all our kit set up and rigged. About an hour or more later we were in the vicinity of the wreck and as Clark slowed the *Seacraig*, I jumped into the wheelhouse to watch the echo-sounder. The bottom trace was showing a uniform 64 metres, but then suddenly it leapt up to 48 metres. Something big was down there.

Clark dropped a large shot on a buoy and then we made a few passes over the wreck, clearly picking out the rises and falls of the wreck which appeared to be sitting upright. We thought we could even make out its superstructure. There was only one way to tell what it was really like – by going down and touching it.

With the sense of excitement mingled with anticipation that assaults your senses on any deep dive to an unknown shipwreck, I wriggled into the harness for my twin set as I sat on a step between the bridge and gunwale of the boat.

I was diving today with Ewan and Jim Burke in a threesome. We planned a bottom time of 20 minutes with a total run time of about an hour. The best result would be to find that the ship was sitting beautifully intact and on her keel. If that was the case, then we would be able to stay shallower, increasing our bottom time and lessening our decompression stops, whilst we explored what I pictured in my mind's eye to be a Hollywood-style intact wreck.

If the wreck were lying on its side – or upside down – then we would have to go to the bottom, our maximum calculated depth. One by one we all jumped from the safety of the gunwales of the *Seacraig* into the unknown.

As soon as my head went beneath the surface, I looked directly down the shot line, which ran almost vertically down nearly 70 metres below. The underwater visibility seemed good out here, with clean deep ocean water and no silt. I could see about ten metres of the line before it disappeared into the inky blackness below.

We descended down the line to a depth of six metres and then halted. Ewan had by now acquired a Buddy Inspiration Rebreather, which he had rigged for mixed gas diving. But it was still relatively new to him, and to us. I got level with Ewan and he did a slow 360 degrees pirouette to let me check for any bubbles coming from his unit. If there was a problem brewing, such as evidenced by a telltale bubble stream, it was better to identify it here in shallow water where it could be easily dealt with in the bright ambient light. A small problem left undiagnosed here could become an insurmountable problem on the bottom.

There were no problematic bubble streams, so after another exchange of OK signals our group of three divers started the main descent.

As we pressed on downwards into the depths, the water gradually filtered out all the red colours. We barely noticed that both we, and our kit, had started to blend with our surroundings. As we pressed further downwards the ambient light faded and our surroundings started to get progressively darker.

As ever, I felt the increasing weight of water above pressing on me in a number of ways. My ears sensed the increasing pressure in much the same way as in a plane. Quickly and frequently I used one hand to grip my nose, and by blowing into my closed-off nose, clear or 'pop' my ears repeatedly as I went down.

My membrane drysuit started to crease and wrinkle as the water pressure compressed the free air trapped inside it. Soon I could feel a pronounced 'squeeze' and I bled Nitrox from the stage cylinder under my left arm into the suit via a hose that led from the tank to my suit inflator. This equalised the pressure inside the suit to the water pressure outside and relieved the discomfort.

At 20 metres down I felt that I was suspended in a void, floating in open ocean. All around was a beautiful deep, dark blue, slightly lighter above, yet merging imperceptibly into an inky darkness below. There was no visual reference for me, save for the shot line, which still seemed to plunge for an eternity down below into the depths.

I could feel the familiar adrenalin rush now as my senses altered. Time seemed to pass even more slowly and, in the silence of the depths, the only sound I could hear was my own breathing magnified a hundred times in my altered state. Normally unnoticed in the topside clamour of noise, here in the depths, the bubbles from the exhaust valve on my demand valve seemed to scream their presence as I exhaled and they started their long billowing ascent to the surface.

Spitting the demand valve of my travel Nitrox mix from my mouth and stowing it in its bungee cable wrapped around the stage tank, I thrust the demand valve for my back mounted 'bottom mix' into my open mouth, which was now completely filled with seawater. I pushed the purge button and flooded my mouth with Trimix, expelling the water from my mouth. I then inhaled deeply. To breathe my Nitrox mix at greater depths than this risked the technical divers' nightmare, an oxygen toxicity convulsion.

It was reassuring to breathe my Trimix bottom gas – I knew I wouldn't have to switch demand valves again until the bottom part of the dive was over and I was well up on the ascent at the 20-metre mark. Here I would switch back to my oxygen-rich 'deco mix' (Nitrox 50).

Pressing on downwards, I soon noticed that the blue-green of my surroundings was now turning distinctly dark, ominous and foreboding. The eternal blackness of deep North Sea and Atlantic water was starting to envelop me, in its uncaring grip. I realised with a start that I had been too wrapped up in the pleasures of the descent. This was a hostile environment – man was not welcome here, only tolerated.

I looked around and above me and could see that Ewan and Jim had already switched on their powerful dive torches. I realised that without my light on, they would not be able to see me below, my form blended in with the uniform darkness around. They would only be aware that I was still down there below them by the regular stream of my shimmering and expanding exhaust bubbles as they rose inexorably towards the surface.

Larger exhaust bubbles from our group expanded in size as they searched for the surface and impacted onto the second group of divers above us, exploding into smaller bubbles which made their scurrying way over their bodies, frantically reaching for the surface.

I was now at a depth of 30 metres and yet, even though the dive seemed to have lasted for an eternity already, the actual time elapsed was only just over a minute.

I was getting heavier and heavier in the water as my suit and undergarments were compressed by the increasing water pressure and lost buoyancy. If I got this wrong I could sink like a stone into the abyss. I bled some 'bottom mix' from my back-mounted twin set into my buoyancy wings and trimmed myself to neutral buoyancy.

Everything still seemed to be functioning properly, so I continued pressing downwards, looking backwards and upwards from time to time to check the progress of my dive companions. Their bright single torch beams pointed straight down at me, a reassuring sight in this hostile environment.

At 40 metres down pitch blackness now enveloped our dive team. I couldn't see anything of myself, my kit or even my arms directly in front of me. All I could see was the intense beam of my UK 800 appearing from the darkness beyond me, seemingly out of nowhere. The thin pencil beam of my head torch swept around like the beam of a lighthouse as I moved, cutting the darkness like a knife. A few feet ahead of me, the white shot line flared in the bright lights but still plunged unrelentingly below.

At 50 metres down the white shot line still led me below. Plankton and particles in suspension fluoresced as they streamed past me.

The 'squeeze' became more pronounced and I bled some more gas into my suit to relieve the momentary discomfort. A Lion's Mane jellyfish, its body orange and nearly two feet wide, was lit up as it passed before the beam of my torch, its many translucent stinging tentacles ten feet long and spread out like a fan, drifting silently in the gentle current.

At 60 metres down I reckoned that I could see an improving clarity to the water, common with the deeper more settled layers of the sea. The plankton seemed less abundant down here and visibility seemed to be better. The wreck trace on the echo-sounder when Clark had first located the vessel had shown that the wreck rose more than 15 metres up from the seabed to about 48 metres – I hoped to see some evidence soon.

But the wreck failed to materialise out of the gloom, and it became clear that we weren't coming down on, or near, its shallowest parts. By now the wreck would be towering above us tantalisingly close by, but out of sight and in what direction?

At 65 metres down my torch beam suddenly lit up a sandy seabed. There was the end of the shot line and then the actual shot itself sitting on the sand with not a piece of wreckage around. After the early morning drive to Arbroath and everything that had gone into this dive, was it possible that we would miss the wreck?

The shot had obviously bounced off the wreck or failed to snag it, and been pulled gently over the side of the wreck by the current. But it was a heavy shot and I guessed it wouldn't have moved far. The huge wreck was still close by.

As I stood on the seabed I looked up the shot line and could see Ewan's torch approaching me, followed by Jim's torch above. As I waited momentarily for them to arrive I looked again at the seabed and saw the telltale marks where the shot had dragged and scraped over the seabed. These marks should lead us right to the wreck.

As Ewan and Jim arrived on the seabed beside me, we did a quick round of OK signals before I gestured the way we would go. We started to fin along following the tracks in the sand.

At first, I thought it was a trick of my mind or torch beam. It took me a few seconds to realise that my night vision had started to kick in, and what had seemed like impenetrable darkness when I hit bottom, seemed now not quite so dark. I sensed a large presence towering above us, dwarfing us as if ants. Then suddenly we were right upon the wreck. A solid, vertical wall of rusted steel blocked our way, rising up beyond the limit of our torch beams – it was the massive bow section of a 5–10,000-ton merchant vessel.

The wreck sat on its keel and we were on the seabed on the port side of the very tip of the bow. The huge flared bow rose up and almost curved back over our heads.

Relieved to be able to rise up to a shallower depth, all three of us at once started ascending the rusted wall of steel which rose up to about 55 msw. As we did so, we saw the torches of the second group of divers flickering as they made their way down the shot line into the blackness. They were some distance away from us and probably completely oblivious of us. We hollered as loudly as we could through our regulators and flashed our torch beams at them, but to no avail. They continued their descent to the seabed.

We moved over what had been the fo'c'stle deck, the top of the fo'c'stle, one deck level above the main deck. Mooring bollards were set here and there and a couple of sturdy cargo winches were fixed on the deck. The main anchor winch was still *in situ* and large linked chains ran out forward to either hawse.

When we had at first reached the port side of the wreck, as we ascended its side I had passed the massive anchor, still held snugly in its hawse. It crossed my mind what would happen if that anchor were to come free as I went past.

Dropping down from the fo'c'stle deck, we arrived on the main deck. As we did so I could make out the torches of the second group working their way towards us along the seabed. The holds here were massive, in keeping with a 10,000-ton vessel, but seemingly empty.

This wreck proved to be so big that we never made it beyond the holds to the bridge superstructure before our allotted bottom time was spent and it was time to ascend.

Once we broke surface 40 minutes later I could see the *Seacraig* wheeling around to come and pick us up. As it did so, I saw Clark, who was alone on the boat, come out of the wheelhouse possibly to deploy the ladder along the side for us to climb up. One minute he was there – and the next he wasn't.

I didn't see what had happened, but Ewan later told me that he had seen Clark slip and fall. An innocent accident, seemingly innocuous, but if he had banged his head and knocked himself out, then we would all be in big trouble, ten miles offshore. When we talked about it later with Clark we all agreed that for the future we wouldn't leave just one person topside. Anything could happen, from a slip right up to a heart attack. With no back-up it would mean severe trouble for those divers in the water.

Once back on the *Seacraig* we were favoured with Clark's usual good hospitality and humour. But as we motored back he told me that he had just heard the coastguard's weather warning. The anticipated bad weather was moving across earlier than expected and there might well be bad weather ahead of us, which would hit us before we got back ashore. It was hard to believe at first given that conditions were so good out where we were.

Half an hour into the voyage back and the clear blue skies ahead were now flecked with wispy grey clouds, and the wind had picked up. Small waves were now breaking atop a larger swell from the west, directly opposing us. Thirty more minutes later and the storm hit us. *Seacraig,* an ex-pilot vessel, pitched and rolled as Clark deftly teased her into the seas, caressing every rolling mountain of sea and trying to pick the easiest route home.

The nearer we got to Arbroath, the more the waves seemed to increase in intensity.

One particularly large wave hit us, pitching *Seacraig* down to her starboard side with such ferocity that John Quinn's dive gear, which had been stowed on the flat foredeck against the wheelhouse, moved en masse to the starboard side. Before we knew it, John's twin set, wings, stage tank, torch and fins went over the side of the boat and fell into the sea. The wings on John's twin set were partially inflated and kept it from sinking into the depths, but his stage tank, attached regulator and everything else was lost.

Seacraig had a guardrail on her flush foredeck and no raised gunwale. Jim Burke was still in his dry suit sitting on the foredeck with his heavy twin set on his back. He had switched off his breathing gas and disconnected the inflation whips for his buoyancy wings and suit inflation. The same wave that rocked *Seacraig* so hard, also threw Jim flat on his back onto his steel tanks. The steel tanks slid across the foredeck, as though they were on ice, towards the guardrail. Jim realised that in the prone position he would slither right under the bottom rung of the rail and fall into the water. With all his inflators disconnected he would have no buoyancy and the heavy twin steel tanks would drag him straight down. With no buoyancy and nothing to breath he would drown.

'Help, Rod. I'm going over the side!' he shouted. I dashed over and sat down on his chest, holding him in position until the boat stabilised.

Seacraig is a big boat but its bow was now starting to bury itself into the oncoming seas and at one stage green water hit the wheel house window with such force that it nearly stove it in. Clark has a history with the sea and is as familiar with the waters around Arbroath as any man. He skilfully guided *Seacraig* through the seas and into the difficult access to Arbroath harbour before we thankfully tied up and offloaded. We had learned another lesson for the future.

CHAPTER FIFTEEN

At Last – RMS *Remuera*

'And in the lowest deep, a lower deep still threat'ning to devour me opens wide'

John Milton, *Paradise Lost*

That same year, 1999, Ewan and I finally located and dived the RMS *Remuera*. On a blisteringly hot summer's day we towed *Stonehaven Diver* up to Fraserburgh and launched from the small slip there. We had worked out our own search area from the approximate positions shown on the Admiralty chart. With the two of us in sailing gear and *Stonehaven Diver* filled with Dan Buoys, magnetometers and coiled lengths of rope, we headed out on an oily, calm, mid-week day under the hot sun. The target area was about eight miles off Fraserburgh, but in these perfect conditions and the boat lightly laden for once, with no heavy dive gear, the miles flashed by.

As we skipped across the millpond ocean I switched on my Lowrance echo-sounder. We were going too fast for my old Lowrance to give me a proper bottom trace but it still gave a good digital readout even at these speeds. I was focussed on reading the navigation information on my GPS to home in on the first search position for us. Ewan was standing behind me.

'About a mile to go, Ewan,' I called, above the din of the outboard engine.

As we closed on the first waypoint, and were about half-a-mile short of it, I was conscious of Ewan peering over my shoulder watching the echo-sounder. Suddenly he called, 'Wait a minute, Rod, turn and go back – we just went over something big.'

I throttled down the boat and turned and retraced the path we had taken along our wake. The bottom trace of the echo-sounder kicked in now that we were off the plane and we were getting a good trace at about 65 metres.

Suddenly, the trace leapt up to about 55 metres. There was indeed something big down there rising up for about 10 metres – 30 feet. I punched the MOB facility on my Garmin GPS to mark the position forever and then slowed.

We threw over one of our pre-weighted coils of rope with a large pink Dan Buoy on it. The weight rushed downwards and soon we saw that it had snagged. A gentle ripple from it betrayed the current working on the line.

Gradually we motored around the wreck, punching in a couple of other high points on it. We dropped another Dan Buoy and line at the most extreme opposite end of the wreck and the orientation of the two buoys gave us the line or direction that the wreck was lying in. She lay north-east–south-west and was very, very large. Using the GPS to measure her distance we traced along the top of the wreck between the two buoys and kept going until we reached the other end of the wreck. She was in excess of 500-feet long. This could only be the *Remuera* – and we had found it by chance, right on the southernmost limit of the box we were going to search in, without even having to deploy the magnetometer.

We tied off to one of the buoys and ate some lunch. Then I got my mobile phone out to wind up Jim Burke, who had developed a passion for the *Remuera* as well.

'Hey, Jim, Snorkel Command here – what you doing?' I said casually when he answered.

'Ah, Snorkellor Rod, good to hear from you. I'm at the office down in London, stressed and harassed. What you up to?' he said quizzically.

'Oh – me? Why Jim, I'm moored on top of the *Remuera* having lunch with Ewan . . . '

'You bastards aren't diving her, are you?' he cut in.

'No, we've been out doing a dry search and found it by chance straight away. Thought you might be interested in a dive on her next weekend.'

And that was that, next weekend's dive programme was sorted out.

The following weekend three boatloads – almost a full Stonehaven Snorkellors contingent – arrived, gases laboriously mixed during the week, at Rosehearty harbour. We had Chris Allen and his new Tornado, my Humber Destroyer and Richard Colliar who had bought my last RIB off me. We had about nine divers in total.

The North Sea is a very exposed place to be and the very north-east tip of Scotland, around Fraserburgh, is particularly exposed to bad seas and wind from all directions. This day the wind seemed too rough and the seas just a bit too big – but with three boats and the prospect of a dive on the

RMS *Remuera* at stake it was going to take something more than a Force 5 to stop us.

So, our small flotilla set off from Rosehearty and bumped and bashed the nine or so miles along to the wreck site. The journey wasn't too bad at all and my Humber Destroyer seemed to devour seas like this. I was probably making about 15 knots, bouncing from wave to wave and looking ahead to read the seas, when the black back and fin of a minke whale surfaced right in front of my boat about 15 feet ahead. I had to do a quick slow down and swerve to avoid running right over it.

Once we got out on site above the wreck we anchored into it. As we all wanted to dive it, we were going to divide the dive into two waves. The first wave would dive whilst the second wave gave boat cover. Once the first wave was up and back safely in the boats, then the second wave would go in.

The sea conditions were rough with a big swell running. This was right at the limit of small boat diving and it wouldn't be pleasant for those left in the anchored boats. But after we discussed it, we agreed the first wave would go in and then we'd review the situation after they were out of the water. If the conditions worsened then we might have to abort. Ewan and I went in on the first wave, as we had found it, with Dave Gordon and Jim Burke. The others stayed topside.

As ever, no matter how rough sea conditions are, as soon as you are underwater the position settles down. The surface conditions only really affect you for the first five or so metres down. We descended in crystal-clear, greenish water. At about 50 metres I saw the wreck materialising out of the gloom and reaching up towards us, beckoning us down.

However, we were immediately disappointed – we had hoped for a Hollywood-style wreck sitting on its keel. Instead we got a wreck lying on its side, the upmost side of which had largely collapsed downwards. We could tell we were on the collapsed side of a great ship, but even in the crystal-clear visibility of some 25 metres, which meant no lights were necessary, we couldn't tell which way was forward and which aft.

We had agreed topside to return to the line to ascend – in these poor sea conditions and with the large swell there was a possibility that surface cover might not see our delayed deco bags if we did a free hanging drifting decompression. So Ewan and I finned along the edge of the wreck looking upwards at the crumpled ship's side that lay like a mountain range beyond us.

We finned for about 100 feet and still did not get to the end of the ship. It was big indeed, and the side was just lined with rows of portholes, many with their glasses still in them.

We turned and finned back to the starting point, passing the line. Jim Burke and Dave Gordon had gone to explore in the opposite direction and as we returned to the line they arrived back as well. We spent the last few minutes of our bottom time exploring the wreck around the line before making our ascent.

Forty-five minutes later our heads broke surface to find a raging maelstrom with large waves washing past our anchored boats – and there were only two boats.

'Where's Richard gone, Dave?' I asked, concerned.

'His boat was getting swamped and he decided to bail and head for Rosehearty. Conditions too bad for him mate – and it's going to be a bugger getting you guys and your kit in.'

Dave was right. As mountainous waves swept past us, my RIB was rising and falling considerably, the bow lifting out of the water before slamming back down heavily. If I drifted under the hull I would be in serious danger.

'Cast off, Dave, and we'll drift – it'll be easier.'

Dave untied us from the Dan Buoy, Ewan went to one side of the RIB and I to the other. Free from the anchor, conditions were a bit easier for us to dekit. We got our stages off and then our backsets, one by one, but it was still very difficult getting them into the boat.

Once we were in the boat we returned to the anchor line. Dave and Jim were already in Chris's boat and it was clear the second wave weren't going to dive – caution being the better part of valour. I tried pulling up the anchor line but it was snagged solid on something. No wonder, when it had had all four of us ascending it and a boat tied to it in these conditions. Chris motored over in his Tornado.

'Did you guys see the minke down there? It surfaced right beside my RIB as I was tied off and stationary – I leaned over and could touch it.'

Dave Gordon chipped in, 'Sorry, Rod, you're not going to get that anchor back I'm afraid. Seeing the conditions, to make sure we didn't pull it off the wreck on our ascent – to fix it for the second wave – I popped the anchor through an open porthole. There is no way that anchor and its open flukes is coming back up through that porthole – sorry, but it's gone.'

I wasn't aware he'd done that down on the wreck, but could understand his logic. He didn't know the second wave would abort. I took out my knife and cut the rope and pulled the Dan Buoy inboard.

'We'll find it easy enough on our next dive.'

In the event we didn't return to the *Remuera* until 2002 when we had a couple of fantastic dives on it in glorious visibility. By now we had all purchased Aquazepp underwater scooters – long, thin bright-orange torpedo-like scooters with a propeller at the stern. These clip to your harness and can drag you through the water very comfortably at speeds of just over two knots. On our Zepps, we were effortlessly able to tour the *Remuera* and get a feel for her layout. She lies on her port side, bows facing to the west. Her hull is collapsing but large sections of it remain intact. At the stern her giant starboard side propeller stands half buried in the sand.

As we have explored this wreck, our initial disappointment at her somewhat collapsed remains has been replaced with wonder, as we have become familiar with her. She is truly one of Scotland's finest wrecks.

In 1997, for the third edition of *Dive Scapa Flow* our group of technical divers had spent a fantastic week's diving back at Scapa Flow. Part of the purpose of the week was to survey two wrecks which now fell within the ambit of technical diving: the boom defence vessel, HMS *Strathgarry*, sunk by collision in 58 metres in Hoxa Sound in 1915, and HMS *Hampshire* on which Lord Kitchener died en route for Russia on 5 June 1916. The *Hampshire* lies in 68 metres in difficult waters one-and-a-half miles west of the towering cliffs of Marwick Head.

Of Lord Kitchener and his staff and the crew of 655 officers and men, only 12 lucky souls would survive. The *Hampshire* was so deep that she had been traditionally off limits for air divers although there had been several salvage attempts over the decades since she sank – efforts to recover the rumoured, but never officially admitted, two million gold sovereigns aboard her. With the advent of technical diving she was now a perfect wreck, with a huge history, in a perfect depth, in crystal-clear Atlantic waters.

In the first two editions of *Dive Scapa Flow*, in my air days, I had narrated the story of her loss but never surveyed her nor had a painting of her wreck on the seabed made up. For the third edition I was going to extend the book to have a full description of diving her.

The *Hampshire* had received her sailing orders on 4 June 1916. She was directed to proceed to Archangel in northern Russia, a journey of 1,649 nautical miles. Initially, she was to pass up the east side of the Orkney islands along a route regularly swept for mines. She would have a protective screen of two destroyers, *Victor* and *Unity*, as far north as Lat. 62° North. From there she would proceed alone, zigzagging at 16 knots to avoid torpedo attack.

On 5 June, however, the weather worsened and by the afternoon a gale was blowing from the north-east. A heavy sea was running along the east coast making mine-sweeping difficult. This would also make it difficult for the two smaller destroyers to keep up with the far larger and more seaworthy 10,850-ton battle cruiser.

The plan was therefore changed and at the last minute the small flotilla was sent up one of the western routes where it was felt that the Orkney islands would give some protection against the easterly gale.

The group left Scapa Flow and started to battle up the west coast of Orkney. The weather had however been wrongly forecast, for within an hour of the group's departure, the storm centre had passed overhead and the wind backed to the north-west. The conditions that the *Hampshire* and her escorts faced were exactly the opposite of what had been intended.

Soon the two smaller destroyers were struggling in the mounting seas to keep up with the larger *Hampshire* at the predetermined speed of not less than 18 knots. This minimum speed was set to allow the group to outrun any U-boat (which would be far slower), that might dare to attack.

First the smaller *Victor* signalled that she could only make 15 knots. Then just a few minutes later *Unity* signalled that she could only make 12 knots. Shortly after that she signalled that she could only make 10 knots. The group could not be allowed to slow up because *Unity* could not keep up – the *Hampshire*, the raison d'être of the group, would be placed in danger. *Hampshire* signalled that she should return to port.

Another 10 minutes later and the *Victor* faced the same problems, signalling that she could not maintain any speed greater than 12 knots. She too was ordered to return to base and the *Hampshire* struggled on alone into the fury of the north-westerly gale.

An hour later found the *Hampshire* herself only able to make 13.5 knots. She fought and struggled up towards the north-westerly point of the main island, Marwick Head. She dipped and crashed in the raging seas with her bow burying itself into the waters, the bow splash billowing up high and washing back along the decks and bridge.

Suddenly a rumbling explosion shook the whole ship, tearing a huge hole in her keel between her bows and bridge. The helm jammed and the lights went out as the power faded. It was 7.40 p.m.

With no power, she could not make radio contact with shore to call for assistance. The ship immediately started to settle into the water by the head. Clouds of brown suffocating smoke poured up from the stoker's mess forward making it difficult to see on the bridge.

The crew streamed aftwards, away from the onrushing water. An officer was heard to call out 'Make way for Lord Kitchener!' and he passed by clad in a greatcoat and went up the after hatch. He was last seen standing on the deck of the ship.

The cruiser settled quickly by the bows. There was no power to work the lifeboat derricks, and none of the larger boats could be hoisted out. Those smaller boats that were lowered into the water were smashed against the side of the *Hampshire* by the force of the storm. Not one single boat got clear intact.

A number of men took their places in the large boom boats, which could not be lowered, in the hope that as the ship went down these boats would float off. The suction created by the *Hampshire*'s passing pulled these boats under with her.

At about 7.50 p.m., only ten to fifteen minutes after striking the mine, she went down – bows first, keeling over to starboard. Smoke and flame belched from just behind the bridge. Her stern lifted slowly out of the water and her two mighty 43-ton phosphor bronze propellers were seen clear of the water, still revolving slowly as she went under.

Only three oval, cork and wood Carley rafts got away from the sinking ship, one of which had only six men in it. The desperate survivors in it faced severe sea conditions. It was bitingly cold and they were drenched. The wind chill gnawed at them and soon they were suffering from exposure. In the storm it was flung over twice, pitching its human cargo into the seas, before it was finally washed ashore in Skaill Bay. Only two men in it were still alive.

Forty-five to fifty men clung to the second larger Carley raft. When it made the shore more than five hours later at 1.15 a.m. only four of them were still alive.

The third raft had about 40 men in it. When it was finally washed ashore on rocks north of Skaill Bay there were only six men alive.

The legendary story of the sinking of the *Hampshire* and the loss of Lord Kitchener is now part of the folklore of Orkney and is still very close to the hearts of many of the islanders. We had treated the wreck with tremendous respect on our 1997 expedition and made sure we got permission from the Ministry of Defence.

From our survey of the wreck, I was able to have a local marine artist who lives near me, Rob Ward of Illusion Illustration, paint the wreck as it lies on the seabed. This was the first time this had been done and his haunting painting immediately reveals at a glance how the wreck looks today.

In 2000 we planned a return expedition with the aim of checking how much the vessel had deteriorated in the intervening three years. We chartered a superb hard boat, the *Three Sisters* from Keith Thomson, the dive charterer at Scapa Flow who I have used since the mid-1980s. Keith is a tall, immensely strong man with a beguiling sense of humour. He has worked the waters around Orkney for more than 20 years and knows them like the back of his hand. I was always immensely confident when Keith was skippering a trip for us.

The first day after our arrival in Scapa Flow, the sea conditions were perfect. We motored out through Hoy Sound to the west, before heading up the western shores and cliffs of Orkney towards Birsay. On the way up, we busied ourselves as usual with the routine of sorting out our dive kit. Somewhat overly eager, Ewan was fully rigged and dressed into his Inspiration Rebreather unit before we had got out of Stromness harbour!

On the drive up, the seas were calm, glistening and oily in a slow languid gentle swell. As I stood at the gunwales of the *Three Sisters* I saw a group of seagulls floating on the surface. Suddenly a grey seal shot up from below and grabbed one of the seagulls in its jaws. An enormous flapping of wings followed as the seagull bravely tried to fight off its attacker. But it was to no avail – the seal pulled the seagull under and it was all over. Seagulls are not tasty birds, even for seals, and aren't part of their usual food. Keith remarked that that must have been a very hungry seal for it to be taking a seagull.

The *Three Sisters* continued its voyage up north towards the last resting-place of the *Hampshire*. Soon, a few dolphins had joined us and started playing in the bow surge, flashing from one side of the ship to the other, seemingly right under the bow, before giving a little jump from time to time. The seas are busy today, I thought.

Further on, and we saw a couple of minke whales. I was very familiar with them after seeing one at close quarters off Fraserburgh earlier that year. Their motion through the water is similar to a dolphin's. As we neared the wreck site, Keith pointed out a pod of pilot whales a mile or so off, their white water spouts dazzling in the bright sunlight.

Finally, Keith picked up the wreck on his echo-sounder and dropped a shot, line and buoy. He then backed off and we finalised getting into our dive kit. Once we were all ready, the eight divers clustered around the starboard side gunwale as Keith took a final run in to the shot line before we would jump in.

As he approached, four large black and white-coloured objects surfaced beside us, water cascading off their backs with the unmistakable tall dorsal fin of Orcas screaming danger to us. A pod of four Orcas – 'killer whales' – was passing by us, en route for an unknown destination. Killer whales are seen in Orkney waters and in the North Sea offshore from time to time. They can get aggressive with divers and it is unsafe to be in the water with wild Orcas. As I looked carefully I could see that one of the pod of four was small, an infant sticking close to its larger parent, dipping and diving in unison.

'Bloody hell – those are Orcas,' Ewan ejaculated.

Someone else piped up, 'Aye, but you've never heard of a diver being taken by an Orca – only Bo Derek's leg in that horrid film.'

The attempt at gallows humour didn't work. All of us froze in our tracks at the gunwales and we all just sat down on the side benches. No one was going in the water when these guys were around.

We kept an eye on the pod of Orcas as they moved away from the *Three Sisters* heading towards the shore a mile or two off. Once they were about a mile away Keith turned the boat and took us back in and we all jumped into the water for the dive.

When I had surveyed the *Hampshire* in 1997 I had done it just using my own leg power to fin around. She is a big ship, some 500 feet in length, the length of two football pitches.

But this time we all used our Aquazepp underwater scooters.

Ewan and I headed initially to the stern where Ewan shot off a reel of film trying to get the perfect shot of me on the prop of the *Hampshire*, perhaps one of the most photogenic and easily recognisable pieces of underwater heritage around Britain.

Unfortunately after setting up the shot, in itself difficult at about 55 metres, Jim Burke unknowingly wandered into the picture and, back towards the camera, starting examining and obscuring a large section of the prop itself. Ewan was later able digitally to completely remove Jim Burke from the shot and morph back in the full prop.

The second of her twin props was illegally removed in 1983 and sat at Peterhead harbour for a long time before eventually being repatriated to Orkney, where it is now on display in the Naval Museum on Hoy. Not many people are able to dive the *Hampshire* in the morning, touch her submerged prop and then visit the Museum and see the other prop all in the same day.

We found that the *Hampshire* is deteriorating significantly. She is fracturing along a series of fissures that run in a straight line along the point where the upturned keel meets the sides of the hull. Eventually the keel will collapse downwards into the wreck, the internal decks collapsing like playing cards.

The *Hampshire* is a magnificent wreck; certainly one of Scotland's greatest. The whole bow area has been removed down to the underside of the main deck. This was, however, only partly as a result of the original mine explosion. In the decades following her sinking there were various official attempts with hard hat, deep-sea divers, to recover the alleged cache of gold sovereigns. A salvage consortium of German businessmen put together another salvage attempt in the 1980s and hired, at great expense, an oilfield diving support vessel. Blasting by this succession of salvers hunting for the strongroom and the gold has all but completely removed the entire bow.

An interesting competition between Jim Burke and Ewan enlivened the voyage back to Stromness. Technical divers spend an inordinate amount of time actually underwater. With bottom times of half an hour it is common to find yourself having to hang around decompressing for an hour or more depending on the depth.

It is known that dehydration encourages the onset of the dreaded bends. So, part of our training is that we must hydrate as much as we can before a dive. Drinking lots of water before a dive is fine – but what goes in, must come out. In a wetsuit there is no problem – just let go and you get instantly warmed up. You can't do that in a drysuit as your inner garments get soaked and lose some of their thermal ability. The mess runs down and fills up your watertight boots, from where there is no escape. It is not pleasant.

Some American technical divers use adult diapers – but you're not going to see proud Scotsmen, accustomed to wearing the kilt, donning a big nappy before a dive. We are meant to be hard men after all.

So Jim Burke and Ewan had 'pee valves' fitted to their suits to allow them to urinate during a dive. A condom-like cycle tube, a sheath, fits over the male member. A thin plastic tube connects into the head of that and runs to a brass one-way valve embedded in the fabric of the dry suit. When you want to pee you can let go and the urine is forced out of the pee valve to the sea. Well, that's how the theory goes – but I have seen Ewan and Jim soaked in their own mess more times than I care to count.

Jim must have been experiencing some, uh, technical problems with thermal shrinkage of the male member, to be polite. His sheath kept coming off. (Perhaps he'd bought the wrong size?)

Jim tells me that no one ever told him that these sheaths have a type of soft glue inside them and are only designed for a single use before being replaced. He used his once and then tried it again the next day – the glue spent, it leaked and he got wet. Once out of his suit, he noticed the remnants of the glue inside and thought that the gunge was the problem. He washed it out and, not surprisingly, wearing it the next day with no seal, it leaked again.

The following day, to get round this problem, Jim got the used sheath on and then wound some electrical tape around himself, to keep the sheath tight on. That seemed to do the trick – until he tried to urinate inwater on the dive. He found that he had wound the tape too tight onto himself – no matter how hard he tried to pee, he couldn't!

Jim's actual pee valve also didn't seem to be functioning correctly on the *Hampshire* dive so Ewan, our technical expert on pee valves, decided to investigate. Rolling down the upper section of their dry suits they disconnected the plastic tubes from the brass pee valve and stood there proudly with the plastic tubes dangling, still connected to the sheaths.

Before we knew it, they had a little competition going with the tubes held out over the gunwales of the boat as far as they could, to see who could pee the furthest. Then the competition evolved and they connected the free ends of both their tubes into a junction and then simultaneously let go – trying to see who had the strongest bladder and who could force their urine back up the other's pipe.

After that Ewan took Jim's malfunctioning pee valve out of his suit to see what the problem was. He thought he would blow it through to make sure the one way valve wasn't leaking. Forgetting about the small reservoir of pee still in it, he put it in his mouth but subconsciously took a deep breath and sucked in – before the intended blow through. Bad move – the sort you only ever do once. He was immediately down on the deck, coughing and spluttering, the remnants of Jim's pee having a most terrible effect on him.

CHAPTER SIXTEEN

HMS *Prince of Wales* and HMS *Repulse* – The Death of the Battleship

'Cannon to the right of them,
Cannon to the left of them,
Cannon in front of them
Volley'd and thunder'd;
Storm'd at with shot and shell,
Boldly they rode and well,
Into the Jaws of Death
Into the mouth of Hell'
            Alfred Tennyson, *The Charge of the Light Brigade*

Just three days after the stunning raid by Japanese forces on Pearl Harbour ushered America's involvement into the Second World War, the brand-new, state-of-the-art, British battleship, HMS *Prince of Wales*, and the mighty battlecruiser, HMS *Repulse*, were attacked and sunk by 85 Japanese torpedo bomber aircraft about 200 miles north of Singapore.

The two mighty British warships had been left tragically exposed, denuded of any air cover, whilst racing to try and repulse a rumoured Japanese invasion further north up the Malayan peninsula. Both ships were hit by a series of torpedo attacks and sunk with enormous loss of life.

Until this moment, the battleship had ruled the waves. It was the supreme embodiment of a nation's sea power and majesty. Heavily protected and heavily gunned, the sight of the tall tripod mast of an enemy battleship appearing over the horizon had struck fear into the hearts of both merchant and naval sailors for two centuries. They were considered invincible.

The loss of HMS *Prince of Wales* was the first time that a battleship had been sunk by air attack in modern warfare. The sinking marked the end of the era of the battleship – and the rise of the era of the modern aircraft carrier, projecting immense air power wherever it went.

Major Guy Wallis of the Parachute Regiment had been with me on our 1997 trip to Scapa Flow, to dive and survey HMS *Hampshire*. A tall, strong and immensely capable deep diver, now in his 40s, his military knowledge and his ability to pick his way through the corridors of power at the Ministry of Defence had been hugely helpful. We had kept in touch and dived and drunk together on a few occasions since then.

In 2001 he was in touch again with a very serious proposition. The British Armed Forces were very keen to encourage their service personnel to embark on adventure or 'on the edge'-type expeditions in the belief that it develops mind and body. Guy was now Assistant Chairman of the Army Sub Aqua Diving Association, which had yet to embrace and accept the new technical diving revolution. Air diving was OK, but not the deadly 'killer gas' that crazy civilian technical divers were breathing. The Association however was moving towards accepting the use of 'mixed gas' and he had an idea for a two-week expedition out to dive and survey the wrecks of HMS *Prince of Wales* and *Repulse* in the South China Sea. An ITN TV crew would be aboard filming for a BBC *Timewatch* programme to be entitled *The Death of the Battleship*. Would I be interested? I thought about it for all of two seconds – before leaping at the chance of getting out to dive these two fabled deep wrecks.

On 13 September 2001, I flew down from Aberdeen airport to London with all my main dive kit and my Aquazepp underwater scooter broken down into bits for transport in a large green plastic box. For good measure I had also prevailed on Chris Allen to lend Guy his Aquazepp for the trip, so I had his scooter in bits in another green plastic box. The amount of gear I was pushing around on my airport trolley was immense, and I was concerned about excess baggage charges when I turned up at Aberdeen airport. BA, bless them, never blinked. My kit got loaded and I was off.

Less than an hour later, I had landed at Gatwick to be met by one of my old dive buddies, Corporal John Quinn, a Royal Marine who was part of the 1997 *Hampshire* team and was also coming on this trip. We loaded all the kit and he drove us along to RAF Uxbridge where the whole team would be meeting and where we would be spending the night.

Once there, after being allocated a bunk and locker, I was introduced to the rest of the team: Captain Greg Wilson, a couple of Paras – Paul Carvel and Stuart McFarlane – Squadron Leader Martin Payne, Sergeant Dave Taylor of 1 Para, who would be in charge of the dive schedule for the trip, a civilian diving doctor from the Institute of Naval Medicine, David Adey, and the underwater cameraman, the charismatic, unique, one and only Dan Burton.

To get into the base to stay overnight as a civilian, I was allocated a nominal rank for the night. Suddenly I was Major Macdonald (seconded from the Tartan Army). I had really wanted to be allocated a rank one higher than Guy's so I could push him around – but sadly it was not to be.

The tragic terrorist attack on the Twin Towers in New York had only happened two days before and there was a heightened state of security everywhere, at the airports and also at the barracks. Service personnel with sub-machine guns kept guard at the entrance.

After Guy arrived and we had had a briefing, we headed off into town for a gallon of Guinness and a curry – just the right mixture for a long haul flight the next day.

Oceanics had sponsored the expedition with an array of gear. We were allocated their new state-of-the-art split fins, full 3-mm tropical wetsuits, regulators and polo shirts embroidered with a military crest and a logo for the 'Joint Services Sub Aqua Diving Club, Trimix expedition to *Prince of Wales* and *Repulse*'. The whole team, as part of the sponsorship deal, was to wear these shirts to travel and throughout the filming aboard whenever possible. The Twin Towers attack two days before however made this impossible for the flight out. The shirts emblazoned with the military crest would give us away instantly to any terrorist and make us a target. Guy ordered that we not wear them for the journey out.

What seemed like days later, after transiting in Kuwait City, we landed in Singapore and were met by a British Embassy driver and a couple of vans, sufficient to take us and our large cargo of dive kit and scooters down to the docks.

When we arrived at our allotted pier we saw our home for the next two weeks, the MV *Mata Ikan* bobbing in a stiff tropical breeze, tight on her mooring ropes. Despite the breeze, the all-pervading, year-round heat of Singapore, a steady 32°C, soon made its presence felt. Working in the direct sunlight to load heavy crates and kit, we were all immediately breaking into sweat and seeking shade where we could.

The *Mata Ikan* had a comfortable lounge and galley with an upper open, but covered, deck with fixed chart tables and chairs. Down a tight stairway from the lounge were four small, spartan bunkrooms, about six feet square, which had four bunks crammed in each. The ship was an old ex-Royal Navy survey vessel and wasn't designed as a luxury ship. The bunks were covered in shiny PVC covers, which brought sweat out of you as soon as you touched them. The walls were plain white formica sheeting. A rickety old air-conditioning unit was mounted up one wall which made one hell of a racket when it was on, and made the room as cold as a freezer.

Once all the dive kit was loaded aboard we added essential provisions, like enough Tiger Beer to last all of us for the whole fortnight. This worked out at a vast amount of Tiger Beer, which we had to trolley aboard. The ITN crew came aboard: Louise Osmond the director and Noel

Swindbourne, a charismatic cameraman, who had started off during the Vietnam War.

Late in the afternoon we cast off and headed out into Singapore Bay, which was jam-packed with merchant ships of all sizes and shapes, all waiting to pick up cargoes destined for every corner of the world.

As our small 75-foot *Mata Ikan* wound its way through these anchored monsters of the deep, we all moved inside into the lounge and discussed the planned diving with the ITN crew. They had just come straight from the Atlantic where, in the immediately preceding weeks, they had been filming a Channel 4 series of documentaries on the battle between *Bismark* and *Hood* and the subsequent search for and filming of the two wrecks.

Some hours later, I went outside and up onto the foredeck to phone my wife, Claire, on my cellphone and touch base. We had set off in daylight but now a tropical night had fallen. Even though we had been on the move for a few hours we were still threading our way through anchored, although less dense, shipping. Everywhere I looked, a forest of anchor and navigation lights blinked back at me. I was mesmerised and sat at the bow for an hour letting the balmy breeze of a tropical evening wash over me as the regular hum of the diesel engines pushed us further north towards our target wrecks.

Like the other members of the team I had a basic idea of the history of the sinkings of these two famous vessels but that was it. The ITN director, Louise, came up to me and told me that Guy had offered me up as the sacrificial 'talking head' for the documentary. This was a surprise, and I was suddenly galvanised out of my jetlagged sub-tropical reverie into picking up a couple of the historical reference books we had aboard to study the sinkings in more depth.

The dimensions of the *Prince of Wales* were staggering. I had dived and surveyed the German First World War battleships at Scapa Flow many, many times for *Dive Scapa Flow*. They are giant wrecks lying in the dark, still depths of Scapa Flow. The battleships there are all about 575 feet in length and displaced about 26,000 tons. If you haven't swum round a sunken battleship from that era it is hard to convey the scale of them. As divers, we see the whole ship, including the part of the hull normally submerged. These ships are the length of two football pitches, with their hulls rising up for some 25 metres – a wall of steel, 75 feet high. Whilst afloat, their upper superstructures, their top hamper, extend upwards for more than a hundred feet, their masts even higher still.

If the German High Seas Fleet battleships at Scapa Flow are impressive, the *Prince of Wales* was a quantum leap ahead again. She was 745 feet long compared to the 575 feet of the German First World War battleships. She weighed in at a massive 35,000 tons displacement compared to the 26,000 tons for the Scapa Flow sunken leviathans. Part of my role was to survey these ships as best I could, to try and get a picture of how they lie on the seabed today. I was daunted by the sheer scale of the undertaking.

The *Prince of Wales* was a brand new battleship, barely completed at the beginning of the Second World War when the *Bismark* broke out into the North Atlantic to start terrorising Allied shipping. The order went out from Churchill that the *Bismark* should be sunk. The *Prince of Wales*, Britain's newest and most formidable battleship with massive 14-inch guns was assigned to take part in the search for and subsequent destruction of *Bismark*, even though there were still civilian contractors aboard, finishing her off.

The *Prince of Wales* and Britain's most famous warship, the massive battle cruiser HMS *Hood*, engaged *Bismark* in a legendary battle in which shells from *Bismark* struck HMS *Hood*, completely destroying her in a cataclysmic explosion which killed all bar three of her full ship's complement of around 1,000 men. The *Prince of Wales* went on to land three crucial shots on *Bismark* even though one by one her guns, which had not yet been made fully operational, went out of action to the extent that at one point she only had five functioning guns left.

As history records, *Bismark* was subsequently sunk and in May 1941, the *Prince of Wales*, along with the battlecruiser HMS *Repulse*, sister ship of HMS *Hood*, was thereafter assigned to Singapore as a deterrent against the possible Japanese invasion of Malaya.

Two weeks earlier Japanese forces had advanced into Indo-China and were now just 300 miles away from Malaya and Singapore. The Royal Navy was stretched to the full by the war against Germany, but Churchill feared for Singapore, which protected vital trade routes from the Empire. To try and deter Japanese aggression, Churchill demanded a battleship fleet be sent to Singapore as a symbol of the might of the British Empire and her legendary sea power.

Churchill insisted that his much beloved and newest battleship, *Prince of Wales* be sent, and chose Admiral Sir Tom Phillips to command her. An aircraft carrier was also despatched to provide air cover for the two mighty British warships but it ran aground en route. The *Prince of Wales* and *Repulse* were ordered to go on alone – but without air cover they became very vulnerable. As they reached and entered Singapore amid great fanfare, the two capital ships were in fact exposed and almost indefensible.

On 7 December 1941 the Japanese carried out a daring air attack against Singapore and suddenly British command wakened up to the fact that the Japanese would not be deterred from an invasion campaign by the presence of two British ships, no matter how powerful they were. At the same time the Japanese fleet crept up on the American base at Pearl Harbour, Hawaii, and delivered their savage early morning attack. This devastatingly successful surprise attack crippled the American Fleet at anchor and ushered in America's involvement in the war. Churchill now realised how exposed his two ships were, even within the confines of Singapore harbour.

Three days after the daring Japanese strike at Pearl Harbour, British intelligence learned that the Japanese were rumoured to have started a land invasion 200 miles further north up the Malayan peninsula at Kota Baru. At 5 p.m. on 8 December 1941, *Prince of Wales* and *Repulse*, escorted by four destroyers, set out to locate the invasion forces, if any, and repel them. They headed out into the South China Sea, hoping to surprise the Japanese forces at dawn. The series of events, which would lead to the end of the battleship era, now started to unfold.

En route to the possible invasion site, a signal was received advising that shore-based air cover, on which the naval commanders had depended, could not be provided as a result of a large force of enemy bombers further north. It transpired that the invasion intelligence was inaccurate – there was in fact no land invasion taking place at Kota Baru. The poor visibility, which had cloaked the British warships as they sped to investigate, cleared and the British ships were spotted by a Japanese reconnaissance plane and a submarine. They reported back and a Japanese attack force of torpedo bombers was scrambled together. Without air cover and now lacking the element of surprise the two British ships turned and headed back for Singapore.

A fleet of 85 Japanese torpedo bombers was sent out to attack the British warships. They soon located their prey and swooped down on the two exposed ships, dropping wave after wave of torpedoes. The commanders of the two British warships threw their charges about as though they were destroyers, twisting and turning the ships to face into the waves of torpedoes streaking towards them. If they could 'comb the tracks' of the torpedoes, the torpedoes would pass harmlessly down the side of the ship.

The sheer number of torpedoes in the water and the inability of the anti-aircraft defences on the ships to knock the planes out of the sky finally overcame the ships. A single torpedo hit the *Prince of Wales* right at her most exposed point, her Achilles heel around the propellers and rudder. The most vital parts of the ship were protected inside the armoured 'citadel' and almost invulnerable. But like any ship, to function, the propellers and rudder have to be free and exposed to the sea. The single torpedo strike blew a hole in the hull right beside the unarmoured outboard port-side propeller and destroyed the A-bracket, which held the free section of the shaft in position. The propeller and shaft, no longer fixed to the hull, corkscrewed around and shook the propeller clean off.

The thrashing of the shaft inside the ship caused massive damage internally. The outboard propeller was driven by the forward engine and so the shaft ran more than 250 feet along inside the ship. The hull plates around where the shaft entered the hull were buckled and torn open by the thrashing shaft and tons of water started flooding into her. She soon took over a heel to port and her rudder jammed.

To trim the vessel her crew tried flooding the starboard side but this couldn't be done quickly enough. Slowly, the water rushing into her port side caused a list to that side.

The second wave of this attack now swarmed at the *Prince of Wales* from the starboard side. With the rudder jammed she could not manoeuvre and three torpedoes struck her side.

The foremost hit her bow about 20 feet back from the stern. This hit however, would not have been fatal to the *Prince of Wales*, as bows are designed to survive collisions and serious damage while leaving the main structure of the ship, further aft, watertight.

The second torpedo hit slightly forward of amidships and the third torpedo hit the aft section of hull. She now had four massive holes in her and a large section of her hull had been opened up to the sea.

The end was inevitable. She slowly turned turtle and sank, with huge loss of life.

Repulse, however, also had to fight her own battle for survival. At one point, there were 16 torpedoes in the water and her commander valiantly tried to manoeuvre his ship to comb the tracks. Finally her fate was sealed when a mass of Japanese torpedo bombers attacked in a pincer or star formation. Torpedoes streaked towards her from every direction. She couldn't comb these differing tracks and she was hit by five torpedoes in rapid succession and by several 1,000-lb bombs around her bridge superstructure. She too rolled over and sank with great loss of life. Two centuries of faith in the invulnerability of the battleship had just been blown away.

We woke from our night's jetlagged slumber early, to the steady throb of the ship's diesel engines, which had been a constant companion for us through the night as we had steamed northwards. I got up from my cramped, sweat-drenched bunk and went up on deck. Even though it was early, the sun blazed down with incredible force. The water was an oily calm and there was nothing to be seen in any direction.

The *Mata Ikan* surged on remorselessly through the oily sea, her bow wave and wake sending out a bubbling foam, which dissipated slowly behind us as it spread out to leave a white trail stretching into the distance.

As the day wore on, the *Mata Ikan* continued its northward passage as we set about rigging our kit, building up our Aquazepp scooters, fixing back plates and harnesses to twin sets of large aluminium dive tanks. A palpable sense of anticipation filled the ship as, after lunch, we neared the site of the battle. The skipper eventually galvanised his crew into action with a simple shouted order. From the immediate burst of activity we knew we were very close to the scene of the tragic sinkings. The last resting place of the *Prince of Wales* and those of her crew who perished lay nearby. I tried to visualise what the wreck might look like, far below us on the seabed.

We crowded into the wheelhouse, eyes straining to see the LCD display on the roof-mounted echo-sounder. We were 50 miles offshore in mid-ocean with nothing around us, yet we all knew that not far away on the seabed beneath us lay two relics of man's attempts to conquer the seas. A sense of history pervaded our ship. We all knew that we were approaching the scene of a great tragedy.

I looked up into the azure-blue skies and thought what it must have been like for those young British sailors so far from home, to see those same skies teaming with hostile planes intent on destroying their ships and killing them. I imagined waves of torpedo bombers peeling off into an attacking run and closing on the ship. Survivors reported that the *Prince of Wales*'s anti-aircraft guns were seemingly unable to hit the bombers before they had loosed their deadly cargoes. A single torpedo from each plane came streaking towards the ship, the only sign of impending doom being the silent telltale track of bubbles left by their passing. It is hard for those of us who have not experienced war on this scale to truly understand what these brave British sailors went through.

The bottom trace on the echo-sounder showed a flat seabed at 70 msw, but then suddenly the trace jumped straight up to about 50 msw. We had just passed over the wreck of the *Prince of Wales*. The ship's diver did a solo bounce dive with a mooring rope down to the wreck and tied off to a mooring cleat on the wreck itself. The engines of the *Mata Ikan* were turned off and we swung at our mooring in the steady southerly two-knot monsoon current. There would be no comfortable period of slack water to dive at, just an unrelenting two-knot current.

The boat crew rigged up a decompression station and deployed it beneath the boat. Long aluminium bars roped together were set at depths of 3 msw, 6 msw and 9 msw. Spare Nitrox 50 cylinders with regulators attached were fixed at either side of each three-metre step and a guide rope was run from the deco station to the down line, our anchor line.

We had mixed our dive gases on the way out and so were ready – and eager – to dive that afternoon. We would be carrying twin manifolded 12-litre tanks on our backs filled with our 'bottom mix' which we had chosen to be a Trimix of 16 per cent oxygen, 45 per cent helium and the balance nitrogen. On the bottom at 70 msw, this mix would give us a reduced narcotic air equivalent depth of 29 metres, easily manageable.

We would travel down from the surface to a depth of 33 msw breathing our 'travel mix' of Nitrox 32 (32 per cent oxygen, balance nitrogen) before switching over to our 'bottom mix'. On the ascent from the bottom at 70 msw, we would change from our 'bottom mix' to our 'travel mix' once we had got up to 33 msw.

For final decompression from 20 msw to the surface we would be breathing a 'deco mix' of Nitrox 50, (50 per cent oxygen, balance nitrogen). Our travel and deco mixes were slung in large aluminium ten-litre cylinders, one under each arm, so in total we would be carrying four tanks. In addition to that burden we would be using our Aquazepp LT 30 scooters to get around the massive 750-foot-long wrecks.

My task, in addition to being the sacrificial 'talking head' for the program, was to survey the wrecks and produce accurate impressions of the wrecks on the seabed. We planned a bottom time on the wreck at 70 msw of 25 minutes with a total dive time of about one and a half hours.

Even though the water was a tropical warm, we wore full 3-mm wetsuits. We would be inwater for a long time on each dive and chilling was still a factor. In addition, a full wetsuit would give us protection against the multitude of invisible stinging organisms and the poisonous sea snakes of which there had been much talk.

Sgt Dave Taylor of 1 Para and I were the first divers into the water. As soon as I jumped from the stern gunwales of the *Mata Ikan*, the steady two-knot current washing along the side of the boat got hold of me. We had run a line from the stern of our boat to the down line at the bow and I grabbed this and started to pull myself hand over hand along the side of the ship, through the surge of white water rippling against me. At this stage I dared not let go of the safety rope. The top speed of my scooter was two and a half knots so I wasn't sure on this initial dive how it would perform against the monsoon current. Once down on the wreck, its massive bulk would give me shelter from the current. Up here, in the full force of the current I feared that if I let go of the rope my scooter might not be able to make any headway and I might be swept downstream from the down line.

Once I had moved up the line, perhaps halfway along the ship, I felt I had got the measure of the current. Pointing my scooter forward, I gunned the go switch of the scooter with one hand, whilst holding onto the grabline with the other hand.

I found that my scooter coped well enough with the current and I moved slowly and effortlessly up the side of the *Mata Ikan* until I reached the anchor line, which plunged down into the seemingly bottomless, deep oceanic blue. There was no sign of the wreck below even though the visibility in every direction laterally looked astonishingly clear.

We started the descent and I soon found that my scooter could easily make way against the current and I could dare to let go of the anchor line and scooter down beside it. I knew from other reports that the *Prince of Wales* was upside down and I strained my eyes down into the gloom looking for a first sight of the upturned whale back of her keel.

I got to my 33-metre switch to my bottom mix and I found that there was still no sign of the wreck below, just a gloomy murkiness. Other dive reports had talked of poor visibility on this wreck caused by silt washed up against it by the currents. If the visibility was going to be any good the wreck would have been in sight by now. This didn't augur well for an attempt to survey the wreck.

As I pressed on down I got to 50 metres and then entered a huge milky cloud of disturbed sediment. I realised that I was close to the *Prince of Wales*, and that its position broadside on to the prevailing current was causing a massive cloud of scour debris to be thrown up, reducing the visibility from 200 feet to about 20 feet.

As I pressed forward through the milky cloud, the huge hull of the *Prince of Wales* appeared a few metres away from me. We were able to start our exploration of the wreck and found that the visibility on the wreck varied greatly depending on where you were on it. We were able to move along out of the cloud into some better visibility.

As Dave and I scootered along the starboard side, I was struck by how good a condition the hull seemed to be in. A battleship is very heavily armoured and strongly constructed. Of all the types of ships that end their lives as wrecks, battleships stand up to the test of time the best. The hull of the *Prince of Wales* seemed almost intact and just covered in a carpet of marine growth.

But then we started seeing evidence of the battle and the wounds that sank her. As we motored along the starboard side we saw three large torpedo explosion holes. One had struck at the very bow, forward of the collision bulkhead of the armoured area, 'the citadel'. The explosion had blown right through from the starboard side to the portside, a hole some 25 feet across.

The second and third torpedo impact sites were also about 25 feet across, large enough to drive a bus into. Importantly however the holes were just under (and now above) the armour belt. The torpedoes had struck the soft underbelly of the vessel in the space between the armour belt and her bilge keels. These large strips of steel project a few feet downwards and run along nearly the complete length of the very bottom of the flat hull, at either side, to give the hull a cutting surface for manoeuvring.

The second hole from the front was at the very start of the bilge keel right at the very lowest part of the armour belt. The bottom (now topmost) sections of armour plating had been knocked backwards and inwards into the hull itself. The armour plating was still intact – but just angled inwards.

The blast hole was right beneath the armour belt and occupied the area down to the bilge keel, which was twisted and bent by the explosion. It looked as though the torpedo had just hit the very bottom of the armour plating. The blast appeared to have knocked the lowest section of armour plating backwards slightly and angled the force of the explosion downwards into the soft unprotected area beneath. This unprotected area was effortlessly rent open to the sea by the explosion. I estimated that the hole was also about 25 feet in diameter with the plating at its edges buckled inwards.

The third torpedo explosion site was at the very end of the armour belt but again on the soft underbelly of the ship. As I stared at these torpedo holes my mind queried why her soft underbelly should have been exposed in this fashion. If the explosions had taken place just five or ten feet higher, the full force of the explosion would have been taken by the armour belt without problem – that was what it was designed to do. Why had the torpedoes struck where they did with such devastating effect?

That night I read up on historical accounts of the battle. The Japanese attack on the *Prince of Wales* had taken place in two waves. During the first wave, she had been struck on her port side around her outboard port side propeller. The propeller shaft, which ran for about 250 feet inside the vessel, had thrashed about causing massive internal damage. This first wave had caused enough damage to make her vulnerable to the second – fatal – attack. I determined to explore the site of that explosion on the following day's dive.

The next day we plunged into the water again with the underwater cameraman Dan Burton. After laying a brass memorial plaque, fashioned by the Royal Navy in memory of those who perished in the tragedy, we filmed the starboard torpedo explosion sites as we made our way to the stern. There, we were dwarfed by the sheer size of the rudders and the three massive, remaining propellers.

The outside port-side propeller was, as we suspected, missing from its shaft. There was only a gaping hole and a mass of bent and buckled plating where the shaft had thrashed about prior to the propeller itself dropping out. Nearby was the torpedo explosion hole and the remnants of the A-bracket, which fixed the free section of the prop shaft to the hull. We had now filmed the entire sequence of her sinking.

It was becoming progressively clear how the *Prince of Wales* had succumbed to the vicious air attack. The large blast hole near the A-bracket would have let vast quantities of water into the port side of the hull. The torn and bent plating caused by the thrashing of the propeller shaft would have allowed further huge quantities of water into the hull. Despite attempts to flood her opposite starboard side to redress her trim, the crew couldn't flood her quickly enough. The thrashing of the shaft for 250 feet inside the hull would have damaged internal compartments and allowed the water to penetrate further forward, far inside the hull. She listed to port and her rudder jammed.

As she listed, her port side buried itself deeper into the water. Correspondingly her starboard side was lifted upwards and canted over, not by much, but enough to expose her soft underbelly to the torpedoes of the second wave of the attack. Her fate was sealed.

We remained onsite above the *Prince of Wales* for a full week, diving her each day and surveying her remains. On one dive I decided to go under the upturned foredeck to see if I could glimpse the massive A-turret with its four 14-inch guns.

As I moved under the foredeck I found that there was a gap of about eight feet between the seabed and the deck above. The visibility down here on the seabed wasn't good and when I moved under the hull it was pitch black.

As I tentatively made my way further under the hull, in the distance it seemed that there was a band of light green at the other side of her 100-foot-wide deck. It dawned on me that this was open water at the other side of the foredeck and that the whole foredeck from A-turret forward was off the seabed. The whole bow section for almost 100 feet was held aloft, suspended and defying gravity, by the sheer size of the crumpled superstructure and foredeck turrets, driven down into the seabed. What strength the construction of this ship had to stand like that despite the ravages of more than 60 years on the bottom. I hoped that she would hold up for a few minutes more.

I retreated and got hold of Dan Burton, our cameraman, and with Guy we returned under the hull. The four 14-inch barrels of A-turret must have been 45 feet long at least and were lying on top of the seabed.

We filmed in the darkness of this man-made cavern as we scootered past this famous and recognisable quad turret. This time we kept on going and passed right through to the clear water at the other side of the foredeck. It was extremely disconcerting having the complete bow section of a 36,000-ton battleship suspended above me. If the bow section were to fracture and collapse right now we would be squashed like flies. No one would ever find us. I was hugely relieved once we had completed the filming and could leave this dark, silty cavern.

At the end of the week we filmed as Guy flew a Royal Navy Ensign from the wreck's starboard side propeller shaft in memory of those who were lost. As the Ensign unfurled, it hung on its buoys and the flag waved gently in the two-knot underwater breeze, as it would have topside. It was a visually haunting and atmospheric moment and we knew immediately that that dramatic footage was how the documentary would close.

After our week's diving on the *Prince of Wales* we moved the eight miles over to the wreck of HMS *Repulse*, which lies in slightly shallower water, and filmed and surveyed that wreck as well. Our diving doctor, Doc Adey, conducted Doppler checks on us after most dives. For a team of 12 divers doing repeat deep technical dives for a fortnight, using the latest advanced decompression software, there was not even the slightest hint of a bend.

It was on a dive on the *Repulse* that I had one of those equipment failures that if you don't control them can quickly lead to disaster. It always happens when you expect it least. Thankfully, in Guy, I had an attentive buddy who quickly sorted out the danger.

The underwater visibility on *Repulse* is far better than *Prince of Wales* as a result of her smaller size and her orientation to the prevailing currents, which produce a smaller build-up of sediments. The visibility was a colossal 200 feet.

After jumping into the water and starting the descent, even though the depth to the seabed was just short of 60 metres, by the time I was 5 or 10 metres down I could see almost the whole wreck far beneath me. I was enthralled to see divers ahead of me on the descent scootering freely down towards the wreck far below – small dots, like ants against the massive bulk of this vast ship.

The *Repulse* lies on her port side and is well heeled over – almost, but not quite, turned turtle like the *Prince of Wales*. Way below me, I could see Dan Burton scootering along the keel of the wreck filming whilst other divers moved down the anchor line. Others were already exploring different parts of her. Shimmering bubble streams from the divers billowed upwards, ever expanding and drifting downstream as they sought the surface.

Although the upmost starboard side of *Repulse* overhangs her main deck, her bridge superstructure lies flat on the seabed and is open for exploration. She too is largely intact and as she is not completely upside down like the *Prince of Wales*, there is a lot to see on her. Her jackstay at the very tip of the bow, from which her ensign would have flown, still stands *in situ*, her massive anchors are still snug in their hawse pipes. The twin 15-inch gun barrels of partially buried B-turret project out of the sand, perhaps one of the most moving and powerful images on this wreck.

On one of the last dives on her, Guy and I had been scootering around her trying to find evidence of her wounds, trying to completely circumnavigate the wreck and do some photography. At one point around the foredeck gun turrets, Guy and I were both intent on examining different parts of the same area and had become separated by about 50 feet – not a lot in this good visibility. We knew where each other was and could see our respective bubble streams, but we had lost immediate visual contact with each other.

I was under the overhanging deck around A-turret – Guy was round the other side of B-turret. My kit had been working perfectly for the whole two weeks of the trip and I felt comfortable and in control.

Suddenly there was an almighty 'crack' right beside my right ear. The bang was so loud that I was momentarily stunned and started seeing stars. As I regained my senses I could hear a rushing 'whoosh' of escaping gas from my back tanks right at my ear.

I looked quickly at my contents gauge. Before this my back tanks were almost full, holding about 200 bar. I was already down to 150 bar and was losing my precious bottom mix very, very quickly. Guy was out of sight, and I couldn't breathe my travel or deco mix gases slung under my arms at this depth for fear of a fatal oxygen toxicity hit. Convulsions and death would follow. Not the best result.

The manifold that connects the pillar valves of each of my back mounted tanks together is fitted with an isolation valve for just this sort of emergency. Screw down the central isolation valve and this isolates one tank off from the other. Thus if you are losing gas from one tank or the regulators serving it, the other side is separated and protected. It will leave you enough gas to get back up to the surface.

Unfortunately, in an example of Murphy's Law at work, I had damaged my right shoulder in a sports injury earlier in the summer and it had not fully recovered. The range of rotation of my shoulder had been badly affected and I simply couldn't get my shoulder turned enough to allow my hand to reach the isolation valve and switch it off.

The continuing rush of bottom mix from my tanks had created a cloud of white bubbles around me and in the midst of this, I twisted and turned to try and reach the isolation valve. As I struggled, it was becoming clear that I simply couldn't do it. I was on the point of stripping off my tanks and harness to get at it when I saw Guy, head down, bombing over at speed towards me on his scooter. He had heard the bang and seen the rush of bubbles.

Taking off my harness and tanks would have been a last resort as the complications that could arise from doing that were dangerous in themselves. I needed the travel and deco gases to get back to the surface safely and wanted them well secured to me. I had already decided that if all my bottom mix went then I would have to risk breathing my travel mix whilst doing a free ascent, breathing as little as possible to a safe depth where I wouldn't 'ox-tox'.

As soon as I saw Guy heading my way I got my head down and gunned my Zepp and screamed over to him. He represented an oasis of safety and beautiful bottom mix that I could share. As we closed on each other at a startling combined speed of four knots I ducked my head downwards as I reached him, presenting the pillar valves of my tanks to him and knowing that he would suss the problem and sort it out.

I was aware of seeing him checking my kit and then an outstretched hand turned off my right-hand pillar valve. Immediately the rushing whoosh of my escaping bottom mix stopped. We stood there on the seabed, settled down and assessed the situation.

I checked my contents gauge and found I had 20 bar left – hardly anything at all. My tanks were nearly completely empty and I would soon be on vapours. I had gone from practically a full set of two 12-litre tanks at 200 bar to just 20 bar in a minute or two. I had breathed my regulators down before and knew that I would soon start to feel resistance to my breathing from my regulators as a result of the drop in pressure. After that, they would just stop working, as I'd be sucking at a vacuum.

I gestured to Guy that we had to abort the dive and head back to the line quickly. I gunned my scooter and screamed back from the foredeck to the down line amidships, all the while rising up the wreck to shallower depths to reduce the amount of my remaining bottom mix I was using. Guy stayed close beside me, ready to hand me his spare regulator should I run out of gas.

In the event, I was able to get to the line and rise up to about 38 msw where it was safe to change over from my bottom mix to the ample supplies of travel mix under my arm. The rest of the ascent went without incident.

Once we got back aboard, the ITN crew filmed as I got out of my kit and inspected the damage. The hose that ran from the pillar valve and 1st Stage valve on my tank to the breathing regulator in my mouth had blown out an inch or two from the 1st Stage valve itself, right beside where my right ear was. There was a hole in it about half an inch long and it was through here that all my bottom mix had been flowing freely. When I discussed this incident with a North Sea commercial diver back in Scotland later it turned out that this problem was known about and dealt with in the offshore industry, but we had never heard of it in our sport technical diving world.

Helium is a very small molecule and can work its way though the reinforced hoses that we use to connect our regulators to our tanks, whereas the molecules of the constituents of air cannot. The breathing hoses are coated with a waterproof rubber or plastic covering which helium however cannot penetrate. If there is a weakness in the hose, then the helium can get through the hose itself but can get trapped under the rubber skin of the hose producing an ever-increasing blister or bubble of helium. Eventually, as in my case, the blister goes bang. In the offshore world they use perforated outer skins which have hundreds of tiny holes in them which allow any build-up to escape, thus avoiding the sort of blow-out I had.

The trip was over too soon and we made the long journey back to the UK. The *Timewatch* program itself was first aired on 18 January 2002 and has since been repeated on terrestrial TV and Sky TV on many occasions. The information I gathered from our surveys of the two wrecks enabled me to get the artist I use for my wreck work, Rob Ward, to paint graphic pictures of the wrecks as they lie on the seabed. We liaised closely with the Survivors Associations for the two wrecks who supported the expedition fully. I feel that our work on these two very sensitive wrecks has helped to raise the profile of these two ships – and to bring an understanding of what happened and of the sacrifice of those who perished, to modern generations. It is hard to truly understand what it must be like to have mighty ships like these sunk from beneath your feet so far from land. For those survivors who still gather for a reunion each year, the sinking is still alive within them, very real, as if it were yesterday.

I presented prints of the paintings to Ken Byrne, Secretary of the Prince of Wales Survivors Association, who also featured in the documentary. Ken kindly phoned me to thank me for the prints. He remarked how accurate the paintings were and that he had been staggered to see the gun turret on *Prince of Wales* in which he had been serving at the time of the attack, projecting from the upturned hull in the painting. Right above it (originally beneath) he could now see the second torpedo explosion hole, which he had felt at the time although he was several decks above.

Some of the prints were framed and put up as prizes at the annual Survivors Association Reunion at Scarborough. Other prints were presented to the Admiral who attended the reunion. I felt honoured to have brought something tangible and of worth to these fine old gentlemen who fought in a war ended a long time before I was even born.

CHAPTER SEVENTEEN

Into the Corryvreckan Whirlpool

'And darkness was upon the face of the Deep'

Genesis 1:2

The Corryvreckan Whirlpool is the stuff of legends. I grew up hearing tales of boats and ships being caught in it and sucked down with their unfortunate sailors into the depths of the monster. Although my imagination ran wild, I never knew really where it was then. As my involvement with the sea grew throughout my diving career, I became more aware of it. But I never dreamt for one moment in all that time that I would dive down into the heart of the whirlpool itself.

The Corryvreckan Whirlpool is the third-largest whirlpool in the world. It takes centre stage in the Gulf of Corryvreckan, a small channel of water just over half-a-mile wide, that separates the Isle of Jura from the smaller island of Scarba on the west coast of Scotland, south of Oban.

The Corryvreckan Whirlpool is perhaps the most feared strip of water in British waters. When the whirlpool is in full motion, the half-mile wide channel is a very dangerous place to be. Tales abound of boats and ships being caught in it and sucked down into oblivion. Such is its danger that the Royal Navy has classed the channel as unnavigable and the lifeboat has been called out to over 50 emergencies there in recent years. Currents can reach 16 knots and its roar can be heard 10 miles away. Standing waves 10 feet high breaking endlessly reveal that there is some massive obstruction on the seabed.

To the west of the Gulf of Corryvreckan is the Atlantic – open water all the way to America. To the east of the Gulf is the Sound of Jura, and then mainland Scotland. It seems as though the whole of the Atlantic tries to funnel through this small channel, pushing colossal amounts of water on the flood towards Scotland. This tidal action has scoured out a massive chasm in the Gulf more than 200 metres deep.

In the middle of this chasm, trying to block the might of the Atlantic, stands a pinnacle of solid rock which reaches up from a depth of 200 metres to just 30 metres short of the surface. The top of the Pinnacle is about 100 feet wide and it widens as it drops down towards the bottom of the chasm 200 metres below. The standing waves visible on the surface are caused as the onrushing tide is forced up and over the Pinnacle before dropping instantly back down into the chasm. An underwater waterfall is created with fierce down currents.

A story, now part of Scottish diving folklore, tells of how, many years ago, a brave diver tried to dive the Pinnacle. He made it down to the Pinnacle all right but the down currents got hold of him. He inflated his BCD, normally enough to send a diver to the surface like a rocket – but he kept going down. He dropped his weightbelt giving him more buoyancy – and still kept going down. The current took him down to the incredible depth of 75 metres before he broke loose and reached up to the surface. The Pinnacle has only rarely been dived.

Scientists have been keen to study the Pinnacle but have been denied permission to dive under Health and Safety Executive (HSE) regulations because of the great depths, and the huge currents and associated dangers. But we as sport divers were not bound by those rules. So when an Edinburgh TV director, who had trained Ewan to dive in his early days, wanted a team of experienced divers to dive the Pinnacle for an *Equinox* documentary, *Maelstrom*, part of the *Lethal Seas* series in 2000, Ewan got the call.

Ewan was very quickly on the phone to me asking if I'd be interested. My initial reaction was that this was a crazy thing to do but he persisted and eventually I agreed. Very shortly after that, I found myself arriving at Oban on a Saturday morning to meet a team led by experienced Trimix diver Graeme Bruce, and made up of Ewan, myself, Jim Burke, Dave Hadden, David Ainsley and Jack Morrison.

The plan was to do a work-up dive in the Falls of Lora, almost directly underneath the Connell Bridge in Oban itself. The Falls of Lora take centre stage in a tight bottleneck channel, which separates Loch Etive from the open sea. The seabed at the Falls is scoured with hundreds of canyons and gorges which lead to a massive pit or hole where the seabed drops off to about 45 metres.

I had seen the full might of the Falls in action on many occasions. There is no actual huge waterfall or series of rocky rapids – just the tight bottleneck channel. But that channel is a special place, for here a raging torrent of white water and standing waves reveal the presence of the underwater canyons and waterfalls.

On previous visits to Oban I have looked in awe at the Falls. On one occasion I saw a motor boat trying to make its way through and up in an effort to break through into the upper reaches of Loch Etive. Time after time the motor boat took a run at the Falls, engine roaring, and fought against the currents and turbulence. And each time it failed and was driven back. This was going to be some shakedown dive and I must admit to feeling apprehensive about this dive itself – let alone the Corryvreckan Whirlpool the following day.

The team leader briefed us on the dive as we got kitted up and launched the boat. We were going to be dropped into the water up current to seaward of the Falls, on the flood. We would then descend some 20 metres into an area of canyons scoured by the currents and find ourselves drifting at speed up river until we came to the focus point, the Falls themselves, where the water plunges over an underwater cliff that drops off from a depth of 20 metres to a depth in excess of 40 metres.

We were told that once we went over the edge of the cliff there was no way we could break free from the current. We just had to literally go with the flow. Once it bottomed out we would be able to rise up and would find ourselves in calmer water. I wondered if Corryvreckan could be worse than what I now expected to face.

We loaded our gear into Graeme's well-equipped RIB and headed round from the slip to the Falls. The TV director wanted shots of the boat passing under the famous Connell Bridge so we spent some time zipping to and fro under the bridge whilst the TV director filmed us from up on the bridge itself. After that we picked him up in the boat and he came out with us filming in the RIB itself.

After the initial scenes were shot it was time for the main event – the shakedown dive. David Ainsley was taking in an underwater video camera to shoot scenes of divers working in the fierce currents, although I thought that would be a tough number in the expected currents. We were all going to dive in a group to give him plenty of subjects to film.

And so, heart racing, I now sat fully kitted on the tubes of the RIB, ready to splash. The command was given and one by one we all tumbled backwards into the water.

Immediately I was aware of the strong current pulling me upstream. I dumped as much air as I could from my dry suit and buoyancy wings on my twin set and dropped downwards to the bottom at about 20 metres.

Arriving on the bottom, my buddy for the dive, Dave Hadden, appeared beside me and then, one by one the others appeared. Once we were all together sheltering in a canyon, David Ainsley set himself up and indicated that he wanted each of us to get into the current and drift past him as he filmed.

We all started flying past him one by one. Once down current of him, I turned to look at him for instructions. He indicated he wanted to repeat the same shot. This was going to be a tough number to work our way back up current to get into position. I grabbed hold of rocky handholds and kicked as hard as I could, fighting the raging current. Slowly I drew level with him and was able to drag myself back to our original position to repeat the shot.

After that it was on with the drift. As David Ainsley filmed we all drifted off and gradually the current managed to separate us all into our buddy pairs. It was just impossible in such strong rapids to keep a large group of divers together.

Dave Hadden and I drifted freely with the current over the canyons. When you went into the canyons you got some measure of protection but above them you were exposed to the full fury of the current. We were whipped along, flying over the bottom at speed as if in a plane. I peered ahead, my mind racing with thoughts of the cliff I expected to fall over any second.

Abruptly the canyons petered out and I thought this meant that the cliff was imminent. I don't like being out of control on a dive and had a sense of foreboding about the cliff, the usual fear of the unknown. In any event the cliff never appeared and then quite suddenly, the current started to ease off and drop away. I guessed that we must have passed by on the land side of the cliff and that we were now past it and into calmer water.

After a few minutes it seemed there was little point in going further. I inflated my six-foot-long, red marker buoy and it sped to the surface in a rush of bubbles, my reel paying out the attached line. All the divers were hitting the surface now and one by one we were picked up by the attendant RIB. It turned out that the current where we had been dropped had taken us somewhat inshore to one side of the cliff itself. We had missed the Disney ride over the Falls but had had to work hard in fierce currents. I must admit that I had little regret about missing the Falls.

That night we headed down to a small pub at the Bridge over the Atlantic, a small bridge that connects the mainland to a small island and so bridges the Atlantic. We had agreed to meet there to conduct the briefing for the next day's dive into the whirlpool, and the ever-present TV director would be there to film.

As we went into the pub we found that the locals had been ushered along to one end of the bar to make way for a number of bright TV lights on stands. They eyed us quizzically as we entered. Shots were taken outside of Ewan arriving in his car at the pub, and then we moved inside to film the next sequential shot of Ewan entering the pub. In between shooting the outside shot and coming into the bar Ewan had taken off his jacket. Once the interior scene had been shot this lack of continuity was noticed and he had to put it on, go outside and do his big walk-in scene again.

We all sat around a beaten, circular, copper bar table, bought in some beers and laid out charts of the gulf to study. David Ainsley, who runs the hugely respected charter dive boat *Porpoise*, was taking us out to the gulf the next day. He knew the waters there well.

David went on to brief us on the latest weather forecast and it wasn't looking good. The wind was already gusting strongly and a Force 8 was now expected the next day, which might well put paid to the dive on the whirlpool.

Nevertheless, although there was a real chance that the dive would be off, we still went through the motions of the dive briefing for the TV camera. There was a sense of unreality about the whole thing. Here we were, planning to dive the most dangerous dive in British waters, and now there was a Force 8 forecast to boot. Surely the dive would be called off.

David Ainsley had dived the Pinnacle many times before and knew the waters there extremely well. He explained what would happen once we got on site.

'The moment the ebb starts, the down currents start. What we need to do is get in on the end of the flood. It's likely to be hard work getting down the shot line – there is no getting away from that.'

We all became locked away in our own thoughts of what the next day would bring. Thinking that the weather was going to blow us off we had a few more beers and chatted late into the night before heading to our rooms.

Awaking on the day of the dive, I was immediately struck by the noise of the wind whipping around our accommodation. Getting up and throwing on some warm clothes I went outside and was joined by Ewan. The force of the wind buffeted us and we both looked at each other and agreed that the dive would most probably be off.

Ewan phoned the TV director who told us to go down to the small harbour where the *Porpoise* was berthed and we'd take a decision then after consulting David Ainsley. As I ate breakfast I was feeling a little relieved at the thought of the dive being abandoned.

After breakfast we collected our gear from our room and made the short drive down to the harbour. There, all the divers were arriving and loading their gear into the *Porpoise*. The wind howled about and I was by this stage absolutely convinced that the dive would be called off. I suspected that we were just not being told as yet so that the TV director could film the actual disappointment (or relief) on our faces as the announcement was made on the quayside. Nevertheless I loaded my gear into the boat and got changed in the lee of a fishhouse block into my warm diving undersuit.

Once all the kit and divers were aboard we were filmed as the *Porpoise* cast off and we headed out to open water. The wind still howled around and I thought that if the dive was going to be called, now was the time. But the *Porpoise* headed onwards. David explained that because of the lie of the surrounding islands he could find shelter and run all the way to the gulf without getting into the stormy weather which would be found in exposed waters.

After being convinced in my own mind for the last 12 hours that the dive was not going ahead, I had to come to terms with the fact that, after all, I was now about to be pitched into the heart of the Corryvreckan Whirlpool. Perhaps it was just as well it turned out like that – at least I had slept well the night before.

The *Porpoise* left the small harbour at about 9 a.m. and, although sea conditions were fairly lumpy, we had a surprisingly comfortable two-hour ride out to the gulf. David Ainsley had been right about the sea conditions allowing us to get to the site despite the fierce winds.

At first there was a lot of nervous gallows humour as we headed out across the Sound of Jura. The divers busied themselves setting up their dive gear and doing the usual round of kit checks. It was in the back of all of our minds that if the downcurrents got hold of us, we could be pulled quite some distance down the side of the Pinnacle.

The absolute, maximum recommended depth for air diving is 50 metres. The depth to the bottom of the Pinnacle was 200 metres. If we were to dive it on compressed air and got pulled down the side of the Pinnacle to such great depths, the very air we breathed would become toxic and kill us.

As a result I chose to dive using TDI's Trimix B, a mixture of 16 per cent oxygen, 45 per cent helium and 39 per cent nitrogen. This would allow me to survive being pulled down to about 100 metres or even more. Ewan was going a step further still. He had rigged his much-cherished Buddy Inspiration Closed Circuit Rebreather, now known as Kato, with an even higher helium mixture, which would allow him if necessary to be swept to the bottom of the Pinnacle at 200 metres and survive. No one was intending going below 60 metres, but it was comforting to know that if the worst came to the worst, and things went wrong, Ewan could actually stand at the bottom of the Pinnacle, look up and at least witness the rest of us casting off this mortal coil.

As we arrived in the Gulf of Corryvreckan everyone on the boat fell silent. The gallows humour petered out – an apprehensive and nervous silence enveloped the *Porpoise*. This was a special place, one of the most foreboding and eerie places I have been in my life. The gulf simply seemed filled with doom, broken only by the cries of a few seagulls. We could see the much-fabled standing waves marking the spot where the Pinnacle stood, hidden in the depths.

David Ainsley manoeuvred his boat into position above the Pinnacle and a very heavy shot, made up of two old iron railway grips, was dropped over the side and plunged down to the Pinnacle below. Once the shot landed, the current whipped the rope tight and the buoys strained against the current. White water broke around the buoys as the current worked on them, leaving a huge rippling wake as though they were being pulled through the water at speed.

The *Porpoise* couldn't moor onto the buoys even when the current is at its slackest: there is never truly a period of absolute slack water on the Pinnacle – there is only a short period of about ten minutes as the current turns when it is diveable. The force of the moving water would work on the hull of the boat causing so much force that the shot would be dragged off.

Once all the divers were prepped the first two took their position on the gunwales of the boat. David came out and gave us a final briefing on the conditions and how the dive had to be run. He told us that the tide was dropping away now towards slack water, but that that period of slack water would only last for ten minutes. After that the tide would pick up fiercely in the opposite direction and it was time to get away and start the ascent.

We were told that a warning sign that the tide was about to turn would be when all the small crabs, which we would see on the Pinnacle, darted for cover. They presumably had learnt through experience that if they didn't get into cover they would end up being swept over the side of the Pinnacle for the long 200-metre fall into the chasm.

Finally, and ominously, we were told that when our bubbles started going downwards we should get the hell out of there as the current would be escalating dramatically. We were to put buoyant gas into everything on us we could, by bleeding air into our drysuits, into our buoyancy wings and by sending up a lifting bag on a reel – that should be sufficient to support us and get us clear of the downcurrents.

Finally, David added a sobering warning: 'Conditions today are not ideal – no one is forced to go in on this dive. There is no pressure on anybody to do so.'

But we were all now committed and psyched up for the dive. There was no going back.

David took the *Porpoise* up beside the buoys and was able to assess the tidal flow at that time as being between 2.4 and 2.9 knots. He then took the boat about 30 feet up current to drop us. By the time we were in and had righted ourselves we should be drifting up to the buoys. It was time to go. The dive was on.

The first two divers rolled backwards into the water on David's signal, righted themselves and grabbed hold of the shot line as they drifted with the current. A quick round of OK signals to each other and the boat and they slipped under the water to start the descent to the Pinnacle.

Once they had cleared the buoys it was time for Dave Hadden and myself to go. I pulled myself awkwardly up from the bench where I had got kitted up and made my way to the gunwale. It was hard work in a pitching boat carrying two heavy 12-litre tanks on my back, two 9-litre tanks of deco mix, one secured under either arm, weights and all the other paraphernalia necessary to survive down in the depths.

I sat down on the gunwale and Dave Hadden clumped down beside me. David gave the signal that we were in position again and, heart racing, Dave and I rolled over backwards, dropping over the side of the boat heavily into the water a few feet below.

As the usual explosion of white water and bubbles that greeted us on entry disappeared, I righted myself and looked down current searching for the buoys and line. All my earlier fears and foreboding had disappeared. I was preoccupied with the mechanics of the dive, of getting to the shot line and not missing it.

Sure enough, I was drifting towards the buoys and could see the shot line leading down from them into the abyss. The underwater visibility looked good – at least 25 metres – and I could see the bubble streams rising up from the two divers ahead of and below us.

As soon as I grabbed the shot line, the current which had been my friend in drifting me onto the rope, became my enemy and swung me round to stream out down current. I had to keep a firm grip on the rope – if I let go of it I would be whipped away very quickly. I dumped excess buoyant air from my suit and wings and started to make the descent, laboriously hand over hand.

It took Dave and I just a few minutes to haul our way down to the top of the Pinnacle. Although the top is at a depth of 30 metres, the shot had snagged down one side of it at about 40 metres.

Initially I thought that the Pinnacle was devoid of life, seemingly scoured clean by the current. On closer examination however, I could see that there was a fine mat of tiny organisms, noticeably smaller than their counterparts elsewhere in Scottish waters. Larger specimens are perhaps swept away by the current, or maybe they have just evolved to be smaller to survive. The top of the Pinnacle was clean and unobstructed by any kelp forests due to its depth.

Large, smooth potholes peppered the surface of the Pinnacle here and there, where small stones had lodged in small holes and were then remorselessly ground round and round by the currents. Over a period of time these small stones had carved out these six-foot deep potholes. There was no fish life noticeable – perhaps because there was no life worthy of eating on the Pinnacle. A few small crabs went about their business here and there.

Dave and I circumnavigated the Pinnacle at a depth of about 45 metres. We then headed up, as planned, to its top, conscious of trying to avoid spending too long at depth which would rack up lengthy decompression stops for the ascent. We were keeping a careful eye on our dive computers and could see the minutes ticking away.

In the glorious 25-metre visibility all the divers gradually collected on the top of the Pinnacle. It was an odd feeling to see all six of us there and I imagined how it must have looked if you could have stripped away the water. Six tiny specks of humanity standing on the 100-foot-wide top of a 200-metre-high rock pinnacle.

As we collected on the top, I noticed a change in the direction of the current. It was as if someone had thrown a big switch. One minute the tide was dropping off gently in one direction. The next you could feel it starting to pick up rapidly in the other direction. There are titanic forces at work here.

I looked down to where I was resting and sure enough, as if on cue, the one or two small crabs around my feet just made their way into little nooks and crannies and disappeared. All life seemed to pass away from the pinnacle – the all too brief moment of calm had passed and the residents of the Pinnacle were preparing themselves for the next six hours in the maelstrom. If the locals were getting worried, our team of six divers should be getting out of there.

Dave and I however couldn't resist the temptation to fin over to the edge of the Pinnacle and look down over the side – down into the 200-metre-deep abyss. Of course, in the limited visibility we could only see about 25 metres down the side. After that there was just an ominous uniform black obscuring the bottom.

As we peered over the side of the Pinnacle I suddenly became aware that my exhaled bubbles had stopped going upwards – as they had done throughout the whole of my diving career. For a second, some bubbles were held motionless in front of my face.

With the next exhaled breath my bubbles started to go slowly downwards over the side of the Pinnacle. As I continued to breathe out my bubbles started going downwards more and more vigorously. It was a very surreal experience – but it was certainly time to get out of this dangerous place.

I looked at Dave and gave the thumbs up signal – returned with an OK signal from Dave. We prepared ourselves by pumping gas into our suits and wings until we were almost positively buoyant. We then each inflated our lifting bags and let go of them. Our reels spun and chattered as they paid out the strong thin line as the bags sped up to the surface.

Once the bags were up it was time to go. Pumping even more gas into suit and wings we basically let the current get hold of us and stepped off the Pinnacle out over the chasm. Our bubbles were still going down and we had been warned that the first ten metres of the ascent would be difficult.

As I stepped off the top of the Pinnacle it was as though a thousand invisible hands were clutching at my legs and trying to pull me down. It was quite an unsettling feeling and initially I had to work hard to make headway upwards. The task of managing the ascent however soon absorbed me as I wound in my reel, winching myself up towards the surface.

Once I got ten metres up from the top of the Pinnacle, the current had carried us so far downstream and away from the Pinnacle that we were starting to come out of the whirlpool. As I rose higher and got further away, the water settled down and we were just into a regular free hanging ascent on our bags. We drifted free in the current seemingly motionless but in reality, speeding over the seabed at several knots.

As we all broke the surface and clambered back into the safety of the *Porpoise* a sense of euphoria overwhelmed all of us. There was much manly banter and slapping of backs – a complete contrast to the silent mood that had overcome the party before the dive. We had successfully carried out perhaps the most challenging dive in British waters into one of the last great unexplored habitats on earth. But we all realised that it had gone so smoothly largely due to the professionalism and know-how of David Ainsley and the team leader Graeme Bruce. They had made a potentially terrifying dive manageable.

We had stood on the Pinnacle and peered into the abyss.

Postscript

A second team of scientists subsequently went out on the *Porpoise* and carried out a test. They had a tailor's dummy rigged up to weigh and resemble a human being. They strapped a dive computer onto its wrist and attached enough line to it to let it hit the bottom. Dropping the dummy man over the side of the boat into the whirlpool, the dummy was immediately sucked down beneath the surface. Line was paid out at an alarming rate as the dummy made a very quick descent to the bottom of the chasm.

Retrieving the dummy later the dive computer showed that it had been taken all the way down to the bottom at 200 metres. I wonder, if that dummy had had eyes that could see, what it would reveal about the bottom of the chasm.

As we headed back to our homes after our Corryvreckan dive, the TV crew were off to Japan and Norway to film the other great whirlpools in the world for the documentary. The resulting programme, *Maelstrom*, was aired in 2000 as part of the *Equinox* series.

Glossary

As this is a book about technical diving, wrecks and the sea it has, of necessity, had to deal with a number of concepts, phrases and pieces of equipment out of the ordinary. I have tried to explain these where they first crop up in the text, however it may assist the reader if I set out a brief explanation here of the main recurring points which non-divers may struggle with.

ABLJ: Adjustable Buoyancy Life Jacket. A horse-collar type orange or yellow lifejacket designed for going under water which can be inflated or deflated below the surface to control a diver's buoyancy.

Aqualung: Generic name given to the breathing device fitted to the top or main valve, the pillar valve, of a scuba tank. This drops the high pressure air in a scuba tank (of around 3000 psi or 232 Bar) down to a level exactly the same as the water pressure surrounding the diver in two successive stages – thus ensuring that a diver's air spaces are not crushed by a higher water pressure. This magical piece of equipment consists of two stages or parts; the 1st Stage clamps to the top pillar valve of the scuba tank. A breathing hose leads from it to the 2nd Stage, the part in front of the diver's face with the mouthpiece which is gripped by the teeth.

Bar: A measure of pressure similar to psi (pounds per square inch) – 1 bar represents the atmospheric pressure we all experience on the surface. At a depth of 10m a diver experiences water pressure of 2 bar, i.e. the 1 bar of atmospheric pressure plus another 1 bar represented by the increase in water pressure over the 10m depth. Accordingly, at 50m the pressure is 6 bar, i.e. 6 times atmospheric pressure.

BCD: Buoyancy Control Device. A development of the ABLJ. This is a winged buoyancy device with a back plate or mount, which fits directly onto the scuba tank. Air is bled by a direct feed from the 1st Stage of the aqualung into the wings of the BCD providing buoyancy. Air can be dumped through a Dump Valve to allow a diver to sink.

Bends: A much-feared diving condition which results from ascending too fast and allowing insufficient time for the expanding bubbles of gas flushing from a diver's tissues to escape harmlessly from the body. The bubbles tend to affect the joints of the body such as the knees and elbows. A 'bend' can vary from mild discomfort in the affected area to such debilitating pain that a diver can be 'bent' double by it – hence the slang term. An affected diver requires medical treatment in a Recompression Chamber.

BSAC: British Sub Aqua Club. The main governing body for sport diving in the UK.

Bottom Line Trace: An echo-sounder is a modern device, which shows the depth from the keel of a boat to the seabed on a small screen. The bottom, or the seabed, is usually represented by a line. Wrecks and fish can be shown in a variety of ways on different sounders. They are so accurate that the contours of the seabed and large rocks can be made out from the surface.

Dan Buoy: The large red/pink heavy-duty buoys used by ships as fenders against other ships or harbour walls and used by divers as a marker or anchor buoys. It's very hard to pull these under – except with a number of divers on the line in a strong current.

DWT: Dead-Weight Tonnage. The number of tons (of 2,240 lb) of cargo and fuel coal that the ship could carry when loaded to the waterline; calculated by multiplying gross tonnage by 1.6.

Echo-sounder: An electronic console mounted device with a screen, which depicts the seabed and reads out the depth of water beneath the keel.

GPS: Global Positioning System. This is a highly accurate navigational device, which fits on a small boat's steering console and can accurately read out the user's position anywhere in the world down to a few feet. These devices have a wonderful array of inbuilt features, such as the GOTO function; any number of Waypoints or targets can be pre-programmed into the GPS and by scrolling the index down to the desired target, for example a wreck, divers can simply press the Go To button and the GPS will give the direction, distance etc. to the target. The bearing or route to any target can also be shown in a number of ways on the screen: some users prefer the Highway feature, which shows a roadway leading to the target – you just steer your boat to stay on the Highway and drive straight to the target – others prefer a small chart showing the boats track or simply a digital readout of the target bearing and current track.

Hydrographic Department: A government department responsible for Admiralty charts and records of, for example, wrecks charted.

Incident pit: A diving term to represent how one simple thing going wrong under water can lead in turn to other small things going wrong. Each failure in its own is manageable but it is the culmination of the successive happenings that creates the incident.

LCD: Liquid Crystal Display. The screen on modern electronic navigational tools such as Echo-sounders, GPS and VHF Radio.

MSW: metres of seawater – a measure of depth.

Nitrogen Narcosis: A diving condition also known as the 'narcs' or the 'Raptures of the Depths'. As divers descend, the water pressure around them increases. To avoid that increasing water pressure crushing their air spaces, lungs etc., the aqualung delivers air at the same increased pressure. Thus, the air pressure in their lungs is at exactly the same pressure as the water outside their bodies. This means, for example, that at 50m, to keep their lungs from crushing they are breathing six times as much air in any one breath as they would on the surface. Air is made up of 79 per cent nitrogen and 21 per cent oxygen. Whilst on the surface the 79 per cent of nitrogen is largely inert, in increasing pressures it starts to have a narcotic effect on the diver. Most divers are affected to a small extent at a depth of 25m. Increasingly, beyond a depth of 40m, a diver is more and more disabled mentally by the narcotic effect of the higher pressures of nitrogen.

Pillar valve: The valve that fits into the threaded top of a scuba tank. The valve allows the Aqualung 1st Stage to be connected to it. Air leaves the tank through a small aperture in the pillar valve. The 1st Stage seals onto the pillar valve with a rubber 'O' ring.

Side tube grablines. An inflatable dive boat has large round buoyancy tubes running up either side of the hull. Looped safety grablines are set along the top of the tubes.

Slack water: The short period of time when the current stops moving in one direction before moving in the other direction. On the east coast of Scotland the current runs roughly north for a 6-hour period before turning to head south for 6 hours. The moment the tide turns and pauses is 'slack water'. At weak neap tides, slack water can last for 1–2 hours. During strong spring tides, slack water on our coasts lasts about 20 minutes.

SSAC: Scottish Sub Aqua Club.

Stride entry: A diver can enter the water from rocks, a harbour wall or a boat by a stride entry. The diver makes sure it is clear beneath, looks dead ahead and steps out to drop down into the water.

RAS Mast: Refuelling At Sea mast found on tankers. These 'H' frame masts allowed fuel to be transfered from the tanker to other vessels at sea.

RIB: Rigid Inflatable Boat. The preferred dive boat set-up. The RIB has a rigid moulded hull designed to deal with heavy seas with buoyancy tubes fitted along either side of it – a brilliantly versatile and safe seaboat.

ROV: Remotely Operated Vehicle. A smart box of electronics fitted with cameras and grabs and developed by the offshore oil industry. It is manoeuvred by small props and controlled remotely by a surface operator. Commands are sent to it via an umbilical. Independent free ROVs are currently being developed which have no need for an umbilical and use through-water communications instead.

TDI: Technical Diving Incorporated. An American-based training agency which helped pioneer the development of mixed gas diving in the sport diving community.

Turned turtle: A term usually associated with the sinking of battleships and heavily armoured warships. The incredibly heavy gun turrets and top hamper, or superstructure, of these warships were formidable when the ship was intact. Once damaged however, if enough water got into the hull, it affected the buoyancy so badly that the heavy upperworks would cause the ship to roll completely upside down, such as in the case of HMS *Royal Oak* and HMS *Prince of Wales*.

Zero vis: Where the underwater visibility is reduced to nil – a diver cannot see his arm or hand in front of his face.